NEWTON ABBOT

Newton Abbot

Philip Carter

THE
MINT
PRESS

First published in Great Britain by The Mint Press, 2004

ISBN 1-903356-40-7

Cataloguing in Publication Data
CIP record for this title is available from the British Library

The Mint Press
18 The Mint
Exeter, Devon
England EX4 3BL

Designed and typeset in New Baskerville 10.5/14
by Mike Dobson, Quince Typesetting

Cover design by Delphine Jones

Printed and bound in Great Britain
by Short Run Press Ltd, Exeter

CONTENTS

To the memory of our daughter

Susan Whiting

FOREWORD

Newton Abbot has had a fascinating history and no book, so far, has had half as much information on the subject as this new publication. It positively rushes the reader along in a whirlwind of amusing, poignant and detailed information that has only been available to a dedicated few researchers of Newton Abbot history.

You will read how the town has joined in the spirit of the celebrations over the years, including some that are quite bizarre! It is a picture of a bustling town shouldering disasters and the see - saw of growth and decline. You will not be bored!

Felicity Cole

Curator
Newton Abbot Town & GWR Museum.

ACKNOWLEDGEMENTS

My thanks to Dr Todd Gray, but for whom I might never have started on this project, Felicity Cole (Newton Abbot Museum), Tony Rouse (Westcountry Studies Library), Roger Brien (Devon & Exeter Institution) and the staff of Exeter Reference and Newton Abbot Libraries. I would also like to thank fellow students Judith Farmer, Clare Greener and Margaret Reed. Thanks also to all those named and unnamed who gave information or help including Wendy Carter, Judy Chard, Tony Collings, Roy Grylls, Eric Harcourt, the late Audrey Hexter, Philip Higginson, Matthew and Tony Knowles, Michael Martin, Peter Ruddick and Robert Zaple also to Glenys Loder for information on Loder's Edge Tool Mill, Ian Bulpin for Bulpin's and Colin Willcocks for Beare's. Last, but by no means least, my wife Mary who spared neither encouragement nor criticism when due!

Permission to publish illustrations and maps has been given by Beare's (pages 182 & 183), Bulpin & Son (130, 131 & 143), Mr. & Mrs. Carrett (88, 114, 116, 118, 133 & 137), Dartington Photo Archive (100, 127 bottom, 129 top, 152, 166 & 176), Devon Arts & Crafts (72, 73 & 7 4), Devon Leathercrafts Ltd. (134, 135 & 136), Devon Record Office (20, 24, 38, 40, 42, 57, 95, 96, 110 & 164 bottom), Exeter University (29, 102 & 103), Roy Grylls (140), Philip Higginson (149), Imperial War Museum (123), New Devon Pottery Ltd. (178), Newton Abbot Museum (2 top, 12, 36, 41, 87, 104 top, 106 bottom, 107, 115, 127 top, 129 bottom, 132, 141, 142, 150, 156, 163, 164 top, 165, 167, 171, 185, 186 & 195), Westcountry Studies Library (2 bottom, 9, 10, 11, 18, 19, 26, 34, 39, 45, 56, 58, 59, 61, 63, 68, 77, 78, 80, 81, 86, 101, 104 bottom, 108, 109, 111, 122, 124 & 139) an d Robert Zaple (43). Copyright rests with the owners where appropriate.

INTRODUCTION

Newton Abbot, despite much of its appearance, is an ancient town with a long and interesting history. The interest is heightened in part because the modern town is an amalgam of not one, but two, separate identities. What came to be called Newton Abbot in the parish of Wolborough and what became Newton Bushel in Highweek parish only officially merged as one as recently as 1901. This twin identity has tended to conceal the history of the whole, because some historical references refer to one place and some to the other. For simplicity and brevity the town will be referred to generally by the term Newton. Only when there are points to make about the different parts will the more specific names be used.

The town has had its moments of national importance, such as the first declaration of William of Orange as king, but generally it has been concerned with more everyday affairs and this it has done successfully over a very long period. During the nineteenth century Newton was very much atypical of other inland towns in Devon. This period is particularly fascinating.

Whilst having nothing like as much general literature as a city such as Exeter, Newton has been fortunate to have more written about it than many other Devon townships, though the last three-quarters of the nineteenth century, the period of the town's most spectacular growth, has no contemporary chronicler.

The earliest known work is D.M. Stirling's *A History of Newton-Abbot and Newton-Bushel,* printed and published in the town in 1830. Stirling was a schoolmaster and gave no bibliography though he mentioned *Magna Britannia* of 1822. He wrote at a time when the Newfoundland trade, which had sustained the town for many years, had just had its final flurry during the Napoleonic Wars. He ascribed a less active spirit of improvement in the town to this cause.[i] Yet this was written at the start of a decade in which Newton would grow at about 18% compared to the county's 8%. Considering the date he wrote, towards the end of his book he made a most percipient remark, stating that a canal or rail road to communicate with the navigation of the Teign would be an infinite advantage.[ii] Stirling's book also contained an early directory.

The next work is *Newton Abbot Its History and Development* by A.J. Rhodes, a journalist, again published in the town under the aegis of the *Mid-Devon Times* in about 1904. W. G. Hoskins commented 'Useful for the nineteenth 19th century development of the town' [iii] when Rhodes wrote, 'the prosperity of Newton Abbot may be traced to many causes' and then went on to list the four most important in his opinion. These were a railway and an industrial centre, the market for a large agricultural district and that the town was endowed with clay. He also said "Newton Abbot has been somewhat aptly termed the *Swindon of the West*" [iv] a term used earlier in *Morris' Directory 1870*.[v] Unfortunately again there was no bibliography or indeed references. More recent is Roger Jones' *A book of Newton Abbot* written in 1979; it is the most scholarly work with both references and a good bibliography though he admitted to have done little original research.[vi] Jones was the town's librarian and therefore had a unique knowledge of local material. Since his time, possibly because of Devon County Council's Library restructuring, some material he mentioned has gone to Torquay and other items seem no longer to be available. Two other books have since been published and add to our knowledge: Derek Beavis' *Newton Abbot, The Story of the Town's Past* (1985) and Harry Unsworth's *A New Look at Old Newton Abbot* (1993).

Because a town does not exist in a vacuum and is affected by what goes on around it, a brief attempt will be made to show Newton in its changing setting. This does not mean that an effort will be made to write an area study, far from it, there will however be brief references to what is happening elsewhere especially when Newton differs from the norm.

Newton's underlying structural factors were important to its development. Its origin was almost certainly due to its position close to the lowest point where it was possible to cross the River Teign and its tributary the Lemon. It was the natural situation for a 'bridge' town and when those bridges were built, they acted as a magnet for commerce and traffic. Newton ceased to be the lowest crossing point in 1827 when the first Shaldon Bridge was built but by that time the road pattern had already been established. Newton's position at the head of a navigable estuary was important in an age when waterborne traffic was the norm for heavy and bulky loads. This natural advantage was later to be enhanced by the digging of an early canal giving employment to bargemen and boatbuilders.

The strip of land here between Dartmoor, the highest land in the south of England, and the Teign estuary was only a few miles wide. Moreover the alternative route around the north of the moor was approximately 20 miles longer, which gave the southern route an advantage. These factors were of vital importance when modern corridors of communication, both by road and rail, were being developed especially as better access was needed to the increasingly important naval base and dockyard at Devonport and the port of Plymouth. The River Lemon is a short river, rising below Haytor on the edge of Dartmoor, but because of its considerable fall in a short distance is swiftly flowing. This river was an ideal source of waterpower for a series of mills ranging from the usual corn mills, to a less common edge tool mill and an even rarer bark mill for the local tannery.

Geology, too, was important. The nearby massive block of Dartmoor is composed of very hard granite. During a significant period of the nineteenth century it was quarried and shipped through Newton. The same granite broken down into china clay, washed down and combined with vegetable matter to form the large deposits of ball clay in the Bovey Basin close to Newton. This proved to be of far more importance over time than the granite itself, because ball clay is a relatively scarce raw material and only found in two other areas in the United Kingdom. Extraction of this clay provided useful employment for at least 250 years and still does today. Newton had intrusions of hard igneous rock that were quarried and limestone used in its numerous limekilns. There were also deposits of sand used for scouring and building.[vii] The small deposits of mineral ores in the immediate vicinity were less important and only provided a little employment for a short period.

The geological provision of good soils combined with a mild climate and sufficient rainfall were the basis for a large hinterland suitable for agriculture. What is more, this Devonshire locality was suited to both arable and pastoral farming. It was, therefore, easier to maintain prosperity when the former faltered from the 1870s onwards.[viii] If this agricultural base is not the most significant factor in Newton's development, it certainly has been the longest prop of its prosperity. For over 700 years the town has been a focus for the countryside around, both servicing its needs and offering a useful outlet for its produce.

The attractive scenery and favourable climate were in time to bring another benefit to the town. It became in a small way a base for visitors; the town advertised itself as 'The Gate to Dartmoor'. More significantly it became an area in which the well-to-do might retire, so bringing an influx of employment in domestic service and a boost to the local retail trade in the nineteenth and twentieth centuries.

A caveat is needed before proceeding further. Because it is essential to know the setting, to paint the background, it has been necessary to list all Newton's advantages. It is easy to look at them superficially and think the town must have succeeded; but other towns had similar factors in their favour, and indeed ones that Newton did not have; yet they failed to prosper. It is therefore essential to delve deeper into Newton's exceptional performance.

Some may question why another book on Newton Abbot is justified. There is obviously the fact that as time goes on there are more years to write about. More importantly, and perhaps surprisingly to non-historians, is the fact that as years pass more information about the past becomes available. Fresh archaeological work brings new evidence to light. Previously unstudied or unconsidered documents can give a new perspective.

CHAPTER 1

THE EARLY YEARS
TO AD 1066

We know insufficient about prehistoric Devon to be aware of any differences between Newton's area and other places around. Later in the Roman era, there seems to have been a sharp divide between Exeter and east Devon compared to the rest of the county. The further west in Devon the later was Saxon influence felt. The various historical ages used to be considered relatively simple. There was the Palaeolithic, the Mesolithic, the Neolithic, the Bronze Age and the Iron Age. There was assumed to have been a progression through from one age to another and from mobile hunter-gatherers to sedentary farmers. Although this overall picture still obtains, there has been much discussion about the rates of change and degrees of overlap.

The most important point to assimilate from the Prehistoric period is what an incredibly long time it was. It was far longer than any period that follows. Furthermore recent work has continued to postulate earlier dates for mankind in Britain. It is now claimed that the earliest traces of man in Devon date back 250,000 years,[1] whereas elsewhere in the country, it has been suggested to have been 700,000 years ago.[2]

There is evidence of very early occupation from Kent's Cavern and Tornewton Caves at Torbryan.[3] Thus it must be assumed that our particular area was used by early Stone Age men. For those ages lack of evidence does not prove lack of activity. However do not assume continuous use; even though our country was not an island then, intervening colder interludes may well have precluded human activity for long periods. One intriguing early find from the Heathfield area was a dug out canoe. This was found in 1881 before there were efficient means of age-dating or even preservation techniques. Sadly, therefore, we shall never know how old it really was.[4] It was made from a hollowed oak tree and was three feet wide and about nine feet long.[5]

There is sound and interesting evidence of Bronze Age activity from the Dainton area, near Ipplepen.[6] Here have been found sword and spearhead moulds and considerable evidence of metal working, more in fact than has yet been found anywhere else in the south of Britain.[7] Two rapier moulds were also found at Chudleigh.[8]

1

Three bronze figurines of a bird, duck and stag; from Milber Camp they could be dated from 1000BC to 50BC, usage unknown. Now at Torquay Museum.

The Iron Age has left a wealth of evidence in our area. The most recent find was a new site at Aller Cross between Newton and Kingskerswell, discovered in 1993 during excavation work prior to a possible Kingskerswell by-pass.[9] This discovery was unexpected and reinforces the notion other sites may be found. Aller Cross also produced later material.[10] At Berry Down, a hill just north of Bradley Manor an excavation in 1926 found evidence of an Iron Age roundhouse.[11] However, quite the most important local Iron Age construction is the well-known Milber Camp.[12] It is in fact the largest erection known from that age in Devon. Generations of Newtonians used to call this the 'Roman Camp' which it was not although recently a nearby Roman connection has been found. William of Orange also used it in 1688 as an encampment.

Considerable debate has continued as to how this type of camp was used; Milber for instance is not a well-thought out defensive site. Did the widely spaced ramparts offer secure accommodation for herds of cattle? Obviously its construction represents considerable human effort, but how many people actually lived on the site we do not know. The Iron Age tribe that lived in the

Milber Iron Age Camp the largest in Devon from a photograph taken c.1900. Newtonians for a long time wrongly called this Roman.

area was part of the Dumnonii which inhabited Cornwall, most of Devon and parts of Somerset.[13] We know something of their primarily agricultural lifestyle but little about their political organisation.

Four particular early finds from the area need mentioning, two were from Milber itself. Firstly, there were three bronze figurines of a bird, duck and stag; they could be dated from 1000BC to 50BC. Their usage we know not, but it is tempting to assume some high status decorative or ritualistic purpose.[14] Secondly there was also a stone spindle whorl cleverly decorated. A similar one was found in Kent's Cavern and may be the work of the same man.[15] The third find of importance were the iron bars from nearby Coffinswell. This collection, originally probably of 100 bars, had been carefully bundled and thoughtfully buried. The assumed date for these is from the second or first centuries BC, and we know from Julius Caesar's *Commentaries* that such items were used as currency. It has been posited that they may have had some other significance as well, or even more mundanely an iron-master's hoard. What we do know for certain and rather sadly is that the only other find of this 2,000-year-old type of artefact, discovered locally in the nineteenth century, was then used to stake cucumbers! The fourth interesting find was a wooden male figure, carved from oak wood, discovered in a ball clay deposit near Kingsteignton. This has been radiocarbon dated to *c.*426–352 BC but its purpose is quite unknown, it may have been a talisman, a toy or have primitive religious or symbolic importance.[16]

As previously mentioned there was a great difference in the Roman period between Exeter and east Devon and the rest of the county. Exeter began as a fortified military establishment and developed into a town. East Devon is a microcosm of much of the rest of Roman Britain at that period; with well made roads and villas. West of Exeter there are the lines of just two main roads, neither made to the usually high Roman standards but little else has yet been found.[17] The most likely explanation is that the Dumnonii submitted early to the Romans and were allowed to order their own affairs subject to overall Roman control.[18] Certainly, life did not just stop beyond Exeter and there is archaeological evidence of people living in the Newton area in the Roman period. It needs to be made clear that this was not an advanced civilization of the true Roman type. Bidwell writes of cultural isolation and comparative backwardness.[19] At Aller Cross there is some evidence of occupation in early Roman times and more in the later Roman period.[20] Near the adjoining Milber Iron Age Camp a small site probably an individual farm existed in the early Roman years.[21] The proximity to Aller Cross should be noted and allows reiteration as to what other sites may yet be discovered. Another minor Roman find was of a Roman coin when the reservoir was being constructed for the growing Milber estate. This was of the Emperor Maximianus 286–305 AD and the coin was struck in Alexandria. It may have been lost at that spot by an early trader, but it could have arrived centuries later. Interesting finds of pottery and other items from the Roman period were also made in 1981 at Kingsteignton.[22]

Of the two Roman roads in west Devon, one left Exeter by the North Gate towards North Tawton. The other left the West Gate and crossing Haldon came to Teignbridge,[23] the bridge of course, not the modern local government district! The Woolners in their study wrote of the geographic importance of this site and thought that the first bridge there was almost certainly Roman.[24] Other work has suggested, and this is indeed logical, that a Roman road continued to cross the River Lemon and probably used the line of the present Back Road in

Newton Abbot.[25] If this is true there was probably a human presence in the area of what is now the town much earlier than was once thought likely.

There was a period of several hundred years between the departure of the Romans and the arrival of the Saxons. The likely time-scale is that the Romans left from about AD 400 and the Saxons were in our part of Devon by AD 700 at the latest.[26] One of the few things we know about the interim period is that Christianity survived. There is at East Ogwell church an early sixth-century Christian burial stone with a Latin inscription.[27] We certainly have no idea how savage or complete was the take over, or replacement, of the British or Celtic inhabitants by the incoming Saxons. It is assumed from evidence of place-names in the southwest that Celtic persisted as a language for a while after the Saxon incursion and before English dominated. This is most evident in Cornwall. It is notable that although Celtic place names are scarce in our part of Devon, there are plenty of them for physical features. 'Tor' a Celtic word for hill features in Dartmoor tors and Torre Abbey. Local Rivers such as Teign, Dart, Avon and Lemon all have Celtic roots. Teign simply means 'stream',[28] Dart is 'abounding in oaks' and Lemon is 'abounding in elms',[29] although several other different origins of Lemon have been suggested. If this evidence of language theory is correct then our area seems to have become firmly Saxon dominated.

The focus of Newton's history moves to Kingsteignton in Saxon times. It was one of the earlier Saxon settlements and probably dates from 700 AD or only a little later. There was a vast Saxon Royal estate of the kingdom of Wessex centred on Kingsteignton that later became the administrative unit of the Teignbridge Hundred.[30] A hundred was a sub-shire administrative unit, there being over 30 in Devon. They were not always whole entities, but sometimes fragmented in separate parts. Towns in Saxon Devon, if not as scarce as hens' teeth, were at least thin on the ground. It is significant that a number of them were at the head of estuaries, for instance: Barnstaple, Plympton (the Plym has since silted up below the town), Kingsbridge, Totnes and Kingsteignton. This enabled these urban places to function as river ports, trading points and distributive centres and, more importantly, as the Viking threat developed, they could act in a defensive role.[31] Haslam suggests that Totnes was designed as a 'burgh-bridge' unit to block access to a major river.[32] It is likely that Highweek, Teignwick as it was once known, was a satellite of Kingsteignton, formerly Teignton, to block further incursion up the Teign. It seems possible therefore that Kingsteignton was royal because of its strategic importance.

Two points need to be made here; we do not know if these Saxon towns were fresh settlements actually started from scratch or whether they were Dumnonian ones taken over and 'promoted' because of their position. They would no doubt have been of significance at that time, but they would certainly not equate with what we think of as a town today. What we do know for sure is that Kingsteignton was at the top of the local hierarchy because the churches in both Highweek and Newton Bushel were chapelries to Kingsteignton. All burials had to be carried out in Kingsteignton until 1427 and Highweek did not become an independent parish church until 1864.[33] Yet over time it was Newton that flourished and Kingsteignton that faltered. Possibly this was because for many years Kingsteignton, apart from the ferry to Netherton, was a land route dead-end, whereas Newton was a useful staging point to other places.

The Danes or Vikings caused trouble in Devon in two respects. In the short term they carried out a number of raids. The later ones were in 981, 988 and

1001 in which year they sailed up the Teign and burnt Kingsteignton. The Anglo-Saxon chronicle states that they destroyed 'many other goodly towns that we can not name'. They then assailed, without success, Exeter. Unfortunately, they were back again in 1003 and this time they took the place, aided by treachery, and plundered and destroyed the town.[34] This caused long-term trouble, especially for historians, in that they burnt the library that held the charters which recorded estate ownership of the period. To add to the confusion these documents were considered so important that attempts were made to fabricate replacements![35]

There is evidence from 1044 of salt production in the area of the tidal estuary of the Teign. In these early days it was impossible to feed all animals through the winter, so many were slaughtered in the autumn and salt was the essential preservative. The heating of brine, in what were called salterns, with wood fires to drive off the water was hard smoky work. It continued for many centuries.[36]

CHAPTER 2

THE NORMAN AND MIDDLE AGES
1066–1485

Although the Normans did not subdue Devon for a couple of years after the Conquest and their take-over was not everywhere instantaneous, at the higher levels it was eventually nearly complete. Few Saxons were still in possession of their lands by the end of William I's reign.[37] At the bottom of the heap though, it may not have made too much difference to the way of life. The Middle Ages were troublesome times. Nationally there were civil wars such as those at the time of Stephen, the Barons' War and later the Wars of the Roses; there was also The Hundred Years War against France, and the Black Death. Although it was a long and turbulent period, key formative events took place, which were to shape the town's history for many centuries to come.

The first evidence of change in our locality is the motte and bailey, Castle Dyke in Highweek, situated 250 ft above sea level on a commanding position looking down the estuary. It is possible that as at Exeter and Totnes it was built after the Conquest as a Norman stronghold to overawe the local inhabitants. It is likely that there was a Saxon settlement thereabouts but there is no date for the castle. Pevsner suggested it dated to the eleventh to thirteenth centuries, and others posit it as late as the reign of Stephen 1135–1154. Maybe it was erected illegally in that turbulent reign. There is no evidence to support the suggestion that the lords of the manor lived at Castle Dyke before later moving down to Bradley Manor; they could well have been absentee lords.[38]

Domesday, as with other parts of the country, is one of the points of contention in Newton's history. It is evident that not all places that existed in Devon in 1086 are included. It was normal practice to name a specific manor and sometimes omit constituent villages or hamlets. There are places recorded that are as yet unidentified. Therefore, whatever theory we propound we cannot be sure we are right. The cachet of inclusion is not definitive.

Set out roughly clockwise are the manors in the immediate area that do feature. These are Teingrace, Teignton (Kingsteignton), Gappah, Ideford, Haccombe, Buckland, Coffinswell, Wolborough, Aller, Abbotskerswell, East and West Ogwell, Holbeam, Ingsdon, and Staplehill. Some suggest Bradley but the case for the one with the same name nearer Tiverton seems stronger. Others offer versions of Neweton or Newtone but it seems unlikely to be our Newton, that as far as we know only obtained the name later. An actual translation of the entry for Wolborough reads as follows 'Ralph of Bruyere holds Wolborough from Baldwin. Siward held it before 1066. It paid tax for 1 hide. Land for 8 ploughs. In Lordship 2 ploughs: 4 slaves 1 virgate, 6 villagers and 7 small holders with 4 ploughs and 3 virgates. A mill which pays 5s. Meadow 15 acres pasture 30 acres woodland as much, 12 cattle and 100 sheep. Formerly 20s value now 40s'.[39] This means that Ralph of Bruyere, whose name later becomes more familiar as Brewer, held his lands from Baldwin, who held the most land in Devon with other estates elsewhere. Baldwin came from what is now Meuilles in the department of Calvados. He helped build Exeter Castle, had his own castle at Okehampton and became Sheriff of Devon.[40] Brewer would have owed allegiance and service, military and other, to Baldwin and so under the manorial system allegiance and service would have gone down the chain. Siward would have been the former Saxon owner now dispossessed. A plough in those days was a large and important item pulled by six or eight oxen. Ox ploughs were still being used in our area nearly 800 years later in 1840!

It is difficult to compare land areas because both terms, hides possibly 120 acres, and virgates, maybe 30 acres, varied with the quality of the land and it is not known how the assessment was made. Ploughs have been considered by some to be a unit of land measure, others regard them as an implement. Teignton (Kingsteignton), if counting ploughs is a fair estimation, was still considerably more important having 16 to Wolborough's 8. Its manpower figures are also greater in Saxon times and for some years to come. Teignton included Teignwick (Highweek).

A silver penny of William II, William Rufus, who ruled from 1087–1109, was found in 1944 in a garden on Newton's Ashburton Road. It was minted in London by a moneyer with the name of Edwi.[41] Unfortunately one coin proves little; it could for instance have been brought and lost centuries later.

Both parts of our modern town, Wolborough, which was to become Newton Abbot on the south bank of the Lemon, and Highweek, which was to become Newton Bushel on the north, developed as new towns. It was a common 'real-estate' speculation in that period to develop a new town because of the extra revenue that would accrue to the owners, the lords of the manor. There is sometimes a tendency to see a charter date as literally the starting time for a particular township. This is usually not the case because the majority grew out 'of more ancient villages or hamlets'.[42] Considering the particular sites on each side of a river crossing, and remembering that the river before it was channelled would have been wider, it seems highly likely there would have been habitations there. So, although the dates are recorded below, the actual beginnings of the towns may be long before then.

In Newton Abbot the town plan does lend more credence to a new development. It was apparently laid out along Wolborough Street at an angle to the then assumed road, Back Road. In Newton Bushel it seems to follow the line of the old road, Highweek Street and Old Exeter Road. On that basis maybe Bushel is older than Abbot! There is the additional factor south of the Lemon in that some believe the original urban settlement must have been immediately around Wolborough Church and then moved down to what is now Wolborough Street. This could be true, on the other hand not all Devon churches were apparently built close to their original settlements for example

Honiton or Okehampton. The only written evidence is far too late in date to be definite proof; what is needed is an archaeological dig on site, such as the recent one around the old church at Buckfastleigh.

It is likely that the new town's burgage plots, laid out along Wolborough Street, conformed to the original field boundaries. This meant that with their narrow frontages later extensions of the properties and indeed the development of the system of courts all proceeded behind the original street line. Later building would normally fill the site of an earlier house. Therefore the urban plan of the Wolborough Street area as seen on nineteenth-century maps was in effect a fossilized field system.

Two other points are worth making here, firstly, Devon was rich in medieval market towns but some succeeded better than others. For instance Bow, Denbury, and Kennford were all once in the same category as Newton but their growth has been rather different. Secondly, in recent years we have more archaeological evidence available to confirm that both Wolborough and Highweek streets did have medieval buildings. This clearly means that though we have no definitive date, both parts of our town started early.

By the time the new towns were under way the ownership of both manors had changed. Lord William Brewer had given Wolborough to his new foundation Torre Abbey in 1196 as an endowment.[43] Thus for centuries to come, up to the Dissolution of the Monasteries, the lords of the manor of Wolborough were the abbots of Torre. This was not uncommon then, other abbeys in Devon such as Tavistock acted in a similar capacity. Highweek's situation is more complex. At Domesday it had been part of Teignton (Kingsteignton), it then probably went into private hands and afterwards again became a royal possession. The lands west of the Teign, including what is now Highweek, then emerge as a separate entity, for a while called Teignwick, and are granted to Theobald de Englishville by Henry III in 1237.[44]

Development dates of the two towns are also uncertain.[45] Furthermore, it seems to have been a common practice in early times, to try and claim an even earlier foundation date. If the abbots of Torre founded Newton Abbot, and the evidence suggests that was so, they must have moved smartly. This is because the abbey was only founded in 1196 but by approximately 1200 there is documentary evidence of a *nova villa* (new town). The earliest extant market and fair charters date from 1269. But they could have been earlier, there is for instance mention of a fair in Wolborough in the Close Rolls of 1221. The fair date was changed at this time to St Leonard's from St Mary's feast day. There is also a reference to a market at Wolborough, rather than Newton, in the Pipe Rolls of 1230.[46]

The borough charter for Newton Bushel is missing, but the grant of a market and authority to develop the town dates from 1246.[47] This type of document is rare giving the specific right to make plots and to let them.[48] Thus originally both towns had a market, Newton Abbot on Wednesday and Newton Bushel on Tuesday as well as annual fairs. It was customary for the lord of the manor to provide the market place. Newton Abbot's was held in the east end of Wolborough Street, wider then than now. Not everyone agrees on Newton Bushel's market place but Jones opts for the triangular-shaped land behind St Mary's in Highweek Street, suggesting that over time 'triangle' became corrupted to Treacle Hill (Chapel Hill).[49] The continuity of Newton Abbot's Wednesday Market stretching over 700 years invites consideration.

An engraving of Highweek Church drawn in 1858. Still at this date a chapel of ease to Kingsteignton, that status continued until 1864.

Much has been made of these towns being remarkably close together. Such a set up is not unique. There were for instance East and West Looe, or Kingsbridge and Dodbrooke. The interesting point maybe, is that both survived and flourished for so long. Newton Abbot was at first Schireborne Newton and several different meanings have been suggested. 'Clear brook' from the Saxon scirburne seems the most likely. More certainly Sherborne Road derives from this earlier name. However, the name later became Newton Abbot, the new town of the abbots of Torre. Newton Bushel derives it name from the Bushel family who were the adopted heirs of Theobald de Englishville.[50]

Neither of the old principal churches have a firm date, Wolborough is mentioned in a taxation document of Pope Nicholas IV in 1292 and Highweek

Wolborough Church, 1856. King Charles I attended service here, both John Lethbridge, the diver, and John Paton the elephant keeper are buried in the churchyard.

Copyright.

Newton Abbot.   The Tower.

St Leonard's Tower, c.1900. Luckily it has survived several proposed demolitions.

features at much the same period.[51] Once the new towns were established the townsfolk found they had a long way to go to their respective churches. This led to the building of two chapels of ease or minor churches, in the newly populated areas. The date of old St Leonard's in Newton Abbot is not known but it was built by 1350.[52] Its tower still stands as the well-known landmark. The date of old St Mary's in Newton Bushel is just as elusive but is probably thirteenth century.[53]

Early information can be gathered from taxation records. For instance, the names of taxpayers in both Highweek and Newton are available for 1332. In those days a differential tax was payable for rural areas, which was a fifteenth, and in urban areas a tenth. Highweek had 22 taxpayers and Newton 14.[54] Fox posits a population figure for Newton at this period of some 500 people. He suggests the occupations would probably have been: bakers, weavers, smiths, tailors, tanners, painters, carpenters, cordwainers (shoemakers), cobblers, glovers, and sellers of salt, coal and pottery.[55] The plague of the Black Death in 1348 may have killed nearly half our island's population; it is unlikely that Newton could have escaped. One record available is that of the clergy in the Archdeaconry of Totnes, which includes Highweek. No less than 40 incumbents in the 70 parishes had to be replaced during the plague. This is obviously a higher percentage than the national average but conscientious priests, who attended the sick and buried the dead, were particularly liable to infection.[56]

Bradley Manor is Newton's oldest inhabited residence but there is no certain date for the first building on the site. Of what is now standing, a small part dates from the thirteenth century, and most of the rest from two major building operations in the fifteenth.[57] On this basis it was probably the Bushel family who built the first part. In 1402 the manor passed through the female line to the Yarde family. The first of these, Richard and his wife Joan, were great builders. Apart from the major part of Bradley Manor including the chapel, they built a new church of All Saints on the hill in Highweek, they added to St

10

Lower Bradley House (Bradley Manor) the house in its setting but the artist has used licence with the background.

Mary's at Newton Bushel and seem to have helped out at St Mary's at Wolborough.[58]

In 1342 Highweek church had an inspection the report was not very flattering. 'The chalice lid is lost, an altar-cloth of the high altar is unembroidered some others are lost. The missal (service book of mass for the year) is mean and deficient. The week-day epistles and gospels are not in it. The Gradual (service book) is monastic. A cruet (small vessel used to store water or wine) is lost, one is cracked. The pax-pole (pax was usually a picture of the crucifixion, kissed by the priest at mass and circulated) is badly painted'. There was also a complaint about a broken window and the parishioners were threatened with the fine of one mark if the defects were not put in order before the next visitation.[59] In May 1427 Pope Martin V granted the right of people living in Highweek to be buried there.[60] Formerly, corpses had to be carried all the way to Kingsteignton church which could present considerable difficulties in wet periods across marshy ground. The old church path coming down to Whitehill Lodge is a reminder of those early times. In 1428 the present All Saints church was consecrated,[61] though there are records of a previous church on the site in the thirteenth century. It was a chapelry to Kingsteignton until late in the nineteenth century.

The remains of a medieval clinker-built boat was discovered in 1898 by clay-workers in Zitherixon pit at Rackerhayes just outside Newton. It was over 20 feet long, made of oak and had been caulked with hair and pitch. At the time it was found it was thought to be 'Viking', but scientific work nearly a century later established it was medieval and built after 1305. It was an undecked vessel, probably designed for river or coastal work.[62] It may have been of a fairly common type in its time but few have survived to provide evidence. The find is also a reminder that the course of the Teign has altered over time both by natural and artificial means

At this period most of the larger merchants of the area were from Exeter. There were a few in other places and one with a widespread trade came from Newton. He was a Gilbert Smyth who imported through Exeter 152 tuns of wine between 1382 and 1399. He also brought in some cargoes via Teignmouth and sold both sturgeon and wine to the Courtenay household at Tiverton.[63] As early as 1395/6 there are records of cloth production at Newton Bushel. At

Medieval ship found 1898 at Rackerhayes. This was originally thought to be 'Viking', there is a display at Torquay Museum.

that time it produced more cloth than Ashburton, but less than Totnes and considerably less than Exeter.[64] Gilbert Yarde who inherited Bradley Manor after the death of his father Richard in 1467 had no less than three fulling mills for washing wool, as well as three corn mills.[65] Clearly the Lemon was being put to good use.

In 1411 the then Abbot of Torre brought a case before the King's justices against the burgesses of Newton Abbot. He alleged amongst other things they had committed trespass and had prevented his bailiffs from levying tolls.[66] There was also a dispute about the ownership of St Leonard's. The outcome seems to have been a compromise but proves that relations between the lords of the manor and the townsfolk were not always amicable. On the other hand it should be appreciated that it would have been the white-robed Premonstratensian canons from Torre who provided the services in Wolborough parish.

Bishop Lacy made the grant of an indulgence, a remission of sins, for 'the building, repair and maintenance' of Teign Bridge in 1452.[67] Two things may surprise us here, firstly, that sins could be forgiven for those contributing cash for good works, secondly, it was a bishop taking the lead in bridge building. In fact a number of bridges were erected thanks to the initiatives of medieval bishops.

CHAPTER 3

THE TUDOR PERIOD
1485–1603

The Tudor period was one of great reconstruction, significant see-sawing religious changes encompassed the Dissolution and the foundation of the Church of England. Seafarers widened the nation's horizons; the Armada and Drake's circumnavigation were the most notable events, but other voyages were to Africa, the Americas and the Far East.

Highweek once had a church house we know this because Richard Yarde in 1513 rented it to Owen Babb and others for one penny.[68] Church houses sometimes served as almshouses, schools or alehouses that held the fund raising church ales.

The Ashburton rolls of the Stanneries in 1523 recorded a John Benat of Highweek paying duty on some 2,000 lbs of tin. There is no evidence of where he obtained the tin, and one might be tempted to think it was Dartmoor. There are however, reports of tin streaming in the Stover area, so the tin may have well come from a nearer source.[69] This is possibly confirmed in a list of the lands of the Marquis of Exeter 'certain tynn workes called . . . Hethefeldes, Dynbridge' which are recorded next to the Manor of 'Newton Abbett'.[70]

Tudor House, one of the few survivors of old houses in this historic street. An exceptional small window on the side might have been used for counting cattle going into the pound before a market.

In this period the form of taxation, known as a subsidy, continued based on a person's wealth either in lands, goods or wages. Hand-written rolls were kept in Highweek and Wolborough of who qualified in 1524 and 1525. In 1524 Wolborough had 104 names and total assessment of £19.10.9d, Highweek had 61 names and a total of £13.3.6d. Interestingly, this proves that although the former was larger in numbers, those in Highweek were somewhat better off. In part this was because the status of the richest inhabitant was different. The lord of the manor in Highweek,

Richard Yarde was resident, whereas the lord of Wolborough, for assessment purposes, was an absentee namely the abbot of Torre Abbey. Kingskerswell makes an interesting comparison having 85 persons and a liability of £8.10. which shows they were obviously less affluent still. Wolborough had three individuals designated 'frenchman', it would be interesting to know why they were there.[71]

The oldest almshouses in Newton Bushel were originally set up by John Gilbert in 1538 for lepers, a so-called lazar house.[72] The almshouses were erected at the end of Wain Lane, at what was then considered a safe distance from the town and originally included a chapel. The old name for Wain Lane was Wen Lane, so the basis for the origin of the name may not be agricultural as in waggon, but medical as in 'wen' a tumour. There were still 3 lepers in 1704 but they were all gone by 1740 when the lazar houses were converted to ordinary almshouses.[73] The Gilberd (name slightly varied), almshouses from that old foundation, rebuilt at least in 1852 and 1979, still stand in Old Exeter Road.

Later in 1576 Robert Hayman gave and endowed houses for the 'maintenance and relief of poor people of the said parish,' Wolborough, in East Street.[75] They were rebuilt in 1845 and still stand at 137/147 East Street.

Henry VIII set in train the Dissolution of the monasteries and amongst these was Torre Abbey. William Petre suppressed it on 23 February 1539;[76] Wolborough had been abbey property for well over 300 years. John Gaverock the last steward (estate manager) for the abbey, had an annual salary of £3.00. In 1545 he and his wife Joan bought the Wolborough estate for nearly £600.00.[77] Gaverock soon tired of living at the more humble Manor House and moved to Forde House. Whether he rebuilt it, is not certain but seems likely, it would have been smaller and less ornate than most of what we see now, but his move surely proved his speculation had not gone amiss. He also took over the cartulary, or book of charters, of Torre Abbey because his signature ' Johannes Gaverock generoso', meaning gentleman, is to be found in it.[78] He did not purchase the advowson, the right of appointing the incumbents, at Wolborough; this stayed with the crown. Neither did he purchase Newton Abbot, which together with its market and fairs were bought by the Yardes of Bradley.[79]

In 1569 there was a fear, some years prior to the Armada, that the Spanish Army was preparing to invade England. The Privy Council ordered a list or

Manor House, built in Henry VIII's reign. It has in its time been used, as a private residence, for courts, a school, lodging house, manufacturing, car dealership and British Legion Club. It is now the offices of the Newton & Mid-Devon Advertiser.

Gilberd's Almshouses, Orders & Directions

This printed notice is held in the Devon Record Office. It is undated but may be around 1900 or thereabouts.

Gilberd's Almshouses

Near Newton Bushell, Devon.

Orders and directions for the government and observance of the poor people occupying the four almshouses as established in A.D. 1538.

That each house shall be occupied by two poor aged or impotent persons, parishioners of the parish of Highweek, being a man and his wife, or two single women; who shall, during their abiding there, use themselves virtuously both in words and deeds, so that by any contrary occasion there shall grow no division amongst them; and that such amongst them as shall have ability to labour shall not be in idleness, but shall assist those that shall be impotent, and also as their power will extend shall labour in the herb garden for their sustenance. And that as many of the said people as shall be able shall attend Divine Service at the Parish church or Chapel and in case of default by any of them, as well for that, as for any other reasonable cause. It shall be lawful for the feoffees for the time being to remove any of the said poor people and to appoint others in their stead, according to the true and charitable intent of the donor.

That the occupants shall keep their houses and premises clean and in good order and condition, and not permit any other person or persons to sleep in or occupy the same, nor keep any poultry or cattle thereon.

That twelve shillings per annum from the feoffees and four pounds per annum from the chamber of Exeter, and paid to the poor people quarterly, by even portions.

That a copy of these orders and directions shall be placed and kept in each of the said houses for the observance of the poor people to be appointed at all times forever hereafter.

Hearder & Son Printers Newton [74]

Gilberd's, in Old Exeter Road, the oldest almshouse foundation in Newton. Originally set up in 1538 as a lazar house for lepers. They have been rebuilt several times.

'muster' of all men over 16 to be prepared. Unfortunately the Highweek records are missing but those from 'Wolborough Parish and Newton Abbot' give us another insight into Newton at that time. The basic list consists of 15 archers, 10 harquebusiers (they had an early type of firearm three feet long), 21 pikemen (their arms were a 15 foot single spiked pike), and 35 billmen (the bills were used for infighting; they were similar to an agricultural billhook on a six-foot handle but usually had a spike on the end). There were some 22 others listed who were to provide other arms and equipment; twelve of these provided caliver (a more developed firearm which followed the harquebus).[80] Later in 1588 Spain made its abortive attempt, the Armada, to invade England. Preparations were made to forestall them and Newton became one of the mustering points. In July horses and men were sent to Chudleigh to collect muskets and the next month money was paid to men on stand-by there.[81]

Events in Newfoundland had a great impact on Newton's economic future for nearly the next four hundred years. In 1497 John Cabot sailed from Bristol to his 'new found land'. Some time after this, English fishermen were working there in some numbers. Sir Walter Raleigh even claimed it was the 'main stay' of the South West. By the early seventeenth century it is estimated that there were as many as 10,000 sailors employed in the trade.[82] Devon ports, and Poole in Dorset were the front runners in the trade. Newton was never a great port, but it was an important supply point to nearby Teignmouth and Dartmouth. The industry required men and these would be recruited in Newton. It also required rope, sea-boots, fishhooks and fishermen's knives, all these and more were made in Newton. Present Newton has St John's Street, Newfoundland Way and the old ropewalk in East Street to remind us of the trades' past importance.

In 1580 the churchwarden's accounts of Stoke Gabriel recorded a payment of 40 shillings towards the 'makynge of Tengebridges'. Presumably that not only means that Teignbridge needed replacement or major repairs but also, and more interestingly, it was of sufficient importance for contributions to be levied from a wide area.[84]

John Gaverock's three daughters sold Forde probably in 1599,[85] there is argument about the date, as possession did not pass until 1604, their mother having a life interest in the property. The purchaser was Sir Richard Reynell, although originally from the Ogwell family, he became a rich London lawyer married to Lucy Brandon, daughter of a goldsmith and City of London official. Shortly after his purchase he commenced major building operations at Forde House. Rhodes wrote this was 'towards the end of Queen Elizabeth's reign' but that seems unlikely if Reynell did not yet have possession. Certainly the operation was not finished until the reign of James I.[86] The house had considerable work done later, but much of what we see dates from that period.

Rope Walk, East Street. Rope was made in Newton for many years for the Newfoundland trade. When this trade declined the owners of the walk diversified into steam packing. It finally closed in 1959.

Newfoundland Trade

The Newfoundland cod fishery trade was important to Newton for centuries. The earliest record of Devon involvement seem to be of ships from Plymouth in 1544. In the latter part of the seventeenth century Devon ship-owners sent 150 ships a year. At the end of the Napoleonic war, 1811–1815, there was a final boom in the trade. After that there was a steady decline and the regular fleet had gone by 1844. The occasional ship still went out mainly to Labrador through the rest of the century.

The way the trade was conducted altered over time. At first it was what was called a 'migratory' business. Ships left England in the spring where crews would fish and process the cod during the summer and return in the autumn. Later some men started to over-winter overseas and indeed to set up more permanent 'sedentary' fishing operations. Devon merchants established fishing stations. In time this 'sedentary' fishing was to become more important than the 'migratory' and eventually replaced it altogether. In the early years much fishing was also done along the coast of the North American mainland as well as Newfoundland. Later, much trade was done on a three-way basis. The trip out from England was the same, but the homeward voyage would be to Iberia or the Mediterranean, here fish would be sold, and fruit, salt or wine loaded to bring back to England.

The business was labour intensive, so that labour was recruited each spring at places such as the *Dartmouth* and *Newfoundland Inns* in Newton. It is known that applicants would attend from other inland small towns and villages to try to sign on. Men came from Ashburton, Bovey, Chudleigh, Hennock and even as far as Okehampton. The trade was generally looked on with some favour by government because it was regarded as a good training for potential sailors for the Royal Navy in time of need.

The other aspect of the trade that affected Newton was the furnishing of supplies. This facet was to endure long after 'migratory' fishing had ceased. The settlers in Newfoundland needed to sell their fish and wanted supplies so that they could continue the business of fishing. Devon traders had long furnished the needs of the men going out to fish, so they had the expertise and the supply knowledge to provide settlers needs. These included leather aprons and sea-boots; this meant tanners, curriers and cobblers and Newton had plenty. Ropes and twines were made at ropewalks and fishermen's knives and fishhooks were also made. There is indeed the oft-told tale of the Newton fisherman's knife manufacturer Stockman, who sued a Sheffield firm for plagiarism and won substantial damages in the High Court.

It was the arrival of steamships, operating from bigger ports that proved the death knell of the centuries' old Newfoundland trade. Yet even then a legacy of the trade, once so important to Newton, remained. In the 1851 census there was for instance a 'Newfoundland Commission Agent' whose 12-year-old son had been born there. There was also a 'Brewer, Malster, Wine & Spirit Merchant' whose 17-year-old daughter had also been born in Newfoundland. In the 1891 census there were 4 people born in Labrador as well as 5 more who had been born in Newfoundland. Three of these were boys at Newton College. They may well have been sent over for their education but the one time trade connection would have almost surely been the reason that Newton was chosen. [83]

The Dartmouth *and* Newfoundland *(now demolished) inns were used for recruiting men for the Newfoundland trade.*

CHAPTER 4

THE STUART PERIOD
1603–1714

Great and stirring events took place in this period. There was the English Civil War, the execution of Charles I, the Protectorate, the Restoration, Monmouth's unsuccessful rebellion and the Glorious Revolution of William of Orange. Newton in contrast to its usual bit-part role, was more than once in the headlines!

In 1619 England's Lord High Admiral, the Duke of Buckingham, requested a maritime survey to find out numbers of seafarers in South Devon. It must have been with the idea of gaining extra manpower for the Royal Navy and may have been specifically for a naval expedition that sailed from Plymouth to Algiers in 1621. Teignmouth, West and East, had over 100 seafarers, Bishopsteignton 10, Kingsteignton 17, Newton Abbot 39, Combeinteignhead 66 and Stokeinteignhead 115.[87] In the Newton list were two 16 year olds, James Mann and Robert Whiting, and at the top end of the age scale was John Graye, aged 52. The numbers indicate that Newton at that period had a considerable interest in maritime callings, probably largely because of the Newfoundland fisheries. This is born out by the fact that of the seven ships listed at Teignmouth at the time, the four biggest the *Jesus, John, Talent* and *Vineyard* were designated 'for Newfoundland'.[88] The Admiral later accompanied Charles I when he came to Forde House.

In 1625 England was at war with Spain and a large expedition, which ended in failure, assembled at Plymouth. Charles I, who had only ascended the throne that year, decided to review the fleet before

Charles I stayed at Forde House twice in 1625 as the guest of Sir Richard and Lucy Reynell.

Forde House, a nineteenth century drawing showing a representation of what it might have looked like in the seventeenth century.

its departure. He stayed as the guest of Sir Richard and Lady Reynell at Forde House both on the way down and on the way back. On the return visit he knighted two of his host's relatives at Forde House and attended service in Wolborough Church[89] He is reported to have touched a child for the evil.[90] Jones itemizes a list of foods provided for the King's entertainment, interesting reading but far removed from normal Newton life.[91] There would have been those locals who would not have been so happy; there was a policy of impressment to fill the ranks of the expedition to Spain and three men from Newton and one from Highweek are known to have been pressed into service.[92]

Legitimate shipping had a continuing problem with pirates operating from the north-west African coast over some centuries. Between 1629 and 1640 at least 72 Westcountry vessels were captured. In 1637 a list of prisoners was brought back from Sallee in Morocco which included a great number of Devonians, amongst these was a captive each from Ashburton, Denbury and Newton Bushel.[93]

Thanks to recent work, we now know considerable more about the running of Forde House and its estate. One newly discovered record starts in 1627 and continues after the death of Sir Richard in 1633 with some entries up until 1648, four years before the death of Lady Lucy. The Reynells lived in some style having another town house in the Cathedral Close at Exeter, now the Devon & Exeter Institution. They went shopping when there for luxury items, for instance 'my lady's gown, stockings and shoes'.[94] Newtonians shopping in Exeter is not an unfamiliar idea to our modern ears, but the Reynells would have been exceptional in those days. They employed some 15 full-time servants specified as 'two cooks, a chambermaid, dairy maid, buttery boy, kitchen boy, coachman, gardener, ploughman, miller, loader and others' employed on a casual basis. The list is illuminating: 'chimney-sweep, wood-cleaver, blacksmith, helier (tiler), carpenter, tailor, weaver, locksmith, tinker, laundress, glazier, weeder, bean-setter, and the spinning woman'. The Reynells had their own coach and horses, which was then unusual in Devon.[95] There are also records of payments to musicians, fiddlers and bell-ringers at Christmas time. One year for the festive season, 'the Reynells purchased more than 24 pounds of raisins, 10 pounds of prunes, 40 pounds of sugar, four pounds of pepper and a pound each of cloves, cinnamon, and nutmeg'. The range of items bought was impressive – just to itemize one category; in birds they bought domesticated chickens, ducks and geese and wild blackbirds, larks, mallard, partridge, pheasant, pigeon, plover, snipe and woodcock. Two fish used are worth mentioning because of their local connection; one was *capa lunga*, a local mussel from the Teign, and the other one was 'bank-fish' which was Newfoundland cod.[96] Decoy gets its name from the one-time decoy of Forde House, that was situated there. (A decoy was a tunnel like structure used to trap waterfowl; one can still be seen at the Swannery at Abbotsbury in Dorset).

Much has been made about the qualities of Lady Lucy Reynell; indeed a nephew of hers wrote a biography about 'the religious and virtuous lady'. She undoubtedly carried out good works; her almshouses originally built in 1640 bearing witness to these.[97] Their successors stand at the junction of Torquay and Church Roads. She expected high standards from the future inmates. 'That the said wyddows there placed shall bee such as shall 3 days in every week frequent the church and devine service, and shall be noe gadders, gosappers, tatlers, talebearers, nor given to reprochful words, nor

Lucy Reynell, nee Brandon, the wife of Sir Richard, was hostess, at Forde House to both King Charles I and Sir Thomas Fairfax, the parliamentary commander-in-chief. Her almshouses in Torquay Road still bear witness to her charity.

abuse of anye. That none of them keep above one servant maide to attend them, and noe man be lodged in any of the said houses'. Yet, maybe she was not the complete paragon because in 1623 she obtained a licence to eat meat on Fridays, which was granted 'provided that it was done soberly and frugally avoiding public scandal.'[98]

Jane, the daughter of Richard and Lucy Reynell, married Sir William Waller in Wolborough church in 1622. [99] He became a general on the parliamentary side in the Civil War. Indeed, he was one of the instigators of the New Model Army but later fell out of favour, went into exile and suffered imprisonment. Jane gave birth to a son who died in infancy and later to a daughter Margaret in 1633.[100] Sadly, Jane died a few months later.

The impost of Ship Money was an attempt by Charles I to raise funds without Parliament. It was brought in for seaports and maritime counties in 1634 and later extended inland. Newton Abbot had the third highest number of defaulters in Devon after Cullompton and Colyton.[101] This could be interpreted as a sign of anti-royalist feeling; either directly because of political sentiment, or poverty leading to long-term resentment. In either case, it might be assumed that Newton would be strongly Parliamentarian. Another piece of evidence points in exactly the opposite direction. After the Restoration, maimed Royalist soldiers could petition for a pension. Newton Abbot was among the 35 parishes with

Reynell Almhouse, set up by Lucy Reynell of Forde House in 1640, she expected high standards from inmates, see text.

the highest proportion of petitioners.[102] Taking both these pieces of evidence into consideration, it can only be assumed that Newton was as divided in its loyalties as places elsewhere.

Immediately before the Civil War, King and Parliament were both man-oeuvring for position. In 1641, Parliament, to show its own solidarity, made a Protestation, which was an affirmation of loyalty to the protestant faith and itself. This was later extended as an obligation to all English men. Those who did not sign were deemed incapable of holding any sort of office. It would be two hundred years before another such complete listing of adult males would be available in parish format. By taking a multiplier of four, to each man, we can arrive at a possible total population figure.

Place	Adult males	Possible total population
Highweek	128	512
Wolborough	270	1080
Total future Newton	**398**	**1592**
Cockington	115	460
St Marychurch	139	556
Tormohun	67	268
Total future Torquay	**321**	**1284**
Kingsteignton	169	676

This table shows that at this period 'future' Newton is well in front of 'future' Torquay. The once far more important Kingsteignton, although still bigger than Highweek is much smaller than Highweek and Wolborough together. The table also provides a useful reminder of how scantily populated the places were then, note these are parish totals, so that the truly urban figures would be smaller still.

War broke out in 1642 and, as far as Newton was concerned, finished in 1646. It has already been shown that there are reasons to think Newton was divided in its loyalties. Life at Forde House may carry this idea further. Lady Lucy, now a widow, who had entertained Charles I and whose late husband had subscribed a 'loan' to his funds, was looking after Margaret, the child of her daughter Jane and the now remarried Sir William Waller, a leader in the Parliamentary cause. It is known that in 1643 Lucy Reynell had a further request for another loan for the King's cause, but there is no record whether it was met or not.[103]

Although there was plenty of campaigning in Devon, Newton was seldom in the news; however, in 1643 Prince Maurice stayed at Forde House while his army camped near Buckland Barton. During the final campaign, in Devon in late 1645 and early 1646, a certain Joshua Sprigg, who was with Fairfax's Parliamentary Army, kept a detailed diary. He recorded that in October 1645 'our spies' reported that Goring, a royalist general had 5,000 horse 'quartering at Totnes, Newton Bushel and as near as Chudleigh'. A little later, in January 1646, there was a raid, Sprigg calls it a 'snatch', on Highweek. Parliamentary dragoons took a lieutenant, some prisoners and colours bearing the motto *Patientia vietrix*.[104] Roughly translated this means 'those that bear suffering attain the victory'.

This is the campaign when on a snowy evening Oliver Cromwell made a surprise attack on Bovey Tracey. Sprigg recorded, the oft-told tale, of the stakes from a game of cards being thrown into the street allowing some Royalists to escape. Afterwards the Parliamentary army fought its way into Ashburton then marched via Totnes to storm Dartmouth. The army then back-tracked because Exeter was still in Royalist hands. On his return Sir Thomas Fairfax, the parliamentary commander-in-chief, stayed at Lady Reynell's Forde House; a company of horse accompanied him. The following day, being the Lord's Day, after sermons he departed for Chudleigh.[105] Some writers claim Cromwell also stayed at Forde. This could be true, they had been together shortly before, but evidence seems lacking. There are also reports that Fairfax stayed in Newton Bushel but this may only be a reference to his stay at Forde and just one of the many occasions when Abbot and Bushel were confused.

Several historians have written about William Yeo, the Church of England curate of Wolborough, and how, because of his strong beliefs, he was in 1662 ejected from his living and had at times to leave his home and even preach in Bradley Woods at night. The Puritan Pit is still there and used annually. It is sometimes called Preacher's Pit or more illogically, unless so called by the opposition – Devil's Pit![106] There is another side to Yeo's personality which has not always been recorded. He had been, during the Civil War, a chaplain to Colonel Gould's regiment,[107] a position that surely went with a pretty hard-line stance. When he came to Newton, as Jones tells us, he patrolled the town with a constable and as Bath adds, armed with a stout stick, to prevent any 'profanation of the Sabbath'.[108] Calamy wrote 'He had a great authority . . . and was a terror to loose persons'.[109] However, he was never arrested and under Charles II's indulgences of 1672 was licensed to preach once again,[110] which, it is recorded, he did with 'competent supply'.[111]

Before the war the textile trades had been in partial recession. The war made matters much worse, by 1645, both weavers and woolcombers in Newton Abbot were dependent on poor relief.[112]

Probably in 1648 Margaret the daughter of William Waller and his wife Jane, nee Reynell, married William Courtenay.[113] They were to have no less than 19 children, several of them being baptized at Wolborough parish church. More importantly, this was to bring the extensive Wolborough estates into the hands of the Courtenays who were later to have such an enormous influence on Newton's development. Margaret Courtenay died in 1689, and her husband just over a decade later in 1702. He left £50 to the poor of Wolborough in his will.[114]

Wills are a great source of information because for many years an inventory of personal possessions had to be produced to obtain probate. Many Devonshire wills were lost in the bombing raids on Exeter in 1942, however, a few survived (see below).

Courtenay Family

Despite the Courtenays very long association with Newton the importance of the role of the family is sometimes overlooked or at the very least under-estimated. Some have gone on record that the coming of the railway made Newton, others have said that the Victorian development was vastly important. Without the active participation of the Courtenays neither of these things may have come to pass. They were also important in the ball clay industry, another major prop of the economy.

In Chapter 6 both the Courtenay's interest in rebuilding and re-fronting the *Globe* and in the coming of the railway is mentioned. Granted they stood to gain a great deal financially from the route, but many landowners of their day would have baulked at having the railway line visible in front of their house as the Courtenays had at Powderham. Certainly if they had not backed the scheme it would have been difficult, if not impossible, to have had a route which gave Newton a key focal point in the system.

In the nineteenth century the Courtenays were among the largest landowners in Devon with estates around Powderham, near Tavistock, in the South Hams and Wolborough. They owned even bigger estates in Ireland. In 1873 they possessed over 20,000 acres in Devon, a little less than 1,000 in Newton. In the 1870s the decline in agriculture, predicted since the repeal of the Corn Laws in 1846, began to take effect. Agricultural estates became less profitable and with this was a concomitant decline in economic power and status. Landowners looked for more profitable ways to invest money, and sold their estates if necessary. The Courtenays continued to embrace urban development in Teignmouth and particularly Newton, on which they had already started. At the same time they were running down their land-holdings in the South Hams and near Tavistock. Because this urban development was profitable to the Courtenays, the decline in their Wolborough estates was relatively slower than elsewhere. The last landholdings did not go until between 1940 and 1950.

It is important to note that they owned by far the greater part of Wolborough. Thus when they had decided to develop they could do it on a grand and cohesive scale that a series of small landowners could not have matched. Furthermore they expanded in a gracious style, employing more than competent architects and did not hesitate to provide roads, a reservoir and a church. Worth wrote that 'the growth of the new town between the old town and the railway station has been judiciously guided and liberally developed'. They also took a considerable paternal interest.

To remind us of the family's importance we still have Courtenay Gardens, together with Park, Road, and Street, Devon Square, and Powderham Close, Road and Terrace.[115]

Parish accounts make interesting reading. In 1648 there is an item for 10s to carry two offenders to prison; the carriers themselves had 2s 6d allowed for bread, beer and candle light. Thomas Tucker was paid 12s for beer and cider that was drunk at several parish meetings! There was beer too for labourers working on the roads.[117] At the time of the War of the Spanish Succession with France, 1703 – 1713, considerably more money was spent on bread and beer than on powder and bullets. As Bath put it, 'even in those days a soldier marched on his stomach!'[118]

Newton once had its own coinage. Starting in the reign of Charles I until after the Restoration, from 1648 to 1672, there arose throughout the country a shortage of small change. Private enterprise provided some, without government assent, until Charles II forbade its production. From Newton Abbot there are records of Wm. Furneaux's half-penny in 1668, in 1669 Elizabeth Maninge and John Maninge half-pennies and from Newton Bushel there is an undated Richard Reynell *The Mercer's Arms*, farthing, a quarter of an old penny.[119]

Two years after the accession of Charles II, in 1660, a hearth tax was introduced; this involved an annual payment of 2 shillings for every hearth. There were exemptions for the poor, but the tax was never very satisfactory and abolished in

James Langdon, was as were many of his time, a small holder involved in the textile trade. He had: 3 milch kyne and one Calve (3 cows and a calf), 17 sheepe & 9 lambes, 1 sowe, 3 hens & a Cocke, 1 harrowe, 1 shovell & 2 mattockes not to mention, One Iorney of barley (load of barley). His involvement in textiles is shown by: 1 spinning torne (spindle wheel) & seaves (weaver's reeds) 1 payre of lombes (looms) 2 quiltornes (wheels for winding yarn) warping pins & Wyle. Many of the other items are domestic for instance; 3 podgers (earthenware or pewter platters) 1 Iron Crocke (metal pot) 1 kittle & a skillet (covered pot and a long handled saucepan). Thinges unseene & forgotten, sounds a delightful phrase to us but was probably merely a legal safeguard![116] Exon is Exeter and relict means widow.

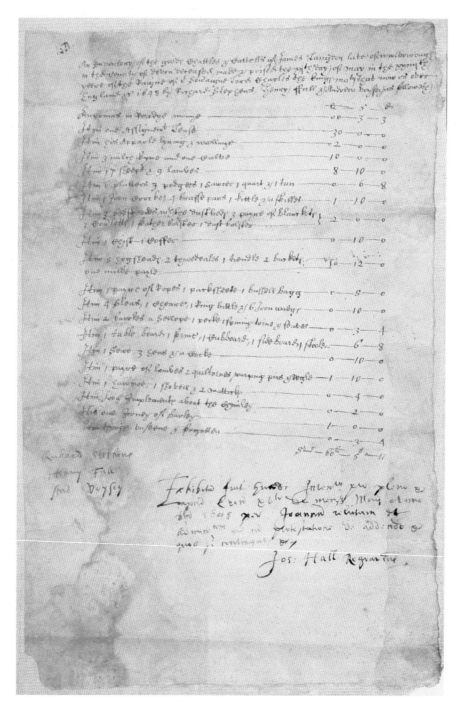

This is a copy of the will of James Langdon of Wolborough who died in 1648. It shows he was a smallholder and engaged in the textile trade.

Part of this old building was once a courthouse. Much later it delighted in the title of 'Ye Old Bunne Shop', and is now a house agent and Italian restaurant.

1689. The local lists for 1674 have Yarde Esq. in Highweek with 15 hearths and 'Sir Wm. Courtney' in 'Newton Abott' with 21, heading their respective lists. Highweek has 31 'Poor' and 'Newton Abott' (Wolborough) at least 21 'Paupers' but the list has been damaged and we cannot be certain if there were more.[120] One projection estimate that 23% of Highweek and possibly 19% of Wolborough were paupers is illuminating and points to a picture of relative prosperity at that period. We do not know the reasons but it could be involvement in the Newfoundland trade.

A series of Wolborough apprenticeship agreements survive for the years from 1673 to 1742. Not all had occupations stated but those that did were 12 yeomen (small farmers), 8 clothiers, 3 tailors, 2 each blacksmiths, cordwainers, mercers (textile sellers), weavers, and one each butcher, chandler (a seller of corn or maritime gear), cooper (barrel maker), currier (leather dresser), fishery in Newfoundland, glove maker, maltster, mariner, mason, woolcomber and inn holder. Information such as this is never exhaustive but gives us some idea of activities in Newton over those years.[121]

A survey of religion in 1676 shows every adult over 16, the number of conformists (Church of England), papist recusants (Roman Catholics), and protestant dissenters (nonconformists). The contemporary expression was 'the telling of noses'.[122] Unfortunately the figures are not comparable in those places which had chapels of ease, because of doubts whether the figures are the whole or only part, and this applied to both Highweek and Wolborough. However, we do get some insight into religious leanings.

Place	Conformists	Papists	Nonconformists
Wolborough	600	-	10
Highweek	296	-	-
Ashburton	200	-	3
Chudleigh	635	-	4
Coffinswell	17	2	5

It would be possible to argue that this local group varies little one from another, they are all staunchly Anglican; that is until you reach Coffinswell, which although small certainly bucks the trend.[123]

On the 5th of November 1688 William of Orange landed at Brixham and Newton was very much involved. William arrived at Newton on the 7th and was proclaimed King William III for the first time at the tower in Wolborough Street. It was market day so there would have been a crowd to listen and the bells were rung in his honour.[124] A stone at the tower commemorates this event but the inscription is erroneous on two counts. It has the wrong date, the 5th not the 7th, and the incorrect reader for the proclamation. There is still argument as to who made the proclamation, some

William of Orange, was well entertained at Forde House on his way from Brixham to London. His host, however, had urgent business else-where!

suggest the Rev. Whittle who was with William's army but it was almost certainly not the Rev. John Reynell. Some also argue that this was only a proclamation not a declaration of kingship. Be that as it may, there can have been few doubts amongst those who heard it that they were witnessing an attempted revolution.

William, with the upper echelons of his entourage and bodyguard, stayed at Forde House but Sir William Courtenay, having told his staff to entertain him, thought of urgent business that needed attention elsewhere on his estates! No doubt, he remembered a number of his ancestors had lost their heads in the past by being on the wrong side and did not want to risk making the same mistake himself. Part of William's army was quartered on Milber Down. One description of William's army was almost certainly based on a sighting at Exeter but there is not likely to have been much difference. Surely never before or since can there have been a sight in the locality to equal it.

William set out on his slow and circumspect journey to Exeter and then London. Thereby the opposition to him largely faded and the kingship he had first claimed in Newton Abbot became his in reality. Possibly the last words on the subject should be allowed to L. du Garde Peach who wrote in his *Unknown Devon* 'for one brief glorious hour Newton Abbot basked in the limelight of history; then it went back to work and forgot about it'.

In 1633 Richard Yarde, the lord of the manor of Highweek, living at Bradley Manor, amalgamated the market and fairs of Newton Bushel and Newton Abbot.

'In the van were the Earl of Macclesfield, and 200 horse artillery, accoutred and mounted of Flanders steeds, with head pieces and body armour, and attended by 200 negroes, wearing embroidered caps with white fur and plumes of feathers. Then followed 200 Finlanders in bear-skins, with black armour and broadswords; and after these were 50 gentlemen and as many pages to attend the Prince's banner, which was inscribed "God and the Protestant religion." Then came 50 led war horses, preceding the prince, who was mounted on a white charger, and wore complete armour, with a plume of white ostrich feathers in his helmet, and 42 running footmen by his side. He was attended by 200 gentlemen and pages who were mounted. These were followed in succession by 3,000 Swiss, 500 volunteers, 600 Guards, and the remaining part of the army numbering in all about 30,000.'[125]

Perhaps surprisingly he closed the Newton Bushel market to concentrate on that at Newton Abbot.[126] This may be because it was busier or he considered it a better site. It must have been a profitable speculation because later Sir William Waller attempted to obtain the market for himself but lost.[127] He was a good loser, in that he afterwards wrote 'yet proceeding from a covetous end [I] was justly punished by the loss of the thing sued for'.

Bridewells, are associated in some minds as prisons, but originally were to solve the problems of the unemployed and to separate those who were work-shy from those who were willing, but unable to work. By the 1630s these had been set up in a number of Devon towns, Newton Abbot amongst them. Private enterprise had a role because Thomas Reynell of Ogwell was awarded rent for the site.[128] Bridewells later did become more like prisons and towards the end of the eighteenth century tended to receive those who had lighter sentences, whereas the more severe sentences were served in gaol. It is uncertain when Newton's Bridewell closed, but it has been suggested it was in the early nineteenth century, when a new county Bridewell opened in Exeter[129]

CHAPTER 5

THE EIGHTEENTH CENTURY
1715–1799

In 1712 a John Fox lodged in the town and wrote 'Everything here suited my taste. The situation of the house and gardens surrounded by beautiful orchards, all of which I could command from my apartments, the charming retired walks, beautiful groves full of singing birds and soft streams and rivulets and the variety of rural prospects . . . though I had a horse of my own and was but three hours from Exeter I never rode there once.'[130] Yet another visitor in 1794 wrote 'It is a large but meanly-built town' however, the entry continues that it has a good market.[131] Five years later George Lipscomb passed through Newton Bushel and commented it was 'a miserable dirty, close inconvenient town, which deserves no further notice than that the streets are narrow, rough and ill built.'[132]

This period covers the reigns of the first two George's and over half that of George III. During this time the post of prime minister came into being, and there were the Jacobite rebellions of 1715 and 1745. A succession of wars occurred which added to our overseas possessions, but we lost the American colonies. John Wesley started on his religious revival, and the period ends with the first struggles against Napoleon Bonaparte.

Newton continued with its staple occupations as a market, manufacturing town and supplier to the Newfoundland trade. It was during this period that the extraction of ball clay began to make an impact on the local economy and towards the end of the period the Stover Canal was cut.

Individual Acts of Parliament set up a series of Turnpike Trusts to improve main roads. The first turnpike road in the Newton area was Totnes to Newton in 1759, then came Newton Bushel in 1761 and Newton to Dartmouth and Keyberry to Torquay both in 1765. This last was from Keyberry Bridge on the south side of Newton Abbot to Tor village; it did not go to the quay until 20 years later. The original route passed over Milber and through the hamlet of

Benjamin Donn's Map of 1765. This map shows Newton and its surroundings in 1765. Donn's projection is generally regarded as the first real road map of Devon. Torquay's lack of importance, at that time, can easily be gleaned.

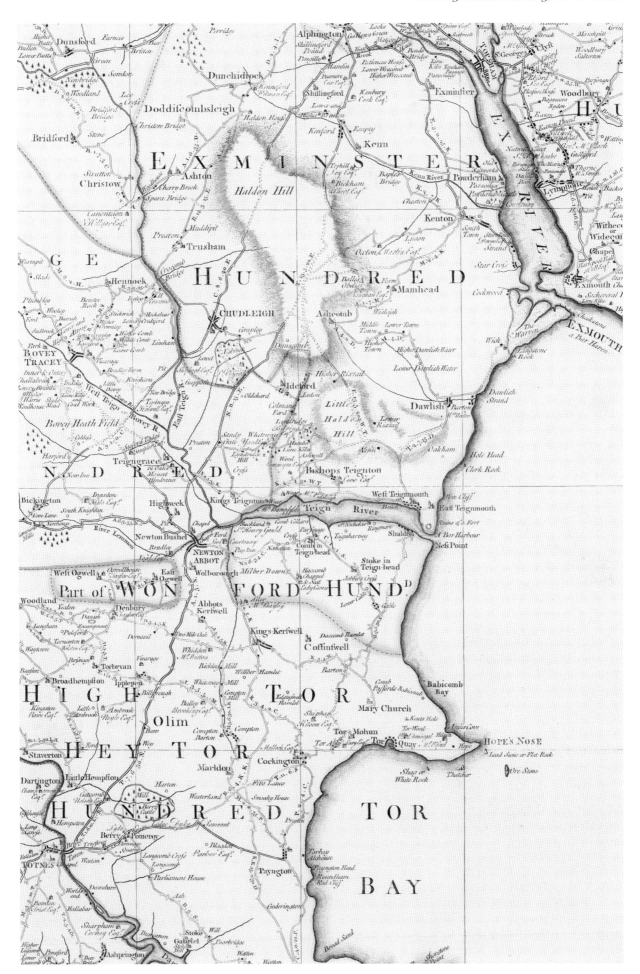

Barton.[133] There was sometimes opposition; Newton Bushel raised a petition against charging tolls on such 'a most incommodious road'.[134] Keepers employed by the trusts might collect tolls but often the collection was farmed out to individuals who purchased the operation for a specific period frequently a year. The outcome of these road improvements was a considerable increase in the speed of travel. For instance the time for a coach travelling from Exeter to London was more than halved. In the 1760s two full days travelling in 1831 was reduced to just 19½ hours.[135] Although at first trusts concentrated on existing roads they later brought new improved routes into being. As time passed a number of the smaller trusts also amalgamated to make bigger units; for instance the Newton and Dartmouth and the Keyberry and Torquay united to form the Dartmouth and Torquay Trust.[136] Despite the enormous improvements in road travel the turnpikes brought most did not long survive the coming of the railways. As Kanefsky put it, the coming of rail caused 'an immediate capture of all but very local passenger and goods traffic from the roads'.[137] A turnpike stone still stands in East Street opposite the Cider Bar, though these days one risks life and limb to get a closer look at it! Early toll-houses remain at Forches Cross, on the Bovey Road, built 1766, and Langford, sadly ruinous, built in 1763, between Decoy and Kingskerswell. The one at New Cross between Kingsteignton and Chudleigh, with its smart repainted tariff board, also still stands, but this is a replacement only going back to 1832![138]

Before the days of rail the carrier's cart was the ubiquitous means of conveying goods. Their starting date is uncertain but there are records from 1760 onwards. There were some long distance routes such as Exeter to London. With the coming of rail long distance routes disappeared, and the short distance tended to focus on railhead market towns such as Newton. Some of the carriers went on a very long time indeed, certainly until after the First World War.

John Lethbridge 1675–1759

Little is known about John Lethbridge's early life. In 1710 along with other Wolborough feoffees, the charitable trustees, he was responsible for improvements to St Mary's, the parish church. At the age of 39 he was living in Newton having been working in the wool trade. He had a large family and, as he himself said, was in reduced circumstances. Quoting his own words 'Necessity is the parent of invention . . . my thoughts turned upon some extraordinary method to retrieve my fortunes . . . it might be practicable to contrive a machine to recover wrecks lost in the sea'. He set to work experimenting in a water-filled trench in his own garden in a prototype barrel-like diving machine. His experiments having proved a success he had a working machine made in London. His problem at first was to find anyone to employ him but he made a breakthrough by obtaining work with another diver, Jacob Rowe. They salvaged together such a rich haul from a wreck off the Cape Verde that henceforth Lethbridge could afford to work on his own. Furthermore, the news spread of his accomplishment, and the Dutch East India Company offered him work on the *Slot Ter Hooge* which had sunk at Porto Santo, Madeira. He was again successful and this led to other work, at home off The Lizard and Plymouth, overseas in the West Indies and at The Cape of Good Hope. He dived on at least 16 wrecks. He certainly retrieved his fortunes and bought an estate at Kingskerswell, although there were at least five occasions when he nearly drowned. He must have been a tough character, still looking for diving work although unsuccessfully at 81 years of age! He was buried in Wolborough churchyard.[142]

Their usual method of operation was to use a particular inn as their starting and finishing point. They would carry passengers of moderate means, as well as goods. In 1760 there were from Exeter four services a week to Totnes via Newton and another four to Dartmouth via Newton.[139] In 1838 Newton services listed included to Ashburton, Chudleigh, Modbury, Moretonhampstead, Paignton, Torquay and Totnes.[140] They would have called at other places en route. A detailed list of 1878 was as follows: Ashburton *Queen's Hotel* daily, Broadhempston *Turk's Head* Sat., Chagford *White Hart* Friday, Christow *Magor's Hotel* Wed., Chudleigh *Bradley Hotel* Wed., Ideford *Bradley Hotel* Wed., Ipplepen *Turk's Head* Wed. & Sat., Torquay *Bradley Hotel* Wed.[141]

Thanks to research of Sun Fire Office inventories, we now know more of serge manufacture in Newton. Serge was a cheap but hard-wearing cloth. The earliest entry is from 1722 of a John Chapple, Wolborough sergemaker, who was insured for £500.[143] Between 1738 and 1766 there were some ten serge makers and two clothiers in the Newton area. The total may be less because some businesses could have been recorded twice for instance if a son had taken over from is father. Often cover was given for stock held at Exeter in the sergemarket or elsewhere. Some of the sergemakers were also shopkeepers. Names such as Pinsent and Rundle recur later in Newton's retail history.[144] For comparison purposes it is interesting to note figures for the trade in other local places: Ashburton 11, Bovey Tracey 2, Chudleigh 4, Totnes 8, but these were all small fry compared to real centres of industry such as Crediton, Cullompton or Tiverton. Daniel Defoe in his *A Tour Through Great Britain By a Gentleman* writing about 1724, mentions Newton Bushel in relation to the woollen trade as a source of serges.[145] Another manufacturing trade which started in Newton later in this period was the manufacture of paper. There is evidence of a Bradley Paper Mill that was active from 1790 to 1848.[146]

Ball clay is china clay that has moved over geological time and become mixed with organic vegetable matter. This gives it certain properties such as plasticity which are absent from china clay. It is called 'ball' clay because it was often cut out in square shape blocks that became rounded in transhipment. In early days it was sometimes called pipe-clay and later potter's clay. The origins of the trade are obscure. It seems likely that such a versatile material must have had its uses from very early times. A clay pipe waste dump was found near Chudleigh dating from 1690–1710.[147] The very first record of a shipment of clay from the area is 1691 when a small consignment was sent to Plymouth.[148] More sizeable cargoes commence from the 1730s; by 1740, 385 tons were shipped in a year and by 1784 it had risen to a considerable 9,428 tons.[149] Most of this clay went to the Mersey to be carried on to the Potteries. By 1777 Sir Josiah Wedgwood, the foremost and most go-ahead potter of his time, used South Devon ball clay from our area. This is known from a letter Wedgwood wrote to his partner Thomas Bentley in London. Perhaps disappointingly he refers to it as "Teignmouth clay".[150] Later in 1791, Wedgwood visited the South West to purchase clay for a group of Stoke-on-Trent potters.[151] The clay was sent down the River Teign to Teignmouth, but despite the fact the previous land journey was short, it was difficult even for pack-horses in a wet and boggy area subject to flooding. Towards the end of the century the problems were largely solved by the Stover Canal.

As with some other happenings in Newton's history there are doubts as to when the Vicarys first came to Newton ranging from 1747 to 1786.[152] What is

Vicary Family

The Vicary family was not only concerned with Newton's history for many years but they also became, at one time, quite the most important family that lived in Newton. They started in the town in business in quite a small way, but prospered over centuries and expanded their interests. They were fell-mongers, wool-combers and tanners. Until the railway complex really grew they were the largest employers in the town, employing over 700 people at one stage. They had the biggest tannery in the West Country, beyond Bristol.

As their business grew their interests spread into other matters that impinged on their affairs. They were prominent in matters of the navigation of the Teign, took an interest in building, promotion of the railway and setting up the gasworks. Several family members were involved with local judicial and administrative affairs. One of them, Mr William Vicary was chosen in 1901 to be the first chairman of the combined Council for Newtons, Abbot and Bushel. They were to the forefront in local charitable matters, they helped set up the local coffee tavern, they assisted in funding the voluntary hospital and hosted, at their home Dyrons, for many years, the annual hospital fete.

The Vicarys may have been in Denbury for a while before owning a business in Newton Bushel, probably in 1747. There seems no reason to disbelieve the family legend; this was that the first to reside here was young Moses Vicary who arrived riding on the back of his mother Elizabeth's horse. When Moses grew up he took over the business and so it passed down the generations to Charles Lane Vicary who was the last of the family to own the business before it was sold to Sanderson, Murray and Elder Ltd. of Bradford in 1939. Mr Charles Lane Vicary died in 1953 aged 69.

Although the wool side of the business was generally the bigger and the longest running, it was the tannery for which Vicary's was better known. They had, what was known as 'heavy' tanning which were principally cowhides at the Highweek Street end of Bradley Lane. This closed about 1929-1930. They also had a leather making up department; this was particularly busy at the time of the First World War making such items as Sam Browne belts, which were worn by army officers. After the war the department was closed and some of the staff became part of the nucleus of the future Devon Leathercrafts.

'Light' tanning of smaller pelts, such as sheepskins, was carried out further away from the town and this continued until after the Second World War. They claimed to be the first firm in England to have tanned ostrich hide with its distinctive large grain pattern. At one period cargoes of pelts of sheep and goats would be landed at Torquay Harbour to be conveyed by steam wagons to the tannery at Newton.

The last part of the business was wool combing including some work latterly on synthetic fibres. This went on until the early 1970s when that too closed down.[153]

certain is that for over two centuries, involved in wool and leather, they were one of the town's largest employers.

For many years in the eighteenth century it was compulsory for tradesmen and others to take parish apprentices. Often, they were welcomed as a cheap source of labour. There is a record of a certain Andrew Bennett who visited Newton in December 1780 to show reason why he should not take a parish apprentice. 'I being not 21 years of age it was agreed I could not make assignment' He then says a little about the visit and gives us one of the earliest descriptions we have of a Newton shop. 'We dined at the *Sun*, one Mumford the innkeeper . . . I bought a common prayer book at Weatherdon who keeps a stationer's shop and sells perspective glasses, and quadrants and maps and Japan inks, pocket books &. &.'[154] It is interesting that in 1785 a list of the forty-four 'most powerful traders in Newfoundland' there were twenty two in Devon including one in Newton Abbot. Dartmouth was well on top in the county, at this date, with fifteen, Topsham had five and the other one was from Teignmouth.[155]

Newton had its watch and clock makers. One of these, James Pike, who worked in the town from 1775 to 1784, was obviously well regarded since he made the turret clock for Powderham Castle.[156] The *Flying Post* started in 1763[157] and in a few years we have records of Newton. An early advertisement appeared in 1773 of John Bussecott, shoemaker of Newton Abbot, for 5 journeymen (qualified workmen who were not masters), and an apprentice. Shoe-making had long prospered in Newton by making sea-boots for Newfoundland.[158]

The earliest extant Newton publications come from this period. Probably the very first is an advertising bill from 1785, for William Baker a 'grocer, mercer, linen and woollen draper, haberdasher, and ironmonger' who claimed that he 'sells at the lowest prices, wholesale and retail'. The next is a poster for 1789 and records a performance of *Hamlet* by the young gentlemen of Weatherdon's School 'by way of amusement, as well as for their improvement in speaking'. Another Newton imprint for 1792 was the Association for the Maintenance and Support of the British Constitution which recorded 'the numerous and respectable meeting of gentlemen, clergy, merchants and freeholders'.[159] The earliest surviving poster for 'Newton Races' dates from this time. It was for the Hunter's Sweepstakes on Milber Down on Monday July 12th 1790 including the 'Gentleman's subscription cup' but this one was printed in Exeter.[160]

Robert Hull extensively remodelled Forde House gardens in 1753/4 and was paid over £300 for his work there. The head gardener at the time was John Lamperry who had three men and a woman working under him.[161] In 1740 the Courtenays moved from Forde House to Powderham.[162] Henceforward the house was let to relatives and a series of tenants until finally sold in 1936. Fortunately for Newton the Courtenays' interest in the town continued.

After nearly 200 years the Yardes, in 1751, sold their manor of Bradley to Thomas Veale.[163] He pulled down the north and west wings which were probably in a bad state of repair. Later the manor passed to the Rev. Richard Lane who is important to Newton's history as the man responsible for moving the market. Because he was the incumbent of Brixton, he never lived in Newton, only visiting it on occasions. Probably because of over lavish spending, Lane sold the house in 1841 to the Rev. Frederick Wall who built Bradley Wood House, which was subsequently destroyed by fire.

Jeremiah Milles, a Precentor of Exeter Cathedral and later Dean, set out in 1762 to collect information about all the parishes in Devon with the intention of writing a county history. Not all responded to his questionnaire. Highweek did reply, so providing contemporary information. Milles questionnaire recorded there were at that time three principle settlement areas in the parish. The largest was Newton Bushel with about 60 houses, Highweek Village was much smaller with 16 houses and the third settlement was Howton, near the site of Seale Hayne, with about 13. There were on average 19 baptisms and the same number of burials a year. The nearest market town was, not surprisingly, Newton Abbot one mile away. Almshouses included Gilberd's, a little way out of town on the Exeter Road. Trees were mostly oak in coppice and elsewhere elms. There is also confirmation once again of woollen manufacture.[164] This trade first heard of two and half centuries before continued for nearly the same time in the future.

In 1765 James Templer senior bought an estate of some 80,000 acres

Stover Canal. The canal at Newton Abbot constructed by the Templers at the end of the eighteenth century, its use spanned some 150 years.

stretching from around Teigngrace up to Haytor Rocks. Some believe he planned the canal. What is more certain is that his son, another James Templer, carried out the project, starting in 1790 and completing it up to Ventiford in 1792. The entrance to the canal was from Whitelake a tidal inlet from the Teign at Jetty Marsh. Whitelake had to be deepened and a basin was built at Jetty Marsh to hold the barges to wait for the incoming tide. The original plan was more ambitious, it should have continued to Bovey Tracey with a branch to Chudleigh.[165] Be that as it may, it was a commercial success and brought prosperity to the area and was used for over a century and a half. Later, for a while, it connected the Haytor Granite Tramway.

In 1788 Hannah Bearne gave money to teach writing and arithmetic to poor children. Thus was founded Bearne's School, the town's oldest extant

Bridge over the Stover Canal another place that looks so quiet now but was so busy once.

Templer Family

Three members of this family were important to Newton Abbot. It was not quite a case of clogs to clogs in three generations but their story does bear some similarities to the adage.

James Templer, was born into a tradesman's family in Exeter. He was orphaned and attended the Blue Coat School. He was apprenticed to an architect and left before he had fully served his time. He went to India where he laid the foundations of a fortune that he enhanced on his return by design projects in London and Plymouth. He bought the big Stover estate and, abandoning the ruinous old Stowford Lodge, built the grand new Stover House, now Stover School. He probably designed it himself. He also laid out the grounds constructing ornamental canals and a lake, now Stover Countryside Park. He paid his former apprentice master the sum of £500. Some suggest this was conscience money because he had run away, others more mundanely see it as a fee for contracts obtained on his return to England. He died in 1782.

His son James Templer, junior, was a lawyer who worked, and indeed came to hold, important judicial appointments in London and he was responsible for constructing the Stover Canal. This was to be economically important for many years because it enabled ball clay to be extracted in bulk reasonably cheaply. He also rebuilt as a memorial to his father, the interesting church of St Peter and St Paul at Teigngrace.

James Templer's son, George Templer, the third generation, constructed both the Haytor Granite Tramway and the New Quay at Teignmouth; he improved the navigation of the Teign. He was also a great sportsman, being a friend of the Rev Jack Russell, whose name lives on with a breed of terriers. Too much hunting, cricket and other leisure pursuits and probably not enough attention to business meant that he had to sell his commercial interests and his Stover estate.

George Templer's death was announced in the *Flying Post*, at his seat Sandford Orleigh in 1844. It added he was formerly of Stover and had been; ' a magistrate of the county and a gentleman of the right character and ancient family'. He was in fact killed in a hunting accident which says something for his enthusiasm for the sport, as he was then 60 years old. [166]

Whitelake. Originally a natural drainage channel, deepened to form the entry to the Stover Canal. The holding basin where barges awaited high tide was a little way up on the right. Up until the 1950s sand-barges unloaded at what is now B & Q's car park, the last water-borne goods traffic to arrive in Newton.

school. Unusually for those days there was no religious preference expressed. The school originally was at the junction of Back and Wolborough Streets. It moved in 1843 to another site in Wolborough Street and then to its present position in Queen Street in1859.[167]

Evidence of bull baiting in Newton was provided by the record of a spiked dog collar inscribed 'Robt. Alsop, Newton 1788'. The bullring was said to have been on the west side of St Leonard's Tower, between there and the old market buildings.[168]

Inns were once used for an incredible range of activities. They accommodated travelling surgeons, and held auctions.[169] They were used for inquests election and political meetings, recruitment, and conduct of business. London newspapers were received and discussed.[170] In addition they served a social purpose as a meeting place for clubs and venues for balls and dances. Newton magistrates presided at the *Globe* for years.[171] In 1779 a Captain Cause was recruiting men, at the *London Inn*, to serve on privateers at the time of the American War of Independence.[172]

In 1791 two brigs, square-rigged, two-masted vessels, *New Providence* and *Friendship* lying at 'Torkay Pier' were on offer at the *White Hart*, the ships advertised as 'Well calculated for the Newfoundland Trade in which they have always been employed'.[173] Note Newton Abbot as the nearest urban venue is chosen for the sale; Torquay's rise is yet to come. This sale was a low point in Newfoundland fishery before the last fillip during the Napoleonic Wars. In 1794, at the *Sun Inn*, the Keyberry Bridge and Torkey (sic) Turnpike Gate tolls for a year were on offer.[174]

In 1795 the Reverend John Swete, the chronicler of the Picturesque in Devon, walked to Newton Bushel, his journey enlivened 'by the parties of Belles and Beaus sauntering at their leisure towards the Downs of Milbourne (Milber) whence in honour of the day the Volunteers of the Town were about to be exercised'. It was Oak Apple Day, 29th May, so all the soldiers had sprigs of oak and Swete thought of 'Birnam Wood moving to Dunsinane'.[175] The next year he pondered why some churches were placed so inconveniently on high hills

Bellamarsh Mill in 1968 prior to demolition. This was the scene of the riot in 1795 that led to Thomas Campion's public execution.

at a distance from their town or village and cites Wolborough church.[176] In the same year, on a journey partly made with his wife and two children, Swete crossed Mr Templer's canal then under construction.[177] Swete's journals have another connection with Newton Abbot. They were kept by his descendants and were in a house at Mount Pleasant when it was bombed in 1942. Martyn Swete, the then owner, and his wife were buried alive for ten hours but then happily rescued. Most journals also survived the ordeal.[178] Sadly one of the volumes that contained information about Newton was lost.

In 1795 low wages and high food prices caused by Napoleon's Continental blockade and a succession of poor harvests brought discontent. In Newton Abbot the justices called in the Cornish Militia Light Infantry.[179] There were riots in other places. Near Chudleigh, led by an Ilsington blacksmith Thomas Campion, rioters wrecked the Bellamarsh Mill owned by James Templer. Escorted by a large military guard, the blacksmith was subsequently publicly executed.[180] The *Flying Post* reported – 'Thursday morning Thomas Campion, for rioting and destroying the mills at Bellamarsh, was taken in a mourning coach, to Bovey Heath, where he was executed according to his sentence'.[181]

CHAPTER 6

THE NINETEENTH CENTURY 1800–1849

In 1800 the Rev. Richard Warner wrote 'another ordeal awaited me in Newton Bushel, a large well-peopled town, whose every face that I encountered exhibited a grin, it was therefore no matter of no small joy to me to be fairly out of the place and on the road to Totnes'.[182] In 1819 a traveller's guide was far from complimentary: 'The houses are poorly built, and the streets badly

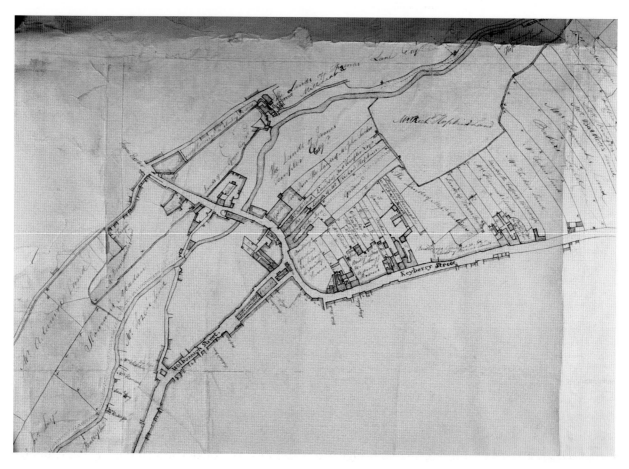

A Newton view in 1828 looking down on the town, barges with square sails on the River Teign in the background.

paved. The principal one is obstructed by an old market-house and shambles'.[183] About 40 years later Doctor Granville, the spa historian, passed through and wrote 'Long ranges of houses of considerable size were rapidly rising and the place exhibited a sprinkling of fine people'. *Robinson's Directory* about the same time stated 'the vicinity affords some of the most beautiful prospects than can perhaps be found in the whole kingdom'. It also tells of Newton's first water-borne tourists 'parties of pleasure from Teignmouth avail themselves of the gratification offered, by an aquatic excursion to Forde House'.[184]

This is a map of Newton probably close to the start of the 19th century. Just three roads meet in the centre at the market cross. Old St. Leonard's has yet to be demolished, the market is still held in Wolborough Street the shambles standing in the middle of the road. The name Keyberry Road tells us that Keyberry is, as yet, more important than Torquay. Lastly it shows you why Exeter Road is where it is, and not where you would expect it!

For the first 15 years of the century the Napoleonic Wars were the main focus of attention. They were followed by a period of hardship and discontent; Peterloo followed Waterloo. Eventually prosperity and stability were restored, the high points being the Reform Bill of 1832 and the Repeal of the Corn Laws in 1846. Other innovations were the abolition of the slave trade, macadamized roads, policemen, railways and cheap postage. Victoria became Queen in 1837 and her long reign was to give her name to an era.

Devon, generally, was no longer a manufacturing county; its tourist hey-day was yet to come, agriculture was its mainstay. Big changes took place in Newton, it became a 'Union Town', with an area workhouse and at the end of the period the railway arrived. Newton had its last fillip of the Newfoundland trade which had been important for centuries. Yet despite this loss it was to do much better than most of its near rivals. In the first 40 years it grew by 63%, Chudleigh achieved 35%, Bovey Tracey 27%, Ashburton 25% and Totnes 22%. There is a mistaken belief that modern Newton started with the railway's arrival. It was already on its way!

Tenders were invited in 1814 from any person desirous of building a bridge over the Teign near Newton Bushel. Plans and specifications were available at, and tenders were to be submitted to, the *Globe*. The bridge was built the following year to a design by the county surveyor James Green and erected by Gregory Weatherdon, a builder from Newton Bushel.[185] A few years later he also built the Dog Marsh Bridge near Chagford. The small Union footbridge was built by public subscription in 1822, on the site of a previous ford.[186] It is suggested the name may be because it served to join the two townships, it sounds logical, but it is not known if this is true. In 1827 the Duchess of Clarence, later Queen Adelaide, opened the splendid new Teignmouth and Shaldon Bridge. This first bridge was only to last 11 years, it collapsed in 1838.[187] The wooden piers of the first structure were weakened by marine creatures, Toredo Navalis (ship-worm), the piers had to be replaced by stone and the bridge reopened two years later. Newton was therefore no longer a strategically placed bridge town but the road pattern was so well established that the town suffered no loss of trade.

In 1815 the newspaper *Flinder's Western Luminary* produced a list of customers.[188] The list included Mr Clement Banfill, spirit merchant, F. M. Bartlett Esq. attorney, Mr J. Beazley, *Globe* Inn innkeeper, Mr Thomas Cowell, *Bear* innkeeper, Dr Curtis, John M. Gill, ironmonger, Hatherley Esq., Fishwick House, R. T. Langworthy Esq. lawyer, Lady Lois Cadwell, dowager, Mr Martin *Globe Inn*, innkeeper, Mr Joseph Murch *Golden Lion* innkeeper, Mr James Passmore, saddler, Mr J. Potter, Lewis Protheroe, Esq., Mr J. Thorne, *Turks Head* innkeeper, and Mr William, innkeeper.[189] Newton had a higher percentage readership than Exeter.

Although it never came to fruition there was a proposal in 1827 to make a half-mile canal from the area of the Town Quay into the centre of Newton Abbot. James Green, who was responsible for both the Bude and Grand Western Canals, drew up the plan.[190] Later Lord Clifford, who brought his clay by land,

This abortive scheme of 1827, for a canal to the centre of the town, never came to fruition although James Green, who was responsible for both the Bude and Grand Western Canals, designed it. It does show though, that Newton was a forward thinking place long before the railway arrived in 1846.

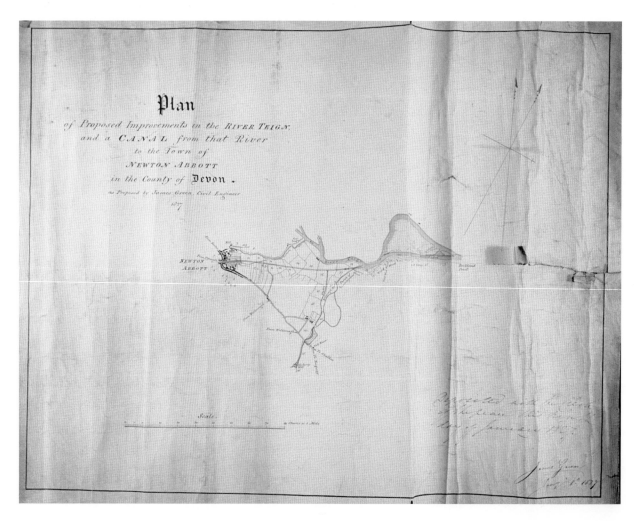

The Hackney Canal was opened in 1843 to enable the Cliffords to compete with the Temple's Stover Canal. The settlement at Hackney grew to provide homes for the bargees working down and back to Teignmouth. The road viaduct opened in 1976 vastly over budget and late.

was not able to compete with the clay coming down the Stover Canal. He therefore constructed his own Hackney Canal from Kingsteignton; it was opened in 1843 and closed in 1930.[191] A vestige of the old canal and the ruins of some of the bargees' cottages can still be seen close to the *Passage* (ferry) *House Inn.*

In 1836 the Totnes Turnpike Trust Act was passed, to improve access to the town of Newton Abbot from Exeter, and this led to the creation of the first direct road from Kingsteignton to Newton.[192] Until then communication between the two places was by a circuitous route across Teignbridge. Not only was a new road required from Kingsteignton but a new way into Newton itself. To accomplish this, various properties were disturbed including two coach houses and three piggeries. The new way, completed by 1842, was called Courtenay Street.[193] One supporter of the scheme was the banker Mr Wise who was shortly to come to grief. This new Courtenay Street, together with the later Station Road (Queen Street) completely changed the configuration of the town. The centre, many now considered, was the junction of Courtenay and Queen Streets, Drum clock, not the St Leonard's Clock Tower. The town had changed its axis and left more modern Newtonians to wonder why Exeter Road did not seem to go in that direction at all!

In February 1838 the *Flying Post* reported 'the populous town of Newton was for the first time lit with gas'.[194] A few years later the *Western Times* offered

Group photographed, early 20th century, outside the Passage House Inn, *at Hackney, the one time bargees' village. The girl's wear pinafores and two of the men are smoking clay pipes.*

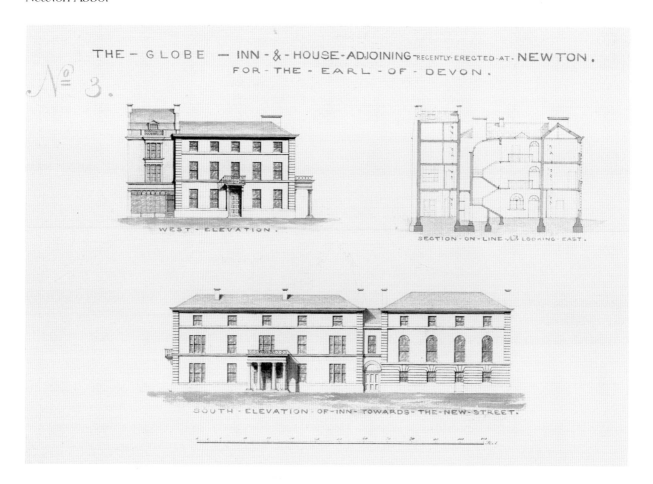

THE - GLOBE - INN - & - HOUSE - ADJOINING RECENTLY ERECTED AT NEWTON.
FOR - THE - EARL - OF - DEVON.

WEST - ELEVATION.

SECTION - ON - LINE LOOKING - EAST.

SOUTH - ELEVATION - OF - INN - TOWARDS - THE - NEW - STREET.

'This town is every night in a most disgraceful state of darkness in consequence of the parish of Wolborough refusing to pay for lighting the streets. Such illiberal conduct is anything but creditable to the parishioners, and may be productive of very serious consequences where so many vehicles are passing and re-passing during the night. Affairs are differently managed in Highweek parish, Newton Bushel being well lighted and affording a strong contrast to its neighbour'.[195] Yet the following month, the paper stated of Wolborough 'The streets once more present their usual appearance at night'. It still was not, at first, at public expense.

Early in the century Mrs Eliz. Cane, who had kept the *Dartmouth* for many years, offered it for sale 'a kitchen and parlour, with 5 lodging rooms and 4 garrets over also a back kitchen, brew-house, and 2 cellars with a good curtilage (surrounding area which was part of the property), and stable and a walled garden and an orchard behind.[196] Thomas Palk, who had kept the *Globe* for 15 years, advertised he 'respectfully begs to inform the Nobility, Gentlemen, Travellers and the Public in general that he has lately made large additions to his house'. He continued that the only coach from Exeter to Plymouth called at his house 'up Tuesday, Thursdays, and Saturdays; down Wednesdays, Fridays and Saturdays'. He offered 'neat post chaises and able horses' with stabling at the house for upwards of forty.[197] Later in 1842 the Earl of Devon instructed his architect Charles Fowler to draw plans to improve the *Globe* which was stated to be 'very inferior and imperfect'. It was intended the rebuilding should match the great improvements effected in that part of the town. Moreover, the front switched from Bridge (Bank) Street to the new Courtenay Street. In May 1843 Mr Beazley, the tenant, moved in but the changes were not completed until

Fowler's plans for rebuilding the Globe, *1841/5, the front was moved from Bridge (Bank) Street to the new Courtenay Street.*

(opposite) These three maps show how rapidly the centre of Newton changed its axis in the mid-nineteenth century. The old road from Exeter came down through Newton Bushel; there was then no direct route to Kingsteignton. There was no need for Queen Street which only became into being as access to the Station. The market cross by old St Leonard's (Clock Tower) was the traditional centre, many would now consider it to be the Drum Clock.

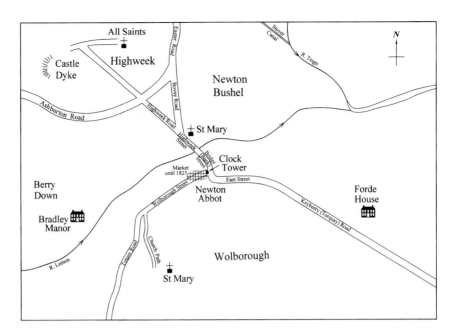

Newton before 1842 pre Courtenay Street.

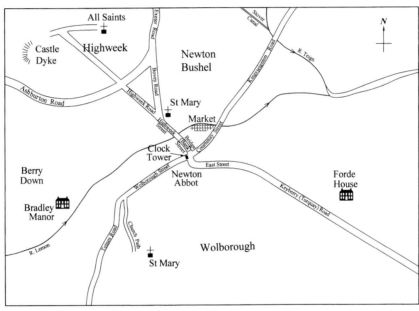

Newton between 1842 and 1846 pre railway.

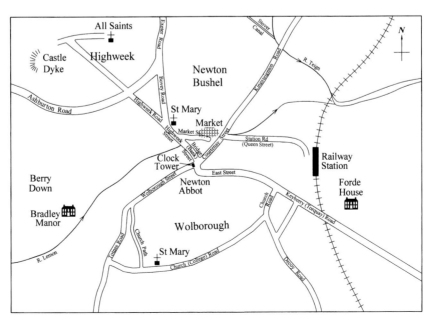

Newton after 1846 post railway.

the next year. It was proudly stated gas fittings were introduced. There seems to have been 21 bedrooms, 4 stables containing 28 stalls, 3 stables without stalls to contain 23 horses. There were 3 coach houses for 12 carriages and there was also a new piggery, poultry yard and dung pit. The number of stables is a useful reminder of the importance of horse-power. One might have thought that Mr Beazley would have had his hands full running such an establishment but he also rented a field in Highweek that grew potatoes![198]

Times were hard and dangerous, two Chudleigh farmers, Joseph Yeo and William Tuckett, returning from the South Hams loaded with corn, were violently robbed on entering Newton. [199] Stones were thrown and Tuckett was knocked off his horse. Yet despite the hardships, Newton was soon advertised as a prosperous place. In 1807 the father of Richard Beard claimed 'Newton Abbot is one of the largest and best market-towns in the West of England, and its trade has wonderfully increased within these few years (when trade in most other towns has been on the decline) on account of its plentiful and well supplied market, which not only draws a great number of people together from the country and neighbouring towns but from a great distance. There are two boarding schools for young gentlemen; and two coaches pass through the said town every day between Exeter and Plymouth'.[200] The other advertisement for letting a druggist shop in 1807 said 'Newton is considered one of the best market towns in the west of England, being situated within a short distance of upwards of twenty villages and two watering places'.[201]

In 1813 James Templer, junior died in Kent. Seven years later his son George, hosted a grand celebration at Haytor to open the tramway that connected the Stover Canal at Ventiford. The *Flying Post* reported 'A long string of carriages filled with elegant and beautiful females, multitudes of horsemen, workmen on foot, the wagons all covered with laurels and waving streamers'. Sadly despite original thought and good engineering the project was only commercially successful for about twenty years. The multi-transhipments tramway, canal and

Richard Beard, 1802/3–1885

Richard Beard's father, also Richard Beard, was a grocer in Newton Abbot. Just to confuse matters, Richard the younger was also to call his son, Richard!

From an advertisement in the *Flying Post* in 1807 it seems the father disposed of his original grocery business, or at least he attempted to do so. Furthermore there are reports of the son working as a coal merchant. Whether this was in collaboration with his father or on his own seems unclear. He lived most of his early life in Newton and moved to London in 1837.

He was soon interested in photography and in 1841 acquired the rights to Daguerre's photographic process. He then issued sub-licences to others to use the process. For instance a man called William Gill obtained the rights for Exeter and showed his daguerreotypes in Sidmouth, Torquay, Totnes and Newton Abbot. In Newton they were displayed by a Mrs Walkes, who was probably an auctioneer and the Registrar of Births and Deaths. Meanwhile in London, Richard set up the first professional portrait studio in England, in Regent Street. *The Times* called it a 'magical process'. Beard himself was more businessman rather than photographer; he employed others for this work. He was at first vastly successful but the business later suffered from disputes over unauthorised plagiarism. He was, though, able to hand the business on to his son Richard Beard III, but as more improved processes became available daguerreotype became outdated.[202]

ship were easily undercut by direct loading onto ships by seaside quarries as at Lamorna in Cornwall. However, for the period it was working barges, some with clay and others with granite, would have been a common sight. It is often regarded as an innovative idea but there was an earlier tramway in Devon that could have inspired it. This was the tramway in use in 1812 at the Oreston Quarries conveying stone for the Plymouth Breakwater.[203] In 1829 George Templer sold his house and estate to Edward Seymour 11th Duke of Somerset. Later he moved nearer to Newton and 'downsized' to Sandford Orleigh. Harris thought 'expenses of his generous and hospitable life-style overtook his fortunes'.[204] This was the beginning of the Duke of Somerset's interests in the locality.

In 1841 the Aller Ochre and Clay Works was for sale. The stock in trade included 2,600 pantiles (roofing tiles), 200 feet of water pipes, 500 bricks, 300 common delph jars (glazed earthenware), numerous casks of ochre and a kerry.[205] Ochre, which can vary in colour, consists of fine clay and iron oxide and is often used in paint manufacture.

In July of the same year the old established bank of Messrs. Wise, Farwell, Baker and Bentall of Newton Abbot stopped payment and it was said the liabilities were heavy.[206] The Newton bank owed money to the Totnes bank for cash advanced but lost on the Newfoundland trade. Later in the same year at Forde House was the sale of the effects of Mr Aylesford Wise, banker, including 'valuable and splendid furniture . . . two family carriages . . .minerals and fossils'.[207] He had obviously lived well and been a man of wide interests, but it all had to go. The bank had issued £5 notes so there were Newton 'fivers'. A second Newton Bank issued them too; this one was absorbed by Capital & Counties Bank in 1891 and became part of Lloyds in 1918.[208]

Robert Goodenough of Newton Abbot, a woollen draper, appeared before the Court of Bankruptcy in Exeter in 1843. He had tried to abscond and was found on a ship in Plymouth Sound called the *Parkfield* that was due to sail the following day for Port Philip (Melbourne area) in Australia. A quantity of property was found on board.[209]

Forde House, c.1832, then the elegant residence of the banker Ayshford Wise who went bankrupt nine years later.

In 1826 Sir Henry Carew chaired a meeting of landowners and farmers at the *Globe* to petition against a repeal of the Corn Laws.[210] Ploughs had once been exclusively pulled by oxen but over the centuries they had progressively been replaced by horses. However, oxen were still in use in the locality in 1840 proved by a ploughing match at Teigngrace where there were three entries. The winner came from Marldon and the second from Bovey Tracey. There was a dinner afterwards at the Assembly Rooms of the *Globe* when some 250 sat down.[211] Next year the annual ploughing match was held at Dornafield Farm near Ipplepen and it was reported that at least 4,000 people attended.[212]

Town administration & development

In 1825 the Rev. Richard Lane possibly realizing the inadequacy of its location for its expanding trade, decided to move the market to what was then a meadow adjoining the town,[213] approximating to the site of the present Butter Market. Alternatively it is suggested that the spur to move the market was compensation from the Totnes Turnpike Trust. As Richard Lane was an absentee landlord, this could be nearer the truth.[214] The *Flying Post* reported 'The shambles in the centre of the High Street are to be pulled down they have long been a great nuisance to the carriages passing through'. Shambles were butcher's shops where animals would have been slaughtered right in the middle of Wolborough Street! The new market was completed the next year in 1826 and was the first of several important changes in the half century.

According to Dell the Wolborough Borough police force was established in 1836, at the same time as several other Devon towns.[215] Yet by 1844 the *Flying Post* was complaining that there were few places, the size and wealth of Newton Abbot in which better security was not provided. Had the Wolborough force lapsed? The *Flying Post* reported Newton was subject to an influx ' of a large number of tramps and thieves of the lowest order and most lawless habits'. 'Yet there is neither policemen, nor watchmen maintained.' It goes on to suggest that if this was not remedied by the time the navigators, i.e. railway constructors, came to the neighbourhood it might prove a costly mistake [216]

In 1841 the Newton Abbot and Newton Bushell Building Company was formed. A notice to this effect is held in Newton Museum. This is significant because it is the first evidence of the development of higher class housing in Newton. The promoters called it 'genteel'. Furthermore not only was it some years before the railway arrived but before it was established that the projected route would go through Newton! The Duke of Somerset was involved with this promotion but the Courtenay's would follow only a few years later on a bigger scale.[217]

Later in time the replacement of Wolborough Vestry by the new Local Board was seen as a great step forward. At this earlier period opinion was against it. A Wolborough Vestry resolution from 1844 stated. 'This meeting considers that the Local Board if established would excite discord, contention & strife and be likely to put at variance the quiet and peaceable inhabitants of the town who have so many years enjoyed harmony concord and peace.'[218] Vestry in this sense was a meeting of parishioners to conduct parish business.

The Seymours, Dukes of Somerset developments on Knowles Hill predate the Courtenays opposite on Wolborough Hill. This grand Somerset Lodge was built for a lady who was a particular friend of one duke!

In September 1847 a meeting of overseers and other townsmen of Wolborough was held to consider building a town hall which would fill a long felt need, The Secretary of State was asked for permission to use the proceeds from the sale of the old parish workhouse.[219] The hall was completed in 1848 and to celebrate a dinner provided by Mr Bradley of the *Globe Hotel* was held, some 90 gentlemen sat down.[220] *Woolmer's Gazette* reported more fully; 'The New Town Hall, this elegant structure, . . . The ground floor contains apartments for the convenience of attorneys, the use of the Reading Club, and the Depot of the Society for Promoting Christian Knowledge. The basement contains the station house. Behind is a lock-up. On the first floor is a spacious and elegant apartment for public business. It will be used by the learned Judge of the District County Court.'[221] Later the premises were increased by incorporating the Wesleyan Chapel next door. The chapel was later replaced by one on the other side of Courtenay Street but this too was in due course demolished to make room for shops.[222]

Workhouse

In 1821 the following advertisement appeared in the *Flying Post* – 'Wanted as Governor for the Workhouse in Newton Abbot a married man without Children. Person capable of keeping a Debtor and Creditor Account and of sober and industrious habits, who can produce good testimonials of character with approved sureties'.[223] This was in the days before Newton became the centre for a 'union' of parish workhouses. The workhouse then would only have accommodated the poor from its own parish. This old Wolborough parish workhouse was not on the site of the later one but on the other side of East Street close to the *Devon Arms* (*The Green Man*).[224] The residue of its lease was sold in December 1837 to a Thomas Carlisle at the *Union Inn*, the street reminds us of the name.[225] Highweek parish had its workhouse in Exeter Road with a lock-up attached.[226]

In 1834 the Poor Law Amendment Act was passed, the idea was to supersede the small parish workhouses with large ones for groups of parishes. The Newton Union was set up in 1836 at a meeting held at the *Globe*. It was decided to build the new workhouse on a site on the south side of East Street. The first paupers were moved in, in 1839[227] and this accommodated the poor from no less than 39 parishes.[228] The fact that Newton was chosen in the first place must have some relation to its standing in the neighbourhood. There is also the interesting thought that had the Unions been set up later in time Torquay might well have made sufficient growth to be chosen instead. Those places chosen became a series of minor capitals, the 'Union' towns of their respective group of parishes. Later 'Union' towns were often used for other functions such as registration and sanitary districts.[229] Newton's workhouse was given the accolade; 'is pleasantly situated on the eastern side of town and is one of the best in England in external appearance and internal arrangements'.[230] Later again it was to be a source of discredit.

Religion

Religious affairs had a higher profile at this period. In 1813 one Mr Clack was appointed Rector of Wolborough. He retained this post with that of the living of Moreton for no less than 52 years and he is reputed to have officiated at Wolborough during all those years just three times! [231] Clack was one of the famous hunting parsons of the day and presumably found the sport better nearer the Moor. A curate was appointed to carry out his duties at Wolborough.

Religious toleration was not the order of the day; speeches were made, maybe significantly on 5th of November 1828, for petitioning Parliament against further concessions to Roman Catholics. Between 1834 and 1836 the old St Leonard's, of which the Tower still stands, was demolished and the new St Leonard's Chapel, now a second-hand furniture warehouse, was built.[232] The old chapel created a traffic problem because it was difficult for coaches to pass. The redoubtable Bishop of Exeter, Dr Henry Philpotts, opened the new chapel in November 1836.[233] The *Flying Post* wrote 'the dilapidated Episcopal Chapel in the centre of the former town was a bar to the completion of its improvement, and we congratulate the inhabitants on its being about to be removed'. It continued that 'the Earl of Devon, who is Lord of the Manor, as well as being a liberal contributor of land on which to erect it, is also a munificent subscriber to the undertaking'. Finally, perhaps with tongue in cheek, it suggests that as the town was in need of a lock-up the Tower could be used for that purpose. Then offenders, like greater men, would have to say 'they had been sent to the Tower'![234]

John Keats arrived at Teignmouth in late 1817 to stay with his sick brother. According to reports he did not enjoy his stay and left in 1818. Whilst there he wrote a poem about the Newton area 'Here all the summer could I stay'. It should be mentioned there are three slightly different versions in circulation. Drouth is thirst, plight in this context array, and prickets are fallow deer.

'Here all the summer could I stay'

For there's a Bishop's teign,
And King's teign
And Coomb at the clear teign head–
Where close by the stream
You may have your cream,
All spread upon barley bread.

There's arch Brook,
And there's Larch Brook
Both turning many a mill;
And cooling the drouth
Of the salmon's mouth,
And fattening his silver gill.

There is Wild wood,
A Mild hood,
To the sheep on the lea o' the down,
Where the golden furze,
With its green, thin spurs,
Doth catch at the maiden's gown.

There is Newton Marsh
With its spear grass harsh—
A pleasant summer level
Where the maidens sweet
Of the Market street,
Do meet in the dusk to revel.

There's the Barton rich
With dyke and ditch
And hedge for the thrush to live in
And the hollow tree
For the buzzing bee
And a bank for the wasp to hive in.

And O, and O
The daisies blow
And the primroses are waken'd;
And the violets white
Sit in silver plight,
And the green bud's as long in the spike end.

Then who would go
Into dark Soho,
And chatter with dack'd-hair'd critics,
When he can stay
For the new-mown hay,
And startle the dappled prickets?[235]

Railways

I. K. Brunel carried out an extensive survey during 1836 for the proposed Exeter, Plymouth & Devonport Railway. According to Kay he worked on two possible routes. Between Exeter and Teignmouth both routes were similar to the current one but more inland in places. From Teignmouth there were two choices, either similar to the present route or continuing along the coast, via Torquay, crossing the Dart and on a lengthy route through the South Hams. Significantly for Newton this second route would have left out Newton altogether. Brunel, though, recommended the inland route with its difficult gradients, not the coastal route that was considerably longer. When a great deal of work had been done the scheme was aborted because of difficulties over money and the opposition, from amongst others, the Earl of Devon.[236] It was not until 1843, seven years later, that the story continues.

In the autumn of 1843 Brunel re-surveyed a route between Exeter and Plymouth. The Exeter, Plymouth & Devonport Railway changed its name to

This was once the Turk's Head *and Brunel stayed here whilst surveying in the locality. It became the Rendez-vous Restaurant and later Pearl of India now Raj Belash. New St Leonard's is alongside.*

the South Devon Railway. This time the Courtenay family backed the scheme. Lord Courtenay, the Earl of Devon's eldest son, became a South Devon Railway director taking a great interest in the project. There was no rival scheme in the offing so the necessary Act was passed in July 1844.[237] Construction on the SDR began at once. The railway, now completed from London to Exeter, meant Exeter was the railhead town for anywhere west. One of the results was a new coach service, the *Tally Ho*, a four-horse coach to Plymouth and Devonport; this was to run from the *Old London Inn* in Exeter and went via Newton Bushel and Totnes. The proprietors announced that 'it will be the best regulated coach between Exeter and Plymouth'.[238] Items on construction work also started to appear in the newspapers. For instance one paper reported material for the tunnel at Marley passed through Ashburton and special equipment had been brought down from the White Ball Tunnel, between Taunton and Exeter, ventilation shafts were being sunk and it was expected 800 to 1,000 men would be employed on the tunnel.[239]

In 1845 a railway company was formed called the Ashburton, Newton and South Devon Junction Railway. The intended route was to be 'through a fine level valley by the side of the river Lemmon'.[240] Although Brunel surveyed the route and the idea was floated for some years, like a number of other schemes of the time, it never came into being. In this particular case, it was probably the rivalry from Buckfastleigh, which was the scheme's undoing. Eventually a rail link to Ashburton came from Totnes via Buckfastleigh. The direct connection to Newton would have been cheaper and quicker but whether in the long run it would have made any difference to the line's survival is a matter of conjecture. The forecasts for the expected traffic survive and although the likely passenger count of 270 weekly is not high, the possible goods traffic gives a guide to Ashburton's local industry of the time. They hoped to carry 6,000 tons of culm (coal dust usually anthracite) for 13 lime kilns, 7,280 tons of coal for house consumption and the forges of 28 smiths, as well as 8,000 tons of slate rags (large coarse roofing slates).

In early summer 1846 the railway reached Teignmouth. From miles around people arrived to see the novelty and if possible have a ride on a train. To get there every available vehicle was used and 'everything approaching four legs was stuck up and made to go'. Six full-grown people in a single donkey cart were seen trotting down the hill into Shaldon. Newton was practically empty: 'six able bodied men might have taken the place so completely was it deserted.'[241] For about seven months in 1846 Teignmouth became the western railhead and many coaches were routed there rather than Exeter[242]

Until the railway arrived the way to travel, for those who could afford it, was by coach. Services operated to and from different coaching inns. For instance the *Golden Lion* had services by Winser's Red Wing Coaches to Exeter twice and Torquay six times daily. Six horses drew each coach.[243] These services did not immediately succumb once the railway arrived because a few people were reluctant to hazard themselves on the new form of transport. It was not long, however, before the train completely displaced the old mode of transport. Horse transport was not redundant; there was an enormous demand for it from rail-heads, around the town and to other destinations not yet on the network. Only long distance coaches could not compete with rail. Isolated areas beyond the railways, such as Hartland, had horse-drawn coaches in operation until the First World War.

The original plan had been to build the Newton station further south. However, some far-sighted persons in Newton could see advantages in having a station nearer the town although it would mean putting in a new road. They therefore approached the directors of the SDR asking for a deviation to bring the station closer to the town and threatened to oppose the Bill in the House of Lords.[244] Some bargaining ensued but the request was granted. Unfortunately one landowner, on the now proposed route, objected and a new Act of Parliament was therefore required. The deviation was combined with the Act for the Torquay branch and passed in August 1846. This delay meant although work proceeded on the line on both sides of Newton nothing could be done there at all. What had been part of a little lane became Station Road and later Queen Street. Owing to the delay, work only finished the day before the opening! Even then there was no direct connection to the market. Another later line of communication was a direct route from Station Bridge to the station. The first station was intended to be a temporary affair but it lasted until 1861. Originally both the up and down platforms were on the same side of the line, but separate. When the Torquay line opened in 1848 that had another starting point nearby.[245]

After a remarkably short period of construction trains started to run on the last day of 1846. Newtonians certainly made a day of it, ending by celebrating the New Year. The day started as early as five o'clock with the firing of salutes and ringing of church bells. 'At ten a procession, consisting of several carriages . . . started from the *Globe Hotel* for the railway station, the Teignmouth Band being in a carriage drawn by eight handsome grey horses, and the whole route being decorated with flags and banners and other insignia of festivity. The long train from Exeter, which had been augmented at Teignmouth, was decorated with flags, banners, ribbons and evergreens. It had a band of wind instruments on board which played, it was said, 'with atmospheric power'! Lord Courtenay MP, Sir Anthony Buller, and Thomas Gill MP, the Chairman of the company were on the train that arrived at ten o'clock, just a few minutes after the arrival of the procession at the commodious new station.[246]

The Portreeve read an address of welcome and Mr Gill 'made a neat and appropriate reply'. 'A procession was then formed to escort the Directors to the town. The Totnes Band led the way and the Teignmouth Band brought up the rear. There were banners inscribed "Brunel and the Broad Gauge", "Success to the South Devon Railway" and other appropriate motifs'. Arrival at the *Globe Hotel* was greeted with enthusiastic cheering. There was a special lunch at Forde House for the directors and evening dinner for inhabitants at the *Globe*. The evening was spent in singing glees and songs.[247] It seems that at first there was only passenger traffic, the goods station at Newton and arrangements for carrying goods, it was hoped, would be ready by the following May.[248]

Railways now featured often in the press. By the first week in February an advertisement for a house property in Wolborough Street, with a detached coach house and stable, stated it was 'within a few minutes walk of the Station of the South Devon Railway.'[249] By mid-May it was claimed that 'the goods traffic at Newton is considerable and daily augmenting.' There was also the announcement of a new early train that would leave Newton at half past six and that would be found ' very convenient for persons having business to transact.'[250] The next stage of the main line to Totnes opened in July. The *Western Times* reported 'in all Totnes, it was shut shop and open house. The good people fell to and feasted their friends as if they had nothing to eat since last famine.' [251] In Newton, the construction of several houses commenced on the new road between the station and the town.[252]

Brunel had planned the line from Exeter to Plymouth, and indeed the branch to Torquay, would be worked by atmospheric propulsion. Work was not far enough advanced for it to be used at the start, so steam-engines were used instead. There were earlier trials but it was not until January 1848 that most trains into Newton were run atmospherically.[253] The story of this inspired failure has so often been told elsewhere that it needs no repetition here, except in so far that it concerned Newton. In early August about 80 workmen, of the atmospheric department, had a celebratory supper at the *Newfoundland Inn* for the opening of the workshops. There were toasts and speeches; Mr Pearson expressed his confidence that the system had got over its chief difficulties.[254] Yet, the next month came the news of the abandonment of the system.

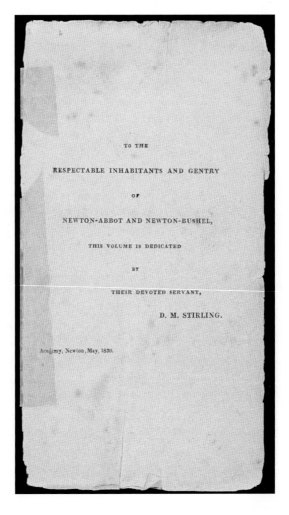

TO THE

RESPECTABLE INHABITANTS AND GENTRY

OF

NEWTON-ABBOT AND NEWTON-BUSHEL,

THIS VOLUME IS DEDICATED

BY

THEIR DEVOTED SERVANT,

D. M. STIRLING.

Academy, Newton, May, 1830.

Dedication, from Stirling, Newton's first history of 1830. Stirling was a schoolmaster in Newton who went on to the headship of Colyton Grammar School.

The experiment had been costly and was to limit SDR enterprise. Indeed, it probably hastened its eventual amalgamation with the Great Western Railway. Why the atmospheric workshops had been placed at Newton does not seem to be on record. However, the fact that empty workshops were available did lead to the later setting up of steam maintenance works, an important factor in Newton's future prosperity.

Newton had its own atmospheric-engine pumping-house similar to the one that was never used, but is still standing, at Torquay. Later this was Longpark Pottery and it now belongs to Frank Mann Wholesale Vegetable Merchants. Newton's pumping house was used for a while as part of the railway workshop complex until it was demolished. Rather more remarkably in 1849, when health authorities were looking for accommodation because of cholera outbreaks, the SDR agreed to it being used if needed to house destitute families![255] Despite this scare in 1849 there was resistance in Newton to the application of the Public Health Act, on the grounds of cost, as the *Western Times* put it, a number of the 'mind your pockets' protested. The opposition was more than verbal because, the paper stated, if it had not been for the superintendent of police 'a breach of the peace would have been committed'.[256]

In November 1847 the SDR's electric telegraph was put to good use. A woman robbed a house in Newton of three gold rings and some money. It was thought she had gone to Exeter so a message was sent there. By coincidence Mr Hobbs, a company's officer, met her in Exeter and she asked to be directed to Milk Street. He said he was going that way and would take her, in fact he took her to the police station. Here she was searched and the articles found.[257]

It has been suggested that the tower of the Market Hall/ Alexandra Hall was copied from the Newton engine-house but there does not seem to be any evidence for this. In the 1840s it was said that an outbreak of cholera at Torquay affected trade in Newton market.[258]

The Torquay branch line opened in December 1848[259] and at first only ran to the present Torre Station site, then described as a 'field in the parish of Tormohun. The present Torquay Station came later. It reached the terminus at Kingswear in 1864.[260] Already by this date there was dissatisfaction that there was no direct access from the railway station to the market. What was to become Queen Street did not cross Courtenay Street. The *Western Times* ex-

Title page from Stirling's book.

A

HISTORY

OF

NEWTON-ABBOT and NEWTON-BUSHEL,

AND ALSO, ILLUSTRATIONS

OF THE

Antiquities, Topography, and Scenery

OF

THE CIRCUMJACENT NEIGHBOURHOOD,

INCLUDING

Teignmouth, Torquay, and Chudleigh.

By The Rev. D. M. STIRLING.

"Where'er futurity may lead the way,
Where in this vale of Life I chance to stray,
Imagination to thy scenes shall turn,
Dwell on thy charms, and for thy beauties burn.—
And the last dream of Earth, that meets my eyes,
Shall be thy lawns and groves, and azure tinted skies."

NEWTON-ABBOT:

PRINTED BY W. F. FORORD.

1830.

pressed it thus 'Much inconvenience is felt that the market is such a distance from the Railway Station, making people as hucksters (pedlars or hawkers) etc have to carry their goods more than a mile and many are therefore kept from attending the market . . .when a road may be cut at a nominal expense through the timber yard opposite Magor's *Commercial Hotel*.[261] Pearl Assurance House now stands on the site of the old *Commercial Hotel*. It was nearly 20 years before the direct connection was made. Torquay newspapers of the time recorded prices from Newton Market e.g. 'Turnips 1d per bunch, Cabbages 1d to 2d each';[262] surely a sign that Torquay customers were in Newton's orbit. Torquay obviously felt they were missing out because they applied to Parliament to open their own market[263] It was never to rival Newton's.

In 1830 the first history of Newton was published. *A History of Newton-Abbot and Newton-Bushel* was written by Rev. D. M. Stirling, a local schoolmaster. At the time he was a little despondent because the Newfoundland trade, a staple for centuries, was failing. Yet Newton was embarking on a decade when it would increase by more than double the county's average. His book also included one of the earliest town directories in Devon. Stirling left to become headmaster of Colyton Grammar School and died there in 1863.[264]

Recreation

In 1823 the Teignbridge Cricket Club, fore-runner of South Devon, played its preliminary game. Sir George Templer had 'A cowshed cleaned and purified a few boards for a table, a sailcloth for a carpet, a round of beef, a salad and home brewed ale', where upon the first cricket party sat down to dine.[265] In the following year the club was founded and claimed to be the oldest in the county. Later it became well known for its dances on 'Ladies Day' when it was said that an invitation was the special ambition of every society girl in Devon![266] The Teignbridge Steeple Chase in 1839 was reported in *Woolmer's Gazette* as set out below. 'The greatest interest was excited to witness the race and at least four thousand persons in carriages, on foot, and horseback had assembled by two o'clock. The ground chosen by Sir Walter Carew for this race was the Marshes at Teignbridge, the distance four miles. The point of starting was at the lower end of the race course towards the New Road leading from Newton to Exeter, nearly two miles up the Teign, towards Bovey forming a circuit, the winning post being in front of the Newton Race Stand, just below the Cricket Ground. There were some twenty leaps in the distance and some awkward fences and brooks'.[267] The description makes it clear that this was the old racecourse on the opposite side of the road to where it is now. The annual summer meeting of Newton Races took place in 1848 but now we are told, the facility of railway travel gave 'increased zest'.[268] In the early summer of 1843 the shooting of a swan was reported at 'Wildwoods situate at Teign near Newton marsh'. A fine specimen weighing twenty-two pounds and having a wingspan of nearly eight feet. It was sold in Newton for seven shillings. There had been a pair but one got away.[269] In July the annual wrestling match lasted from Monday to Thursday, but the attendance was down, 'and it seemed to excite but little interest in the town'.[270]

Victoria was crowned in 1837 and Newtonians celebrated with a sit down dinner for nearly 3,000 people in the meadow that later became the site of the new market. Teas were provided for the women and children. There was a firework display in the evening with an immense bonfire of 700 faggots of furze and twelve tar barrels. The day finished with a Coronation Ball at the *Globe*.[271]

In 1826 a medical remedy was produced in Newton Bushel ' Dr Green's Celebrated Royal Antiscorbutic Drops'. Antiscorbutic is a preventative against scurvy, which is a vitamin deficiency disease commonplace on ships at that time. Why at Newton, one wonders, a throw-back to the Newfoundland trade or a sign of expanding empire? Dr Green lived at Minerva House, still extant, the home later of Pinsent the Newton brewers. There was still a little Newfoundland trade in the vicinity as a later 1847 report proves. The *Haberdine* of Teignmouth arrived with the first cargo of Labrador dry salted cod for that season.[272]

Two great personages came to Newton. The Archduke Nicholas of Russia, on a tour of England in 1828, changed horses at the *Globe*. It is reported he shook hands with a tailor.[273] In May 1846 the Duke of Wellington stopped at the *Globe Hotel* whilst his horses were being changed. He had been expected, so church bells were rung in his honour and crowds gathered to see 'so renowned a warrior'.[274]

In early 1846 there were grumbles about the long delivery time taken to deliver a letter in Ashburton posted in Newton. The *Western Times* with tongue in cheek thought that officials with such 'somnolent propensities' should be complimented.[275] The season was exceptionally mild, before the end of February, Mr Mayne the druggist had large size gooseberries growing out of doors in his garden [276] In the next year an Ashburton woman 'was stung by a viper' when she was gathering whortleberries (bilberries). Thanks to medical assistance, she was reported to be doing well.[277]

Minerva House. A Dr. Green, who sold 'Celebrated Royal Antiscorbutic Drops', lived here early in the nineteenth century. Later it became the home of the Pinsent family, Newton brewers. It was famous for its lovely garden now the cattle market.

CHAPTER 7

THE LATER NINETEENTH CENTURY 1850–1899

In 1851 a handbook said of Newton 'Inn *Globe Hotel*, good clean and cheap'.[278] Six years later in a directory was this description 'Newton Abbot at the present time is in the most thriving condition and its inhabitants, seem to have one common object in view and that is to make it one of the best market towns of the district, and have adopted as their motto that significant word 'Forward'.'[279] By 1870 a directory stated "Newton Abbot, in the parish of Wolborough, is a flourishing market town, adjoining Newton Bushel in the parish of Highweek" and continued "but to the stranger, or the general public, the whole is usually known as Newton Abbot only".[280] A 1879 handbook described Newton thus 'is beautifully situated in a vale, on the Lemon rivulet, which here joins the Teign. The town has been much extended since it became a railway centre. Its market is widely known for its abundant supplies'.[281] James Hussey in 1886 wrote 'An enjoyable drive brought us to Newton Abbot, a very bright clean-looking town', unfortunately he goes on 'through which we drove without halting'.[282]

The new Courtenay Street, an early view, c.1855, the base of the old market cross was then still in the middle of the road. Note Beazley's recently rebuilt Globe.

This period is the high-water mark of the Victorian age when Britain was the richest nation and indeed 'the workshop of the world'. Devon, though its tourist business was increasing, was still very much an agricultural county. Up until the 1870s agriculture still prospered but increasing mechanization and agrarian improvement were already reducing the numbers needed in some types of farming. Where numbers declined they affected not only the viability of villages but also a decline in most market towns in the county.

Newton was exceptional - it boomed. Building was a continuous process. In addition to a market, Newton also had clay for which there was an increasing demand. It was a communication centre and a staging post on routes to other towns, had industries and was a 'union town' making it an administrative centre. It was a railway junction and had the railway works. The town was being developed and the affluent clientele attracted improved shops and demanded good schools. The better shopping attracted folk from further afield. The fact that the town was increasing and had good communications drew in more commercial firms. A 'topsy' factor was at work because undoubtedly, nothing succeeds like success.

So much in fact happened during the period that no attempt has been made to record every event but it is hoped that none of the major happenings have been omitted. Only a cross section of lesser events has been included to show what went on in the town and would have made the local news and social chitchat of the day.

In the first half of the century the two towns had impressively doubled in population from a total of 2,126 in 1801 to 4,625 in 1851 an increase of some 218%. They were, exceptionally for inland towns, to more than double again. The population rose to 10,738 by 1901, this time a 232% increase. Natural increase was high because growing towns attract young people, but natural increase was not enough to sustain Newton's rate of growth. A study of where all the people came from has been made and some of them came a long way indeed for those times. (See chapter 8).

Newton from Powderham Park, not as yet many houses on Knowles Hill.

River Teign, from Knowles Hill once often called Brecknock, or Breakneck Hill. Stover Canal left foreground, new toll-road to Kingsteignton mid-ground. Probably c.1855 though the picture may be a few years earlier.

Administration

Although Newton has been referred to as though it was one, it was still two places with separate administrations, Newton Abbot south of the Lemon was still Wolborough, Newton Bushel north of the Lemon, Highweek. Surprisingly the two separate authorities remain throughout the whole of this period although progress towards amalgamation was well in place right at the end of it. Newton's parliamentary constituency was combined with Ashburton. There was news that a branch of the court would be established at Torquay saving the inhabitants the inconvenience and expense of visiting Newton.[283] Although Torquay was now of considerable size, traditionally it had been of little account and therefore subsidiary to Newton in many matters.

There was still talk of removing the old tower in Wolborough Street. It was suggested that this could be one of 'the finest improvements that could be conferred on the town' and give it 'a rather more civilized appearance'.[284] The channelling of the Lemon made Newton particularly susceptible to floods until the Holbeam Dam was finally erected. The first serious flood of more modern times was in 1851.

There was considerable discussion on the town drains in 1852 and there were three meetings in September and another in October, when it was decided that with a contribution from the Devon & Courtenay Estate, the scheme would go ahead.[285] It is more than surprising to remember that a Mr Hall who called attention to the abomination of the town's open sewers had his effigy burnt and his windows smashed.[286]

In 1852 Wolborough Vestry discussed whether the new Station Road, later Queen Street, should be taken over by the parish. There was opposition on the grounds that it was not of sufficient utility to justify the cost but the majority opinion decided it was![287] In 1853 there was a report on Newton 'this much improving place', that there were to be new roads on the Devon estate and Wolborough Hill. The building land had a southern aspect and views of the surrounding countryside, which were 'scarcely to be surpassed'.[288] By 1854 the Devon Estate had laid out building sites and to celebrate the cutting of the first

Newton view from Knowles Hill, 1860, Shaldon & Newton Railway Bridges are both visible as well as the atmospheric railway tower.

NEWTON

sod, the children were marched from the workhouse in procession up the hillside. Afterwards they were given tea in the street on tables laid from the Tower up to the *Half Moon Inn*.[289] Building plans approved in 1866 included at least 39 new properties from villas to cottages and a new Wesleyan Chapel. A new street was proposed by Lord Devon from East Street to Wolborough Hill. The town was still growing fast in 1869 and there were numerous building applications, one alone from Mr Zealley to build 30 houses. So many new villa residences had been erected in Highweek by 1856 that it was determined if possible to re-pew and warm the church.[290]

A meeting of the ratepayers of Highweek and Newton Bushel in the *Seven Stars Inn* in October considered lighting Highweek village and this was carried by 34 to three.[291] Lighting was installed the next year, 1854, but the gasometer had to be enlarged first to cope with the extra demand. There were complaints that Newton Gas Company were discharging tar gas into the river in 1861, which was not only poisoning fish but also creating an offensive nuisance.[292] Two years later there was an escape of gas in the station waiting room; Mr Hammett the inspector took a light to find the leak. The gas which had collected under the ceiling exploded and he was considerably injured.[293] In 1885 the Gas Company announced their intention to build a new and much larger gasholder and an extension of their works.[294] The Rural District Council asked the Newton Guardians if they could lay gas on at their boardroom and not only did they agree but also they decided to adopt the 'incandescent light'.[295]

During 1858 new roads were opened around Courtenay Park and Wolborough Hill. New houses were let nearly as fast as they were erected and it was anticipated that Newton would become a very prosperous town.[296] An immense reservoir was in the course of construction to supply the Earl of Devon's properties. Torquay Water Company was now laying water mains to various parts of the town.[297] One of the last significant decisions made by the Wolborough Vestry is still in evidence today. Consent was granted to the Earl of Devon's application to make a new road from Courtlands/Torquay Road through Broadmeadow, present Forde Park area, to the top of Decoy Road at

the end of Church Road,[298] then the old name for Coach Road. There had been a somewhat sinuous old road taking off from just above the Station Bridge but this new road provided a new, wider and straighter route.

A preliminary meeting was held late in 1863 towards the adoption of the Local Government Act 1858, to change from a parish vestry to a more powerful local government board. Mr W. J. Watts was appointed chairman. He said he felt 'great pleasure at all times in taking part in anything that would tend to the welfare of the town of Newton'.[299] A resolution in favour was carried by a large majority on a show of hands. However, a Mr Flamark demanded a poll that was held on 23 November 1863 and carried by 325 votes to 50.[300] The first meeting of the Wolborough Local Board was held on 19 February 1864. Mr Flamark interestingly later changed his mind, or felt he was being left out, because he stood for, but unsurprisingly was not elected, to the local board![301] Later still, he requested that Fairfield Terrace should have its named changed to his, but again he was unsuccessful![302]

The first meeting of the local Board in 1864 voted without dissent to admit reporters to meetings. They then started like the proverbial new brooms; in March street lighting was considered and the surveyor was instructed to report on sanitary conditions. In April improvements were detailed for Station Road and the question of naming streets and numbering houses was referred to the Improvement Committee.

In April too there was communication with Highweek asking them to consider a report on joint drainage. The Surveyor was authorized to dispose of the refuse collected by the Scavenger 'as he may deem expedient'.[303] This decision caused trouble later. The Scavenger collected rubbish and was provided with a bell, to advise the townspeople he was coming. When they heard the bell they could put out their ashes and rubbish.

In 1866 the Board bought a bigger water cart, very necessary to keep down dust and help cleanse roads when they were unsealed and there was much horse traffic! They bargained to have 'Wolborough Local Board Newton Abbot' painted on the cart 'without extra charge' and also bought a new muck cart.[304] The Sergeant of Police was appointed as an additional inspector of nuisances. He promptly reported the refuse heaps belonging to the Board which the Surveyor was then asked to move to 'some more convenient place'.[305] Mr Watts made the offer of a drinking fountain to be placed by the Tower if Torquay Local Board would give the water.[306] This they subsequently agreed.

The Board decided to order a smoke-testing machine for drains. Something seems to have gone amiss in Wolborough's finances; it was discovered that

Devon Square. Courtenay developments came after the Seymour's in Newton but they were on a much bigger scale. They used good architects and set high standards. They provided a reservoir on Wolborough Hill and St Paul's Church.

though Highweek had originally paid a third of the cost of the public sewers, they had not been asked for a further contribution for 34 years![307] One householder in Quay Road was instructed to strip the paper from her walls and disinfect her property because cases of diphtheria had recently occurred there.[308] In 1868 there were problems with the drains of Mr Pinsent at the *Plymouth Inn* and the South Devon Railway premises.

Health

In 1853 cholera, came to Newton causing some 57 deaths.[309] Not much is recorded about this outbreak possibly because some local papers refrained from publishing such news. Cholera, incidentally, came back to Kingsteignton in 1866 and 11 died.[310]

A dispensary was started, in 1858 to which was later added a hospital in 1873.[312] Newton Abbot's first cottage hospital was established to hold 13 patients; but was inadequate in size practically from the beginning. It was maintained by voluntary subscriptions and donations. A new hospital was built, on another site off East Street and opened in 1898. Mr Scratton, squire of Ogwell, the long time secretary of the Hospital Board, gave the land. Mrs Fisher of Abbotsbury House provided money for building, but sadly she died before it was opened.[313] Fisher Road was named after this benefactress.[314] During 1894 some 130 patients were admitted and they had dealt with 44 accidents of which 12 were serious. The site of the new Isolation Hospital was finally decided in 1898, in a field on Totnes Road near the old turnpike house at Ogwell Cross.[311] It still stands as Brunel Lodge. There had been early plans to have it at Forches Cross and indeed several other places. A resolution, at an annual meeting was carried asking local clergy to arrange a Hospital Sunday;[315] all the church and chapel collections in the town would be given to the local hospital. Donations came from other sources for instance, in 1893 Mr St Maur of Stover House handed

Harold St Maur, was the last of the family of the dukes of Somerset to live at Stover House, now Stover School.

to the Newton Cottage Hospital £20 realized by a charge for admission to skate on Stover Lake during the late frost.[316] Later there was an annual carnival and a fete at Dyrons, the home of the Vicarys. In 1948 the hospital became part of the National Health Service.[317]

In the 1860s the Board declined to appoint a Superintendent to carry out the provisions of the Vaccination Acts. However, in April 1873 availed themselves of the Public Health Act of 1872 and employed a part-time medical officer provided arrangements were made with other authorities. The five urban authorities in the Newton Union were Dawlish, St Mary-church, Teignmouth, Torquay and

Wolborough. In August Mr Leonard Armstrong of Starbeck near Harrogate was appointed and renewed in 1877, and 1879. The Medical officer and Inspector of Nuisances were told to take 'all proper steps to prevent the spread of fever in Osborne Street'.[318]

It is unlikely that many of us would have wanted to live in the town as it then was. In 1875 the council wrote to a Mr Harris threatening to prosecute if he continued to slaughter cattle and keep filthy dogs on his premises in Queen Street. The owner of the *Turk's Head* was required to construct a drain for the dung pits, privies, piggeries and stables in his yard. The *Turk's Head* was later the Rendez-Vous, the Pearl of India and Raj Belash.[319] Four years later there was a complaint about a Mr Jacobs boiling offensive meat for his dogs. Even worse there were problems with a piggery and manure deposit at the back of the Cottage Hospital in East Street.[320]

Market

What triggered these next events is not known but it may have been a petition from the townsfolk about the state of the market. In May 1864 a special meeting was called to consider the possible purchase of the market properties. The Rev. Lane, the owner, was to be asked his price. At the same time the surveyor and Improvement Committee were consulted as to the best way of making an entrance from Station Road.[321] There was no direct access then by the present 'Drum Clock'. There was opposition, or a least caution, shown by some ratepayers as to their liabilities[322] but the scheme was finally passed in October 1867. The whole matter took some time as an Act of Parliament was needed and a deputation from the Board asked Lord Devon for support.[323]

In February 1870 the Board set out to obtain plans and estimates for laying out the Market Place and erecting new buildings. There were to be butchery, fish, poultry, butter and fruit markets. The Corn Exchange was to 'be so constructed as to be readily available for other purposes'. In August the contract was signed with Mr Harvey a Torquay builder for £5730, and it was stated that stone was coming from Curry Mallet quarry in Somerset. The opening was fixed for Wednesday 20th of December 1871 and decisions were made as to the 'best mode of celebrating', which was to include a dinner for the poor.[324] The press reported that on opening 'the several departments were abundantly supplied' and that the Board would nearly double their tolls that were let annually by auction.[325] In December 1876 the tolls were knocked down at auction to a Mr Pillar for £600 but the *Flying Post* added that it understood Mr Coleridge was the 'real purchaser'.[326] The reason for this is probably because relations between the Board and Mr Coleridge, a long time tenant of the market were not always amicable.

Roads

Several roads, being in good condition, were taken over from Lord Devon in the Devon Square area and plans for erection of dwelling houses in Forde

Park, Queen St., Devon Square, St Paul's Road, were approved, no less than four builders wishing to erect houses in Forde Park. Abbotsbury a modern mansion on a terraced knoll, was up for sale in 1866 with seven acres 'overlooking the twin towns of Newton Abbot and Newton Bushel'.[327] This one time house gave its name to the present suburb. Lord Devon offered Courtenay Park to the town on a 21-year lease.[328] This offer was accepted, the lease was later renewed and finally the town bought the park in 1897.

The Board requested the Gas and Water companies to be more careful about disturbing roads and to see they were properly re-laid. It was decided to name the road through Well Park, Tudor Road. Permission was refused for a slaughterhouse in Queen Street and a reward was offered to try and prevent damage to public lamps. A significant decision was made to cover in the River Lemon from 'the present Fish Market to Hero Bridge'.[329]

There was contact with Highweek asking them to share the cost of repairing a bridge over the Lemon. A Mr Stranger was called upon to restore the turf on the sides of the path leading to the Station and to discontinue running his sheep there! It was decided that the road at the back of the College should be called College Road.[330]

The Torquay Turnpike Trust gave permission for the Board, in 1873, to lay down a footpath from the Railway Bridge to Penn Inn.[331]

The year 1876 began with the rent audit and dinner for some 200 tenants of the Devon Estate at the *Globe Hotel* with the Earl of Devon presiding. This would have been an annual event but some of what was said was very apposite to the town at that time. His Lordship thanked those who had so materially assisted in improving the town. Mr Chudleigh responded saying the 'present prosperous condition of the town' had been brought about by 'Lord Devon's liberality letting the land'. The Earl of Devon in reply, said it was 'difficult to realize the progress of the town in the past forty years. The results were satisfactory to him and he trusted that the progress would continue'. Newton had extended not only in commerce and wealth but the moral welfare of the town had gained in

Penn Inn Bridge, it is difficult to equate this peaceful spot with the busy main road junction that we know today.

all directions. In particular 'they had schools in point of style character and efficiency, equal to those of any town in England'.[332] At the same event in 1880 at the *Globe Hotel*, an excellent repast was provided by the new proprietor Mr R. Pope. Mr Drew, who had been steward for 40 years, said that during that period the Newton tenantry had increased from 10 or 11 to nearly three hundred.[333] Striking proof here, if it was needed, of how the Courtenays had been developing Wolborough and how the tenantry were increasing.

It was decided to number Bank, Courtenay, East, Queen and Wolborough streets with even numbers on one side and odd on the other. Devon Square, Quay road and Quay terrace were numbered with a different scheme.[334]

In March 1877 much dissatisfaction was felt about the state of the roads, due in great extent to the 'recent heavy and continuous rain'.[335] Union Street was cut to link East Street with Courtenay Street in 1883.[336] It was announced in 1887 that Mr Russell of Bank Street was to build an 'extremely new structure', its use unfortunately not recorded, 'of the most modern style of architecture' substituting it for one that was perhaps three hundred years old. Other improvements were taking place at the same time.[337] This is yet more evidence of how Newton was developing and why so little of the ancient town remains. Buildings were not yet listed. Lord Rosebery, later Prime Minister, came to open the new Liberal club in a 'good position' in Union Street, almost opposite the Mid-Devon Constitutional Club. Lord Rosebery arrived from Plymouth by train, he was met by Mr Seale Hayne MP. They proceeded to Broadlands, later an old people's home, currently College House Post 16 Centre and the source of the name for the Broadlands estate built in the 1920s. It was then the residence of Mr J. Vicary J.P. and they were entertained to lunch. Afterwards Lord Rosebery addressed a public meeting in the vegetable market. In April 1888 it was reported that the Newton Abbot Constitutional Club in Union Street was nearly complete and that Lord Randolph Churchill would open it at the end of the month.[338] Something apparently went wrong because, Sir Michael Hicks Beach, solicitor general, opened it on 13th October.

There was a suggestion that St Leonard's Tower should be illuminated but there was opposition from those who favoured demolition. The Society for the Protection of Ancient Buildings came to its defence and a postcard poll was undertaken. The mass vote of some 900 voted for retention and the Tower was again saved, although there was another threat of removal in 1925.

The United Kingdom Telegraph Co. also requested permission, which was granted, to place poles and wires along the roads in the district.[339] In the period there were often requests for more streetlights, one in November was from Major Yates and the inhabitants of Forde Park. The Board wrote to the proprietors of 'Cabs, Omnibuses and Flys (hackney carriage pulled by a single horse)' that it was desirable 'they should carry lamps on dark nights'. They also subscribed one pound to illuminate Mr Uglow's clock in the following year provided the clock was put in good order.[340] Was this an early public private partnership?

The suggestion has been made that Newton was slow to adopt electricity for its public lighting because several members of the Wolborough Board had an interest in the Gas Company. This latter point is certainly true because there was an application in 1888 to the Local Government Board for permission for three members of the Board, Messes Bearne, Vicary and Watts to be allowed to vote on matters concerning the Gas Company despite their interest in it.[341] It is surely surprising to find that one of the very three members who was supposed to be furthering his interest in gas was one of the very first in the town to adopt electric light! The story unfolds thus; there was an application from the Electric Light companies in 1882 but the Board turned this down on the grounds they contemplated applying for a provisional order themselves. The clerk was instructed to write to the Board of Trade as to the procedure to obtain an order under the Electric Lights Act of 1882.[342] In 1888 there was a press report that the tannery of Messes Vicary Bros. was to be lit by electricity. It added that the work would be undertaken by Mr Radcliff 'who lighted Torquay Theatre with his light'.[343] In 1889 there was another application from the Devon & Cornwall Supply Company Ltd. and it was referred to the Lighting Committee.[344] This time permission was given.[345]

The Board considered the purchase of a horse and cart.[346] During 1867 they started moves to shift a long-standing grievance of the townsfolk. The first tollhouse of the Totnes turnpike was at the east end of the gates of what is now Baker's Park. This meant tolls had to be paid by those only going a very short distance out of town. The Board set out to have it removed to the Ogwell Cross area; in this they were eventually successful, but it took some while to achieve invoking assistance from the Duke of Somerset, Lord Devon, Lord Churston and the county members.[347]

The Board was in contact with the Postmaster General in 1865 to obtain better Post Office accommodation for the district. Poor mail service came to the Board's attention, they wanted weekday collections nearer the departure of 'the north bound train' and clearance of pillar boxes in the park on Sundays.[348]

Originally built in the very early 1870s as a corn exchange but designed to be used for other purposes. The name was changed to Alexandra in 1874. It has been suggested that Brunel's Italianate atmospheric towers influenced its design.

A Royal Commission had been set up to inquire into the employment of women and children in agriculture. A meeting in Newton unanimously agreed that in Devonshire legislative interference was unnecessary but it was thought boys under 10 or girls under 16 should not be employed.[349]

The working men of Newton Abbot assembled at the *Globe Hotel* on a Saturday evening to form a constitutional association.[350] In 1873 the plans for the first 13 Mackrell Almshouses were passed by the Wolborough Board, and in approving these, the Board offered thanks to Mr Mackrell and 'warm appreciation of his munificence and benevolence'. These opened in 1874. Thomas Mackrell was born in Newton Abbot and became wealthy as a chemist in Barnstaple. He is reputed to have chosen to build the almshouses in the field where he had played as a child. The remainder of the block was built with money from his sister's estate after she had died in 1894.[351] The design in limestone was by the architect J.W. Rowell. In September 1874 the Corn Exchange had its name changed to the Alexandra Hall, at the request of the tenant, the name is still extant; now the Alexandra Cinema.[352]

The Surveyor was authorized in 1890 to procure two copies of the Ordnance Map of the district.[353] The Clerk to Wolborough Board reported that there had been only five applications for licenses for carriages plying for hire. In 1899 the bridge over the Lemon at the end of the Avenue sank so much that traffic was stopped.[354] DCC decided that a telephone should be placed in Newton Abbot police station. The cost would be £10 per annum and it was thought particularly desirable to be able to communicate with Torquay.[355] In 1851 a Mr Prynn, dental surgeon from London and the sole inventor of the self-adhesive artificial teeth, was advertising his services in Newton every Wednesday, Thursday, Friday and Saturday.[356]

Hero Bridge

The origins of the name are not straightforward. Jones in his book opts for a rescue before the Second World War while the *Mid-Devon Advertiser* suggested it related to an event in 1913. However, it was called Hero Bridge in the Wolborough Board Minutes of 1867. It would be easy to consider there may have been an earlier rescue and bearing in mind the urban nature of part of the river and its speed of flow at times of flood, this is more than possible. See for instance the rescue of Iris Anderson in 1941. But Michael Martin has pointed out that there was a Hero Place, based on the classical figure close beside the bridge. His opinion is that the local name of the nearby cottage row was transferred to the bridge and this frankly seems the most likely but certainly more mundane explanation!

The most well recorded version of the 'rescue'

story is below, but it certainly is not the origin of the name. Maybe, it is a useful reminder of how some well-circulated stories are in fact myths.

A fishmonger, not a footballer, called George Best, jumped into the river when it was in flood to rescue a boy from drowning. What is really remarkable about the story is that he could not swim. His family teased him after the rescue but several townspeople were appreciative of his bravery and a subscription was made to buy him a gold watch. Later, sadly, his sister died and his mother a widow could not afford to pay for the funeral, so, nobly he sold his watch to pay for it.

After the rescue he was to marry and as a matter of interest two of his granddaughters swam for Devon County Swimming Team.[357]

Amalgamation

Some reports give the impression that Wolborough was always for a merger of the towns and Highweek reluctant. That does not seem to be wholly true. Furthermore, it seems unlikely that we see the whole picture from printed records because, presumably, negotiation was also done verbally. Apparently, the first important public comment on possible amalgamation was made by a Newton correspondent with the *nom de plume* 'Johnny' in the *Flying Post*. He wrote 'the idea to amalgamate Wolborough and Highweek is a good one. In fact the only reason they are separate now is that nobody has ever bothered to unite them'. It is extraordinary, he goes on, to share the same gas, same water etc. 'share everything except governing body. Wolborough governed by a local board. Highweek by Sanitary Committee and Rural Sanitary Authority which is about as awkward a muddle as could well be imagined'.[358] In 1894 the name of the Wolborough Board was changed to Newton Abbot, the Board gave way to the Newton Abbot Urban District Council. They shortly approached Highweek about amalgamation but were rebuffed. Highweek considered applying for urban powers.[359] In June 1896 Highweek decided a committee should meet Wolborough to consider amalgamation.[360] In July Wolborough deferred carrying out the coroner's recommendation to provide proper bathing accommodation on the canal on the grounds it should be postponed until amalgamation.[361] By 1898 they co-operated enough for a joint address to be given by Mr Lewis Bearne on behalf of NAUDC and Highweek Council at the County Agricultural Show. In 1899 Highweek presented terms for amalgamation. These were a preferential rate 6d in the pound for ten years, they should contribute nothing to market debt, appoint their own overseers and the joint council was not to control Highweek charities.[362] In 1900 Newton Abbot applied to Devon County Council for an enquiry regarding amalgamation with Highweek and part of Haccombe with Combe.[363] The outcome was favourable, the merger did not take place until 1901. A variable rate, which had been the sticking point for some while, was agreed.[364] We are left to marvel that this amalgamation process, that we now take so much for granted, should have taken nearly a decade. Yet both communities, though living cheek by jowl, had been separate entities since their foundations, perhaps for some 700 years!

Mr R.H. Baker who had been clerk to the Local Board for a number of years died in 1894 and left a generous bequest to provide a public park for the benefit of the inhabitants of Highweek and Wolborough. This was used to establish Baker's Park.[365] It was laid out in 1905 and is still very much appreciated to this day. [366] There is a plaque on the park gate pillar.

Poverty & the workhouse

A cold spell had economic consequences in February 1853 harsh weather threw many 'mechanics and others out of employment'. The poor relief committee distributed meat, soup and coals to 'a large number of poor persons who were highly grateful'.[367] The following year started harshly; there were riots over the high price of bread. The press stated that the 'public are greatly indebted to our resident magistrate . . . for prompt measures to preserve the peace'. The

Newton view, c.1855, showing workhouse in the foreground, atmospheric tower on the extreme right, Vicary's chimney and St Leonard's tower far left. Wolborough Hill was often called Bakers Hill then.

humanity of the Board of Guardians, which increased the amount of outdoor relief, was also commended. Times were also hard in 1869 for some, as plans were also approved for a soup kitchen. Later in 1908, a building was bought, for this purpose, in Union Street.[368] This building is now part of Wolborough Primary School but high on the wall 'parish room and soup kitchen' can still be read. Again February 1881 was obviously a cruel month there were a large number of applications for relief, many of them from farm labourers, destitute 'through the inclemency of the weather and illness'.[369]

Miss Burdett Coutts presented a harmonium and coconut matting to the workhouse chapel. She said the chapel would be too cold for old people. George Coniam, a pauper and former soldier aged 28, died in the carrier's waggon between Bovey Tracey and Newton. The carrier said on arrival at the workhouse 'make haste for there is a man here in the waggon who is either dead or dying'. There were several other passengers and one of the women said it was a shameful thing to remove him from his bed on such a cold and stormy day.[370] Later there was an unusual admission to the workhouse, a Theodore Teame once a physician in Worcester who had lately filled the post of house surgeon at Teignmouth Infirmary but had been dismissed for 'dissipated habits'.[371] By 1878 the workhouse had problems with the number of tramps. In one week twenty-six had been admitted to the casual ward and one of these had been sent before the magistrates and sentenced to seven days hard labour for disorderly conduct [372] In March no less than 27 were reported in the week. The master of the workhouse stated most were decently dressed and in his opinion were intent on work in Plymouth dockyard.[373] A woman from Teignmouth, who had left her husband seven years earlier but was ill and destitute, was allowed to enter the workhouse but the clerk was instructed to proceed against her husband for maintenance.[374] The Rev. H. Tudor asked the Guardians in 1882, to be allowed to give the children an afternoon's holiday with tea at Teignmouth. The Guardians assented and thanked the Rev. Tudor for his kindness.[375] A year later the Board of Guardians tried the Christmas puddings supplied to the inmates and they were 'pronounced to be very good'.[376] The Board announced that the new stone breaking yard was 'completed and in working order'. The yard was sub-divided into compartments and after breakfast each man had to crack half a ton of stones small enough to pass through a regulation iron plate. It was thought this was a useful 'deterrent to wayfarers seeking temporary relief in the house'.[377] Lady Agnes Wood asked if girls in the workhouse could be told about the Girls Friendly Society so that they might join after leaving for service. It was decided to respectfully decline as 'the present system worked well' and there was no need of aid from the Society.[378]

The Guardians also dealt with relief. A woman called Loram, deserted by her husband, had struggled to maintain herself and four children for some years. She applied in 1855 to the Board of Guardians for clothing for her son aged 12 who was to go to sea for a five-year apprenticeship. The Board considered this a proper application and granted £2.[379] Next year the Board granted £2 for a family called Lear to emigrate to Melbourne in Australia.[380] In 1877 the widows of three recently drowned fishermen from Teignmouth applied for relief.[381] There were problems of incoming aliens. The master reported he admitted three Italian children and their monkey with which they travelled the country begging. The Italian consul was approached and assented to repatriate the children to Italy if they were sent to the consulate. The Board agreed, but they kept the monkey![382] At the Board of Guardians Mr Scratton moved that 'King Coffee' the black man who had frequently been before the Board be proceeded against, for leaving his wife and family chargeable to the Union.[383] The Board had obviously driven too hard a bargain over coal purchased in 1883. Whilst it was according to contract, it contained much small coal. One board member suggested it should be made into balls with clay to give a great heat and be long lasting. The master promised to give the suggestion a trial.[384]

At the pre-Christmas meeting of the Guardians in 1887 Mr Creed suggested able-bodied paupers who 'through their own neglect of disinclination to work come to the house' should be supplied with a different diet or work regime to ordinary cases. This was turned down, the chairman said that workhouses were 'not places of punishment'.[385]

The workhouse was later associated with scandal. Numbers grew in the second half of the century and the facilities became inadequate and understaffed.[386] Neither the Guardians nor the master of the house, Mr Cawse, seemed inclined to remedy matters. Everything was subordinated to economy. It was not until a local practitioner, a Dr J. W. Ley, became persistent in his protests that an enquiry was set up in 1894 under Lord Courtenay.[387] This enquiry produced distressing evidence of cruelty, especially to children, the feeble minded, sick and elderly. The matron, who was the master's wife, was condemned as callous. The kindest thing that can be said about her is probably that towards the end, she was ill herself. She died only a few weeks after being forced to resign.

It was reported old men and women were forced to give away pitiful meals for soap to wash verminous clothing. Women were described as covered in lice; one deranged woman, half covered in mud, was kept in a kennel in the yard. Lunatics and the sick were kept with all the other occupants. When a new nurse reported a woman was dying the Matron's retort had been 'Let her die – we have enough of her sort here'.[388] The entire staff was replaced, but what makes the episode even worse is the reluctance of the Guardians after this exposure. The Newton correspondent 'Johnny' wrote 'The sooner the whole place is clean swept out and a fresh start made the better. . . if Guardians only make up their minds to this instead of clinging for dear life to a policy of patch they and everyone else concerned would be much better for it.'[389] In August the Guardians decided single beds would be provided for girls and those as young as 15 should not be required to work in the laundry with women of bad character. Furthermore, and far more importantly, they decided separate accommodation would be provided for the sick![390] By October they agreed to employ a 'trained' nurse because, perhaps, nursing was deficient. One member still thought charges were exaggerated and that 'mountains were being made out of molehills.' The Guardians, having found they could not make Mr Cawse a presentation out of public funds, subscribed to one privately.[391] This was the finally irony; the Board who were in control, rewarded the man who had run it so badly that it had become a national scandal! Even then the Board continued to drag their feet. At a meeting in May 1885 Dr Ley suggested they adopt the motto 'procrastination' because nothing had been achieved of the reforms suggested by the Local Government Board some 12 months previously.[392]

In 1892 the Guardians gave the Teignmouth relieving officer a week's leave of absence 'on the occasion of his marriage'. He was presented with a silver mounted oak spirit case and a pair of nutcrackers as a wedding gift. At the same meeting Dr Colcross requested a straightjacket because of the trouble experienced in removing lunatics. The application was granted.[393] The Guardians decided to obtain a new copper similar to that used at the Plymouth workhouse; the old one could be utilized for making the oatmeal skilly,[394] thin watery porridge made with oatmeal and water. They discussed a couple who lived at Ipplepen named Farley who had been sent £100 by their son from the Cape of Good Hope. It was decided that as they had informed the Board, and that there were two of them to be kept, the Board would not claim back the relief given during the past 12 months.[395] The Guardians resolved to provide two perambulators for the use of babies. There was strenuous opposition from some who said it was 'placing a premium on immorality'.[396]

In 1896 an unusual post-mortem was reported to the Guardians. Daniel Osborne of St Marychurch died and Dr Colcross had found two sovereigns in his stomach.[397] Money found on an inmate would have been taken to help pay for his keep. Had this old man secreted the money but then falling ill feared it would be found, so swallowed it? A case came up before the Guardians of a man who occasionally took off his wooden leg to beat his wife.[398] The visiting committee recommended inmates should have a bun each on Good Friday and Colonel Walcott offered 16 shillings to pay for them. Dr Ley proposed that the workhouse pigsties should be abolished because they were deleterious to general health but his motion was lost.[399] Later the Board tried to move the pigs and was offered a low-lying field subject to flooding. A witty member of the Board suggested they would need to teach the pigs to swim! Three children were admitted suffering from typhoid fever, they were placed in an isolation ward and two nurses employed. Dr Ley now urged the 'necessity of an isolation hospital'.[400] Torbay Hospital, to which the Newton Guardians subscribed 20 guineas a year, refused to take a man with consumption from the workhouse, saying they did not care to take in paupers. The Guardians thought if that was their policy Torbay Hospital should not take their 20 guineas.[401] It was reported the workhouse was short of junk, the short lengths of old rope which had were taken apart by hand, for oakum.[402] Oakum was used for caulking, that is stopping up the ship's seams but its manufacture was very hard on the hands. In 1897 there were a series of complaints that bread was of poor quality. The Board returned some to the contractor and said in future they would specify 'superfine' instead of 'best fine'. Trouble continued with complaints that bread was under-baked.[403] In 1899 the workhouse tried to board out children to make more room for lunatics. There had been delays because it had been difficult to find property near the house. Some queried why this was necessary, but others suggested it was to enable mothers to deal with their children. The opposition faction responded saying that the 'least the mothers were encouraged to visit them the better' adding given the class of mother they should not have too much contact between the mothers and the children.[404]

Education

Schools were used for other purposes, for instance in 1855 some 200 subsidized blankets were distributed to the poor at the National School.[405] An entry in the Bearnes' School logbook lists the educational supplies that arrived in 1857. These were 48 spelling books, 6 slates, 36 pencils, 12 penholders and a box of nibs.[406] Later in 1868 plans by a Mr Babbage for erection of schoolrooms in Queen Street were approved provided there was 'a continuous supply of water for the privies'.[407] A private school advertised, in 1870 itself as a Classical, Mathematical and Commercial School, conducted by T. Hackworth: 'Mr Hackworth's great claim is to prepare pupils for what will probably be their future destination, and to combine the qualities of the Christian, the Scholar and the Gentleman.' Pupils of today might not have appreciated the holidays; Christmas 14 days, Midsummer 21 days.[408] In 1874 the Earl of Devon opened the new Marsh Schools, these held 200 pupils, until then some 120 had been educated in a former dwelling house. The press announced the school was chiefly for 'the poorer class of people who live in the Marshes' and that it would 'confer a great boon in disseminating education'.[409]

The forerunner of Newton College, established in Courtenay Park in 1861, moved to its College Road site in 1864 and went through a long period of expansion.[410] In 1876 a presentation was made, by the Earl of Devon and others, of an iron building to serve as a chapel for some 180 persons. The College also purchased a spacious new cricket ground, now public playing fields. In 1881 the College considered adding eight new classrooms and a new hall because the number of pupils 'has increased so rapidly during the last two to three years'.[411] In its heyday it enjoyed an enviable reputation which was not maintained and the college finally closed during the Second World War. Some remaining pupils went to form 'Newton House' at Kelly College Tavistock.

The Devon Central Chamber of Agriculture sometimes met at Newton Abbot for debates; for instance in 1870 'National Education; Secular v Religious'.[412] In 1872 the Wolborough School children, with the rector, teachers and friends amounting to some 750, had their annual treat in Stover Park thanks to the Duke of Somerset.[413] In 1873 he presented prizes at the Newton Abbot Art and Science School.[414] The Earl Devon presented prizes in 1878 and certificates for the Cambridge Local Examination in the Town Hall. Boys from the town and

Aller Pottery water wheel, the pottery functioned from about 1881 to 1924.

surrounding neighbourhood were there. Not many of the fair sex presented themselves for examination but the Earl had pleasure in making an award to Miss Poulton 'who had passed a very creditable examination'.[415]

The Board of Guardians petitioned Parliament that the age at which children should be compelled to attend school should be reduced from 14 to 12.[416] However, in the same year, 1881, a proposal for a high school for girls was made. A meeting was called to consider forming a Girl's Day School Company Limited in connection with the National Union for Improving Education of Women. The circular that convened the meeting stated there was 'a great demand in Newton for a good middle-class day school for girls there being no public school nearer than Exeter'.[417] Another meeting was called in the Parish Room in East Street, in 1883, to consider a grammar school, the eleventh Earl of Devon presided: 'For a long time the need of a school for the middle classes had been apparent to all interested in education'.[418] The school was established at Woodstock in Courtenay Park and moved to what is now Old Exeter Road. It transformed from fee paying, to entry on merit, and then fell before the fashion for comprehensive education; it is now Knowles Hill School.

In 1889 a meeting decided to form a Newton Abbot District University Association.[419] A few years later Mr A.W. Clayden began a course of lectures on the subject 'Geology' at Newton in connection with the University Extension Scheme. There was a fair attendance at afternoons and evenings.[420] Highweek Parish Council had discussed technical education. It had its advocates but Mr

Aller Pottery kiln, bottle kilns were commonplace in pottery manufacture until the mid-twentieth century. Some small examples still remain at Bovey Tracey.

Segar thought 'people should be made to work in a proper manner instead of attending classes of this kind, which would do them no good'. He continued 'The working classes were very ignorant and common things and he did not think technical education was going to help them.'[421]

A very early advertisement for the High School for Girls featured in Devonshire Antiquities *by John Chudleigh. Indian children then, would have been the English children of parents in India sent to England for schooling.*

High School for Girls

COURTENAY PARK,
NEWTON ABBOT.

Head Mistress : **MISS RIDLEY** *(First Class Honours, Cambridge Higher Local.)*

Assisted by Efficient Mistresses and Visiting Masters.

Pupils are prepared for the various Local Examinations, and the School is examined annually by the Oxford and Cambridge School Examiners.

The Head Mistress receives Boarders in Florian, her private house (connected with the school-house by a covered passage.)

Home comforts, with the advantage of public school training. Arrangements made for Indian children

Tennis, Good Playground, Garden, and Gymnasium

Crime and punishment

Mrs Mary Ann Frost was granted protection of her property from her husband. He had gone to Australia in 1854 and had not been concerned with his wife's welfare since. She had received a windfall from a relative and did not wish her forgetful husband to turn up and enjoy the legacy.[422] A woman called Ann Partridge unwisely tried to sleep in a policeman's outhouse. He marched her off to the station house 'where beds are always prepared for travellers'. The magistrate later awarded her 'seven days board and lodging with the prison-keeper'.[423]

The press complained that there had been so many accidents that scarcely a day passed without serious injury to 'hot-brained drivers'. No motorists then either! A specific accident was reported on the 'Mile-end Cottage – Newton Bushel road'. A gig overturned and smashed, a man and his housekeeper were thrown out. The penalty was a £2 fine and expenses.[424] Drunkenness also had its penalties; one Elizabeth Matthews of Torquay was fined 5 shillings but allowed a week to pay failing which she would 'be placed in the stocks for six hours'.[425] Counterfeit half sovereigns were being circulated in the town. Sovereigns were gold coins worth one pound. It was said that they 'look and ring remarkably well' but are 'light in weight'. Some victims were respectable farmers wives who sold butter and eggs.[426] In 1854 there were warnings of pickpockets operating in the market; 'several persons went home minus their purses and money'.[427] A female swindler, who had not paid for her Newton lodgings and stolen some items, was swiftly arrested in Plymouth in 1856. This was achieved because the police were given a Collodian portrait of her.[428] This was a very early practical use of the then new photographic process that had been invented in 1851. At the petty sessions William Goodenough was charged with wantonly firing a cannon within fifty feet of the Kingsteignton Road; he was fined 1s and 6s 6d. expenses.[429] In 1859 William Brasse, a tramp, was sent to prison for one month

A Wolborough cider-apple orchard, this peaceful scene reminds us how rural the area close to our town once was.

with hard labour for begging.[430] In 1862 a horse-dealer and a pig-jobber settled some 'differences' about a doubtful transaction in the market by a regular set-to. The police interfered when the fight was over.[431] A baker was fined for refusing to weigh a loaf.[432]

Scandal was abroad in 1863 over a farmer and a miller's wife who were supposed to have gone off together. It could just have been an agreeable outing, but both had taken 'sufficient funds with them for a rather longer excursion'.[433] Streetlights were kept burning until four in the morning instead of midnight. It was thought this would keep the town quieter and reduce petty theft.[434] Sarah Cope in the service of Mr Lucas, manure manufacturer, committed suicide. She had gone to a shop to buy oxalic acid, ostensibly to clean brass, but having obtained it, drank a large portion.[435] Four boys, who stole apples from Mr Stockman the miller, were ordered to be locked up until four o'clock and then whipped.[436]

The year 1870 started with a robbery which happily did not have the implications it might do now. A man called Dyer, a stone ripper from Torquay, stole 120 lbs. of blasting powder from a powder magazine near Newton. He and another man broke through the roof and were seen carrying bags across their backs.[437] Vandals were a problem in 1871, as now, the surveyor reported that several boys had been detected breaking lamps.[438] In February 1875, Margaret Crawley, 'a woman of ill-fame' from Plymouth was convicted of drunkenness.[439]

A 'strange scene' occurred at Newton Station. Maria Tucker, the wife of a Torquay man, eloped with a Plymouth fishmonger and took a considerable sum of money. Her husband laid in wait at the station and searched his wife and by cutting open her clothing found 50 sovereigns secreted under her left arm. On securing the money he let his wife go away with the fishmonger. The crowd was obviously on the husband's side because there was 'loud and continued cheering' when he recovered the money. Although Maria had received a cut in the head during the struggle she was subsequently sentenced, at Torquay Petty Sessions, to a month's hard labour for assaulting her husband and a police officer.[440]

An inquest was held on the suicide of a waggoner employed by Pinsent's Newton Brewery. He left a widow and six children, the youngest just six weeks old. The Coroner condemned the practice of brewers allowing their men unlimited beer and landlords for supplying free drinks when the waggoners made deliveries. He said this was 'false kindness'.[441]

A two-day bazaar was held at Sandford Orleigh, the 'pretty little seat of the great African traveller'. This raised funds for the *Mount Edgecumbe* training ship; but as well as money the promoters wanted boys! 'Any boy between the age of 11 and 14 who is found destitute or begging or stealing or refractory or frequenting bad company may be sent under the Industrial Schools Act on 2s. a week being guaranteed by one or other of the local authorities'.[442] A case that excited local interest was Alexander Moffat a much-respected manager of a Newton bank for some 12 years, who was charged with embezzlement. At a meeting at *Bradley's Hotel* a subscription was opened for Mrs Moffat who from what was a position of prosperity, with her family of eight children, was suddenly 'brought face to face with want'.[443]

Charlotte Spry was charged in 1884 with trying to pass off a counterfeit half-crown. There was a police check on milk sellers, a constable bought milk at 14 dairies in Newton and had them analyzed; 12 were pure. The chairman said that it was highly satisfactory that only two samples were adulterated![444] In 1886 a lad in the employ of F.B. Law stole four sixpenny pieces, modern theoretical equivalent 10p, from his master's till. His sentence was 12 strokes with the birch-rod. There was a prosecution by the Inland Revenue of a labourer for shooting partridges without a license.[445]

James Madder, the recent landlord of the *Market House Inn*, was sentenced to 14 days hard labour for assaulting his wife Mary. It was said he was habitually the worse for drink. The bench expressed the hope that after his sentence he would live amicably with his wife.[446] The police station near the top of Union Street was erected. It has long since become a shop but the heavy internal cell doors remain.[447] In 1891 Elizabeth Partridge, a shellfish dealer was found drowned in the Hackney Canal. The deceased, it was stated, was not sober and the verdict was 'Found Drowned'.[448]

Crime, in 1892, ranged from sleeping rough to infanticide. At the police court there were a number of cases, some arising from the recent race meeting. William Gode, a sawyer, was fined 7s.6d. for being drunk, Benjamin Owen 10s. for playing games of chance. Albert Jackman was fined 12s. for obtaining liquor not being a *bona fide* traveller. George Heward who was charged with sleeping under a haystack in the parish of Wolborough at 3 am and assaulting P.C. Adams, was sentenced to ten days with hard labour in Exeter jail.[449] A man trimming trees at Lower Marsh House on the Kingsteignton Road found a brown paper parcel in a dyke. The police were called and found it contained the body of a newly born female child that had been in the water about a fortnight.[450]

George Hamlyn, a lad, pleaded guilty to driving a horse and trap furiously in Wolborough Street. A constable said he was going at 13 to 14 mph and had driven over a child aged two and a half knocking him down and breaking his collarbone. He was fined 10s. or seven days. The chairman said he hoped it would be a caution to others.[451]

Amelia Adams, a woman who was said to be of dissolute habits was charged with sleeping out, she had been found in an outhouse in East Street at midnight. She had previous convictions so was sentenced to two months hard labour in prison.

Robert Small, 13, was before the court for stealing a chick. Fortunate lad, he was discharged under the First Offenders Act; however, his father was advised to 'give him a good thrashing'.[452] A check was carried out on the proof of spirits in public houses, three of them, the *Jolly Sailor, Royal Oak,* and *Turk's Head*, were found to be selling brandy under strength. The landlord of the *Jolly Sailor* thought this was due to the continual opening of the cask.[453] Frederick Crossing was charged at the police court with disorderly conduct by placing himself in a sheet and impersonating a ghost. He was bound over for six months to keep the peace.[454]

Kate Allen of Portsmouth, 'on the tramp' with three children was charged with stealing a pair of boots in Queen Street.[455] A Newton man Harry Grant murdered his wife with a hammer. He was placed in Exeter Gaol under sentence of death, but was respited and later, his sentence was commuted to imprisonment because of doubts about his mental state.[456] He was released and returned to Newton in 1911.

Charles B. King of Newton Abbot 'well-known, as an entertainer' was put on trial in 1897. He was accused of having abducted Carrie Louisa Martin aged 17, of Bishopsteignton. The judge directed the jury to bring in a verdict of 'not guilty' whereupon he was released. It seems to have been an unusual case; there was doubt about the young lady's age, even 22 was suggested. The girl's sister had abetted the elopement and the girl was reported as having 'a condition' before she eloped! She seems to have cared for Charles because when he was arrested in London and brought back to Devon she voluntarily accompanied him on the journey.[457]

William Baggaley, an ex-army man discharged with disgrace, reported having set fire to a rick at Sandygate. He said he had been on the tramp for two years and done scarcely any work. He said 'I'd rather go to prison than continually tramp around the country'.[458] Life at the end of the century continued its steady pace, Robert Smith was charged with driving his traction engine at over two miles an hour.[459]

Railway

In 1852 the inhabitants of Newton Abbot and Newton Bushel determined to adopt London time.[460] Until the coming of the railways it had varied across the country; the railways radiating from the capital though adopted London Time. It was therefore inconvenient to have to cope with two different kinds of time, hence Newton's sensible decision to change. Interestingly, Exeter was much more insular in this respect, at first refusing to change and then coming up with the idea of running two clocks with different times, one for Exeter the other for London time![461] What rather spoils this picture of progressive timekeeping Newtonians is that later, in 1865, there was apparently only one hand on the clock and lack of funds to rectify the matter[462]

Queen Victoria passed through Newton in 1856, although a substantial crowd waited to see her, only some of the ladies were allowed on the platform alongside the train. In 1859 Prince Albert, on his way to Saltash to open Brunel's new bridge across the Tamar, was delayed in Newton. This happened because the signalman was 'napping at his post' and it took loud whistling to waken him.[463]

The tender for a new railway station was accepted in 1860.[464] The South Devon Railway Company employed so many workmen by 1861 that the

Passenger, possibly unwilling, at Newton Junction. Interestingly the suggested date of the drawing is 1880 but the request to change the name of the station to Newton Abbot had been made in 1876 and followed shortly afterwards.

employees found it difficult to procure houses. The company had therefore determined to erect 150 houses themselves for the mechanics to reside in near the works.[465] In 1861 preliminary arrangements were made for commencing the Newton to Moretonhampstead railway;[466] the line, which ran via Bovey Tracey and Lustleigh, opened to passenger traffic in 1866.[467] In 1877 there was an inquest on a fatal accident to John Powesland, a foreman shunter. The jury returned a verdict of 'Accidental Death' but suggested that the railway company should contribute to the local hospital because of its many accident cases. The paper reporting the case said that was 'very well as far as it goes but might not the company be also advised to contribute fewer cases of accident'.[468] The GWR took over the SDR and were requested by the Board in 1876 to alter the name of the station from Newton Junction to Newton Abbot.[469]

In 1882 the first part of the Teign Valley railway line from Heathfield to Ashton was opened.[470] Later there was a railway accident when an unattached locomotive on the down line struck a passenger train going to Torquay, at points. Fortunately, no passengers were seriously hurt, only somewhat shaken, but both engines were badly damaged.[471] In 1885 the GWR claimed, in a re-rating case, that both the Moretonhampstead and Ashburton lines ran at a loss.[472] One day in May 1899 the engine of the 8.30 train from Newton to Moretonhampstead broke down at Lustleigh. A telegram was sent to Newton for another engine and some of the passengers who had appointments had to get carriages to their destination. The train had been delayed two hours before a fresh engine could get there and take the train on.[473] In 1890 railway men in Newton sought a reduction in hours and an increase in wages.[474] There was an accident in 1891 when 15-year-old Thomas Palmer fell and caught his hand in a turntable severely crushing it.[475] Over one weekend in May 1892 the GWR railway system was altered from Broad to Standard gauge, a most amazing engineering feat. There was news, too, of more investment by the railway. The down line through the station was successfully straightened and the hot water house to provide heated foot warmers was nearly finished. Trains were unheated then.

River Teign, undated, but after the Moretonhampstead line was built and before new racecourse. Hackney the bargees' village is visible on its creek.

Goods by water

Newton quay was considerably extended in 1851 which was thought would benefit the town. There is a tendency to think that once the railway arrived at Newton nearly all goods went out or came in by train. This was not so, a considerable quantity was still conveyed by water. There are records of the cargoes that arrived and were despatched from the Courtenay Wharves and there were other wharves as well, so the extracts set out below are only a fraction of the whole. The very last cargoes to arrive in Newton were sand barges coming up the Whitelake to unload by he present B&Q carpark until the early 1950s. There was incidentally a quayside inn, originally the *Passage House* but later *Wharf House*, towards the bottom of Wharf Road.

The Courtenay daybook of exports runs from 1860 to 1906. The greatest single commodity sent out was not surprisingly clay, but the ores are a useful reminder of mining in the Teign valley. The record of imports also starts in 1860 but continues to 1910. The two major commodities brought in were timber and coal. Undoubtedly the trade of carrying goods by water was declining overall throughout the period but in total it was certainly significant.

Some sample years are listed.

The names in brackets are the consignee or consignor.

IMPORTS
1860
October, Bark this would have been for tanning, hides, Valonia, which are acorn cups of the Levantine evergreen oak, again used for tanning (Vicary). Coals (Pinsent) Luggage (Bickford).

November, Sand (Webber), Coals (Exmouth Mining Coy.)

December, Rice etc, Groceries.

1870
January, Coals, Bark,

March, Manure.

June, Portland stone presumably for building, Salt.

July, Pebbles, Valonia, Timber, Coals.

August, Spirit, Gwalia.

November, Groceries, Sand

1880
January, Coal, Pipes, Cement.

March, Culm, usually very small anthracite, 2 Hogsheads and 1 Puncheon.

May, Coal, Hides.

October, 2 pipes of wine.

1890
January, Cement, 49 casks petroleum

February, Coal

August. Slate

September, Coal (Newton Gas co)

October, Pig iron (Beares)

1900
Coals (Newton Gas co)

February, Slates (Devon Trading Co.)

March, Cement (Devon Trading Co.)

June 360 Barrels Oil (Bear Creek Oil Co)

August, 200 Barrels Oil, Coals (Newton Gas Co.)

September, 240 Barrels Oil.

EXPORTS
1860
October, Ochre, Luggage, Clay, Timber.

November, Bales flesh, these would be the tanned inside layers of animals hides used for linings and such like purposes, Copper Ore (Exmouth Mining Co), Clay

1870
January, Lead ore, it is likely that this also came from the Teign Valley because as well as Wheal Exmouth at Christow there were other mines producing lead ore notably Frankmills mine at Hyner which is north east of Hennock, Clay.

April, Clay, Lead ore.

August, Stone

September, Blende, this is sphalerite a zinc sulphide an important source material for zinc (Exmouth Mining Co.)

1880
January, Clay.

March, Stone, Clay.

September, Stone, Clay

1890
Stone, Clay. [476]

Church/Religion

Church matters were of importance to inhabitants of Newton at the time. In 1850 a meeting of the Irish Society was treated to an 'eloquent and very articulate speech on the errors of Popery and Puseyism'.[477] Puseyism, a high-church strand of the Church of England, advocated a return to Catholic practices.

The Bishop refused to ordain a candidate for holy orders who had attended a concert in aid of fire victims organized by a dissenting body. He said that the candidate had committed schism.[478] This became something of a *cause celebre* in Newton causing so much public indignation that a public meeting was called.

There was open air preaching in 1858 near the Tower on a Saturday evening when a Dr Bell preached to a large concourse of people.[479] The Bishop of Exeter finally relented and allowed evening service to be celebrated at St Leonard's rather than in Wolborough Parish Church when the weather was wet. The inhabitants had asked for this for some years, but the Bishop had always turned it down, even though Lord Courtenay had backed the petitioners.[480] The distance of both Highweek and Wolborough parish churches from their main centres of population had been a factor affecting attendance mentioned by both incumbents in the Religious Census of 1851. This census was a one off, because the results were so divisive it was never again attempted. In a footnote to history long past, Highweek finally became a parish independent of Kingsteignton; it had been a chapel of ease, since Saxon times.[481] It was announced in 1867 that St Paul's Church, built principally by the Earl of Devon for his tenants, would be formally opened by Bishop Spencer at the end of October.[482] By 1871 St Paul's, was found to be too small because of growing congregations. An additional wing was added, the Earl of Devon laying the foundation stone.[483] The South Devon Book Hawking Association held its 1862 annual meeting at the *Globe*; hawking had nothing to do with falconry; they sold religious tracts! There had been a marked increase in the sales of bibles, prayer books and church services. The Association had a sales analysis for different social classes.[484]

The 1860s started with a petty argument. The Registrar of the Archdeaconry

St Paul's Church in Edwardian days. From a post card which had been sent for an old halfpenny.

Abbotsleigh House stood on the site that became St Augustine's Priory in 1860. The Priory closed in 1983, and it is now a housing complex.

of Totnes wanted to change the way churchwardens were appointed. The ratepayers of Wolborough however, were satisfied and claimed the system, where the receivers of the feoffees had acted as churchwardens, had been in operation for some 300 years! A change, it was suggested, would inevitably produce dissent between feoffees and churchwardens.[485] It was announced in 1886 that a church institute for young men was to be formed in Newton. This would provide members of the three Anglican churches with a library and rooms for reading and recreation.

The Abbotsleigh estate, near Abbotskerswell, was purchased for use as a Roman Catholic religious house.[486] It became St Augustine's Priory, but closed in 1983. In 1867 Roman Catholics purchased from the Earl of Devon a site 'for the erection of a place of worship and a residence for the officiating priest' near St Paul's Church,[487] still on the original site at the present time. The Congregational Chapel opened in Queen Street in 1875, it held eight hundred worshippers. The architect was Mr J. W. Rowell, by then working in Torquay, and the builders were Parker's of Newton Abbot. To celebrate there was both a luncheon in the Temperance Hall and a tea at the Alexandra Hall. The chapel is now solicitors' offices.

Plans were submitted for a Wesleyan Chapel in 1866. The first meeting of the Salvation Army in Newton was held outside the market in 1882.[488] The next year the Rechabites, belonging to the local tent 'Bud of Promise', had a social tea at the Temperance Hall.[489] Rechabites were a sect of total abstainers. A singular accident was reported in 1893. Mr J. Farrell of Station Cottages was taking off his overcoat before entering the church at his daughter's wedding. In so doing his left arm was forced from its socket. He remained during the ceremony but afterwards the arm had to be reset.[490] There was an interesting gypsy funeral for Robert Burch 43 in 1898, at Wolborough Parish Church, 'a lovely lot of flowers, wreaths and crosses'.[491] It is a tradition in their community to vie with one another in the magnificence of floral tributes. The English Church Union held their Devon branch annual meeting in 1878 at the *Globe Hotel* but 'Not a single clergyman belonging to Newton Abbot was present'.

The committee also went on record that they regretted their inability 'to obtain the use of a church in Newton Abbot for a service in connection with the meeting'. [492] There was a two-day bazaar in 1896 at the Market Buildings in aid of Wolborough church funds. 'The bazaar represented an old Cornish fishing village with St Michael's Mount in the distance'.[493] Mr W Vicary opened a Grand Ice Carnival bazaar to raise funds for the growing needs of Methodism in 1899.[494]

Industry & Retail

During this half century and later there was a great diversity of industry in Newton. In 1854 there was a fire on the premises of Mr Vicary, the tanner, caused by drying bark soaked in the floods.[495] A wagon laden with bark for Mr Vicary's tannery in 1858 came into contact with the shed of the fish market which was totally demolished but no person was hurt.[496] There was an inquest at the *Commercial Inn* in 1870 on William Stevens aged 11, employed by Mr Vicary who had been sent to fetch a horse from his master's stables. The boy was seen being dragged along by a galloping horse and was found lifeless minus an arm and an ear with head and face dreadfully cut. The verdict was 'Accidental death'.[497] At Christmas in 1886 Messrs. Vicary made their 'usual generous' Christmas present of meat to their workmen numbering some 300, men had 7 1/2 lbs. and the boys 3 1/2 lbs. of beef each.[498] The numbers employed show how important Vicary's were to the local economy and for many years before and after. Towards the end of the century there was a strike at Vicary's for an increase in pay and a shorter working week. Replacements were found and 'the most dissatisfied and wranglesome' were not re-employed.[499]

The ironmongers announced that they would close their shops at the earlier hour of seven o'clock in the winter months except on Wednesdays and Saturdays.[500]

John Polyblank, engineers, iron and brass founders reduced their men's hours to 60 per week, a reduction of two, by allowing them to finish work on Saturdays at 4 p.m.[501] Polyblank Road is a reminder of this business of long ago. In 1892 there was meeting at the Dolphin Coffee Tavern of shop assistants to appoint a committee to try and secure early closing on Thursdays during the summer months at two rather than four o'clock which had been the case up until now.[502]

A 'talented townsman' Mr B.J. Webber won first prize at the Bath and West Agricultural show for the 'best four horse-power thrashing (threshing) machine'.[503] Later Mr Webber, an engineer, invented a new pump that was 'capable of lifting from five to six hogsheads an hour'. It was tried out at a Kingsteignton clay works.[504] Hogshead was a variable liquid measure usually around 50 gallons. Two years later it was announced in that C & H Webber's, iron-founders were to erect a sawmill on Jetty Marsh. 'This will be driven by waterpower of which there is an abundant supply'.[505]

During the Crimean War a manufacturer in Newton Abbot responded to a national appeal for tobacco for the troops by offering to present a box of his clay pipes. The article in the paper noted 'Tobacco without pipes is perhaps not quite so inconvenient as mustard without beef'.[506] Later in the war the old tower bells were rung to celebrate the fall of Sebastopol.[507]

The first newspaper to appear in Newton Abbot was called the *Newton Journal* and came out when Stamp Duty was still applicable.[508] It went into liquidation but restarted by Daniel Vile as *The South Devon Advertiser* in 1863. Vile had grown up in poverty and become a farm labourer; however, he went to night school and later worked for the *Newton Journal*. When it failed, there was no money to pay his wages so he was given the business, which he then ran successfully as the *Advertiser*.[509]

During 1872/1873 the Wolborough Iron Mine operated between Newton and Abbotskerswell.[510] It was never a large undertaking but shipments of ore were sent from Newton Quay, to Ebbw Vale and Rhymney in South Wales but some even went to Bilbao in Spain.[511] Another enterprise was the South Devon Waggon Works in East Street. It was sold and comprised 'valuable machinery, tools and stock-in-trade comprising, three new exhibition farm wagons, two harvest wains, four-wheel ditto, butchers' wagons, carts, beverley cart, etc. . . . a large quantity of well seasoned ash plank, and elm board, ash, elm and oak trees, apple tree wood . . . American cloth, carriage lamps and trimmings in great variety'.[512]

Local clay merchants were prosecuted for offences under the Metalliferous Mines Legislation Act. Messrs Watts, Blake and Bearne were fined for not displaying a notice at Preston Manor Mine and not properly fencing shafts at Fountain Pits. There were other fines for insufficient ventilation and failing to furnish enough drying and dressing room accommodation.[513] A 'terrible death' was reported when Charles Wyatt, foreman at Stockman Brothers the millers, entered the grinding room in the dark and became entangled in the machinery.[514] In 1898 the Inspector of Fisheries, on behalf of the Board of Trade, held an enquiry in the town. Should there be a close season, using certain kinds of nets, for flat fish? What size could lobsters be taken? It is interesting there were delegates from all along south Devon coast including Stokenham, Beesands and Hallsands.

Frank Matcham, 1854–1920

Frank Matcham was born in East Street in Newton Abbot, the son of a brewery manager and started work as an office boy in Torquay. Later he was apprenticed to an architectural firm in London. He married Maria Robinson, daughter of the proprietor of a firm of theatre architects, and took over the family firm. He designed over 120 music halls and theatres when they were becoming more popular and seeking to expand in size and opulence. Not only were inland cities growing rapidly, but also there were burgeoning seaside resorts. Among his better known work in London were the Hackney Empire, the Hippodrome in Charing Cross Road, the Coliseum, and the London Palladium. He also worked in Belfast, was responsible for the Blackpool Opera House and the Bristol Hippodrome. He seems to have been highly adept. His work was functional and he worked speedily, often having to contend with difficult or restricted sites. One particular job he did at the Edgware Music Hall was completed in four months, from foundation to opening for a Christmas pantomime! Despite this there were criticisms in the architectural profession which found fault for not adhering to traditional design tenets, even though the results were spectacular. Certainly he must have pleased his clients, because otherwise he would never have obtained the great amount of business.[515]

Fires

In 1859 there was a fire in a detached building behind the *Jolly Sailor*, the building was used for drying feathers, probably for pillows and suchlike.[516] Two serious fires occurred in 1874, one at a draper's shop in Courtenay Street. Mr Horder, who slept over the shop was rescued by means of a ladder. Four females at the top of the house were taken through a window.[517] At that period nearly every shop proprietor would live above his shop and many apprentices or shop assistants would also 'live in'. The other fire, the biggest for some years, was Mr George Stockman's Newton Flour Mill. The steam engine was destroyed and stocks of corn and flour burnt. The mill was reduced to ruins.[518] It was originally water-powered so this news item indicates it had been modernised to steam. Yet, despite all these fires in 1876 the application to form a fire brigade was refused by the Board.[519] By 1879 the Board was obviously looking for protection against fire, six more men were added to the fire brigade. The surveyor was also directed to repair the hose and order an additional standpipe.[520]

In 1881 there was a destructive fire at Messrs. Polyblank the South Devon iron works. The workmen, some of whom had been thrown out of work, lost a considerable quantity of tools and Mr Polyblank lost a large number of patterns.[521] The men would then have largely supplied the working tools in a factory such as this, at their own cost. There was another large fire a year later, in Queen Street. Mr Bentley who was a tobacconist and cricket bat maker, owned the business. The whole of the shop contents was destroyed. Neighbouring tradesmen extinguished the fire because the town water was not turned on until an hour after the fire was first seen! A spark from a train on the Moretonhampstead line in 1887 caught the thatch of the Devon & Courtenay clay cellars, an extensive range of buildings some 250-foot long beside the River Lemon. There was danger of the fire spreading, because running parallel with and behind the clay cellars was the large cider stores of Symonds and Co. of Totnes and at right angles the lofty and extensive stores of Arthur Lee corn and hay merchant. The West of England Insurance Fire Brigade attended as did Highweek parish brigade.[522] There was a fire in Mr Yeo's rope works; the furnace for heating oil became overheated, ignited, and spilt out on to the earth floor of the shed. Fortunately little damage was done.[523] The West of England Fire Brigade presented an engine to the town in 1899.[524]

Leisure

Leisure often had an 'improving' content. A club was formed at Magor's *Commercial Hotel* to enable the working classes to visit The Great Exhibition in London's Hyde Park.[525] In the summer Cock's, an American touring party of artistes entered the town with a 'cortege of horses, carriages, rein-deer and bipeds'.[526] It was reported that great numbers of visitors flocked to the 'beautiful village of Highweek', 'a delightful spot', in which the 'beauty of scenery cannot be excelled'.[527] A travelling theatrical company presented *'How to live without money'*. The paper wittily suggested the company well understood the method judging by the poor houses they received. The same issue recorded the visit of a large number of teetotallers, who had arrived by excursion train to spend the day in the 'delightful retreat' of Bradley Woods.[528] This is evidence of how quickly excursion trains became operative in the area and what a popular venue Bradley Woods was. Only ten years before Thomas Cook the pioneer of excursion trains had run his first train from Leicester to Loughborough in 1841 and that had been for temperance supporters too.[529]

In summer 1852 there was a 'Pic-Nic' that left Barge's *Half Moon Inn* and went in three conveyances to Berry Castle accompanied by the Newton Band. 'The day was delightfully spent'.[530] The fifth of November was celebrated by burning an effigy of the Pope 'amid loud huzzas'. Firework night was then an occasion for anti-Catholic feelings and did not always pass by soberly! In other years there were reports of flaming tar barrels being rolled through the streets regardless of consequences to persons or property. The Newton Literary Society opened their spring session with a concert of vocal and instrumental music at Beazley's *Globe Hotel*.[531] In 1854 a New Zealand chief gave two lectures, which were well attended, at the National schoolroom in Kingsteignton, on New Zealand and Australia.

In 1855 there was a grand summer fete in Bradley Woods with the following bands: The 15th King's Hussars, The New Swindon and Mechanics Institution and Bell Band, the Torquay Subscription, the South Devon Railway Locomotive Band and the Torquay Choral Society. There was an extensive collection of models and a demonstration of electric telegraphy. In 1856 petitions were sent from the town to Parliament against opening the Crystal Palace and the British Museum on Sundays.[532] Hundreds of people flocked to Bradley Woods in 1858 to hear 'the profuse strains of unpremeditated art' of a nightingale.[533]

One summer night in 1850 the 10.45 train arrived at 3 a.m. carrying passengers from the national agricultural show at Exeter with no less than 43 carriages. It was detained at several stations en route and on starting from Teignmouth several carriages were left behind in a tunnel; 'an engine was sent back to relieve the unfortunates from their gloomy position'.[534] At that time there were tunnels on both sides of Teignmouth Station. Then, and for many years afterwards, the County Show had a different venue each year. It was well into the next century before it became a static event on the same show ground each year. A preliminary announcement was made in May 1874 that it would come to Newton provided the town met the Agricultural Society's requirements. The press said there was no doubt that 'such an enterprising town as Newton Abbot will readily do so'. A deputation was sent to Barnstaple, which hosted the show in 1874, to asses what would be required. [535] The *Flying Post* reported Newton inhabitants had worked 'with the heartiest good will to give their agricultural friends a cordial and befitting welcome'. The town was extensively decorated, the streets leading from the railway station were 'lined with Venetian motifs' each of these surmounted by a cushion and crown 'canopied throughout the whole length with festoons of flowers'. There were 'trophies of flags' and 'triumphal arches'. At night St Leonard's and the Market Tower were lit by gaslight, the fuel provided free by the Gas Company. The show yard was at the end of Wolborough Street, less than a mile from the station, on a 15-acre site divided by the River Lemon. Three substantial wooden bridges were provided. As well as the implements at the show field, there were trials of steam ploughs at Wolborough Barton, 'Messrs Beare & Co of Liverton Works Newton Abbot have one of the largest collections of machinery and implements on the ground'. In connection with the show there was a monster fete, two floral concerts, performances by the band of the Royal Marines from Plymouth, a theatre at the *Globe* gave performances nightly, fireworks and other attractions. [536] It was also reported the new town clock in the old tower proved a great boon to the hundreds of strangers visiting for the agricultural show. [537] The Devon County show returned in 1887 and was held on the old racecourse on the other side of the Kingsteignton Road. The weather this time 'was even more unfavourable than on the last occasion'. There were serious accidents and destruction of property. Several tents were completely demolished and a large refreshment tent collapsed. For a while it is recorded visitors were almost panic-stricken scarcely knowing where to go or what to do. Luckily by five o'clock the wind abated.[538] The big event of 1898 was the third visit of the Devon County Agricultural Show. This time it was held on the Ashburton Road opposite Ess Hill and was opened by Lord Clifford. One stand offered 'Stone's butter colouring which imparts a pure rich beautiful colour to butter and cheese and their celebrated Essence of Rennet which will make a junket in three minutes'. Another stand of Plymouth engineers demonstrated what could be done by electricity as a motive-power. No less than 12 motors were driven by one dynamo.[539]

An Exhibition of Works of Art and Industry was held in the Philadelphia Hall in 1870. Prizes were given for models in iron, brass or other metal, wood, plaster, card-board, imitation flowers, best hand-made print dress, patchwork, knitted pair worsted stockings, white embroidery, hand-made lace, straw plaiting, hand-made pair of boots, set of horse shoes, specimen of saddlery, basket work, geological specimens, free hand drawing, mechanical drawing, penmanship, window plants, collection wild grapes, nosegay of wild flowers, oil landscape, photograph from life and specimen bird stuffing by professionals.[540] In 1873 the Newton Abbot Horticultural Garden Society held its annual show at Rose-hill, a big house then, its gateway remains in Highweek Road a little way below the present Dyrons Swimming pool; the paper reported 'It wasn't exactly flower show weather'.[541] A restriction was placed on bathing in the Teign and its

Published by G. Daimond, Newton Abbot.   Lithographed by Newman & Cº 48 Watling Stº London.

Knowles Hill from the South Devon Cricket Ground

Knowles Hill from the South Devon Cricket ground, c.1855. The kit was different then!

tributaries between 10am and 6pm and furthermore 'that all bathers do wear drawers'.[542] In August 1875 there was a great fete run by the South Devon Railway Working Men's Club on a field next to the cricket ground. The 3rd Devon Volunteer Artillery band played some 'capital dance music'. 'There was the magic post-office for lovers' and 'Aunt Sally' and 'Uncle Sam' were both present.[543]

In days when less entertainment was provided commercially, people more often organized their own. At this period in Newton there was a 'Pleasant Evening Committee' which arranged various events; for instance they held a spelling bee combined with musical entertainment in February of 1876.[544] The Board agreed the plans for a Coffee Tavern.[545] This project was to provide non-licensed premises where people could go for social meetings and try to counter the evils of alcohol. The Earl of Devon officially opened the Tavern in October 1880. It later became known as the Dolphin Tavern and the chairman of directors was Mr J. Vicary. It offered wholesome refreshment had a reading room and a bagatelle board.[546] In some towns such as Totnes coffee taverns soon failed, but in Newton it became a financial success and ran at a profit for a number of years.

The 1880 season of subscription dances started in the *Globe* Assembly rooms with music provided by the band of Royal Marines.[547] The annual fair in 1881 was a big one. It filled the whole of the Market Place from the entrance to Courtenay Street on one side, to the other end leading into Bank Street. There were shows, swing-boats, steam-circuses, rifle-shooting galleries and sweet stalls. In the market there was a show of useful horses.[548] In December there was again skating on Stover Lake, 'the ice being in excellent condition'. It was so popular that people coming from a distance, such as Plymouth, were advised that the nearest station was Heathfield on the Moretonhampstead line.[549] There was a meeting of the 'West of England Rowing Association' at the *Globe* in 1882 for the purpose of forming a local association.

Queen Victoria's Golden Jubilee in 1887 was a great occasion. 'Right loyally

Post Office staff in Market Street, not many female employees then, uniformed telegraph boys, who would have delivered telegrams at the front. The building is decorated for a special occasion but which one is not recorded.

did the inhabitants of this town celebrate' the *Flying Post* recorded. The town was well decorated and the day generally observed as a holiday. There was a royal salute from Wolborough Hill; both Highweek and Wolborough parish churches rang merry peals. There was a procession through the town and some 2,000 sat down to dinner in the market-hall.[550] Mr R.H. Baker gave a personal donation of £10 as a Jubilee gift for the poor of the two parishes. A carillon machine capable of playing 21 tunes was placed in St Leonard's Tower.[551] The plaque is still on the west side of the Tower.

A meeting was held at the Town Hall to consider inviting the Devonshire Association to hold their 1888 meeting at Newton Abbot. Mr Cotton spoke saying how advantageous this would be whereupon it was unanimously agreed and a subscription for funds was set up.[552] There was a lecture at the Great Western Mechanics Institution on the Free Libraries Act by Mr Wright, the public librarian of Plymouth. It was hoped a library would be set up as the result of his visit, but it did not happen.[553] Cock-fighting was reported in the neighbourhood. The police made a raid causing a general stampede; those identified included 'several publicans and other well-to-do persons'.[554]

During 1892 a Primrose League dance was held in Newton, about 80 members and friends attended.[555] Primrose League was a public association to foster Conservatism and named after Benjamin Disraeli's reputedly favourite flower. A meeting was called at the Town Hall for the purpose of setting up a tennis club. Attendance was 'fairly good' but 'much interest' was shown. Grounds had been secured in Forde Park and it was decided to call it the Forde Lawn Tennis Club. A concert, held in the Alexandra Hall in aid of the Athletic Fund, was provided by the pupils of the Grammar School. They presented Coleman's comedy *The Heir at Law* and the well-known farce *The Area Bells*. During the interval there was an exhibition of dumb-bell and swordstick drill by junior

Jubilee at Newton Work-house, almost certainly the Diamond of 1897. No one would have chosen to go there but all have clean pinafores for the special occasion.

boys.[556] The first run of Newton Rovers Cycle Club was announced for April. A smoking concert would follow and members of other clubs were being invited.[557] It was decided to form an association football club.[558]

The Diamond Jubilee was also a time of great celebration. Inhabitants were woken by a salute of 60 guns from Wolborough and Knowles Hills and hundreds turned out for a service at St Leonard's Tower at 7 o'clock. The press reported Newton prided itself on its processions but this time 'it eclipsed itself' thanks to the tradesmen and continued 'few towns in England made a finer effort in this direction'. Over 1,000 poor and aged had a 'sumptuous repast' at the market buildings. There were Old England sports at the Recreation Ground, juvenile sports and maypole-dancing in the afternoon, and evening dances in Courtenay Park and the Alexandra Hall. Songs of the West were performed in the Butter market and a procession of illuminated cyclists went to Wolborough Hill where there was an immense bonfire.[559] Some 600 infants each received a penny and some confectionery. As a permanent memorial an endowment fund was set up for Newton Abbot Hospital.[560]

The cabman's annual supper for 1888 was held at the *Union Hotel* and with friends the numbers came to 70. The party was obviously a good one because it did not break up till three in the morning. This was despite the songs they sang which included 'Dear old pals' 'The soldier's grave' and 'See that my grave is kept green'![561] The various churches of Newton Abbot held their annual harvest tea in the Pannier Market and the Alexandra Hall; an unprecedented number of some 1,400 sat down together. The Pleasant Evening's Committee had made the arrangements and the ladies of the town had prettily decorated the halls.[562] At the end of the year the tradesmen held their 'show' night and was said to be equal to the previous year. The drapers laid out their windows in 'charming style representing different scenes'; the butchers showed immense carcasses of beef, mutton and pork. Grocers and confectioners paid special attention to their decorations and crowds paraded the streets to admire the displays.[563]

In 1891 an interesting lecture on the Channel Tunnel was given in the Town Hall, to a large and appreciative audience.[564] The employees of Mr George Hicks builder of Kingskerswell, in 1898 had their wayzgoose, correctly a printer's picnic but here used for a workmen's outing, journeying to Princetown in a break supplied by the *Globe Hotel*.[565]

Towards the end of the century Newton seems to have been moving to more modern entertainment; the Council called the market lessee's attention to insurance requirements for cinematograph and biograph exhibitions.[566] In the very last year Newton Abbot Flying Club flew a pigeon race from Templecombe on 19 August.[567] Wolborough Harvest Tea was held in Market Buildings, the entertainment included a musical bicycle ride by 14 ladies trained by Sergeant-Major Tommy and a gymnastic display on the horizontal bar.[568] At the end of that year and despite bad weather, a large number witnessed a meet of the South Devon Hunt at the Tower.[569]

In May 1875 Sir Samuel and Lady Baker took up residence at Sandford Orleigh. The 'noble traveller' sailed up the Teign in a steam vessel made especially with a shallow draught. 'The church bells at Highweek rang a merry peal' and there were 'other demonstrations of hearty welcome'.[570] Some years later General Gordon stayed with Sir Samuel. Sandford Orleigh had a reputation for gracious living; at Christmas orange trees were brought into the house so guests might pick their own oranges!

Lady Florence Baker 1842–1916

Florence Baker was born Florence, possibly von Sass, of a German speaking family in Transylvania. She was orphaned as a small girl in the Hungarian uprisings, and took on the name of Finnian. She was exhibited for sale in the slave market in Widdin, in the Ottoman Empire, now Vidin in Bulgaria. Quite how she arrived there is uncertain, the most exciting, but possibly the most unlikely, version, is that she was at sea and taken by pirates and then sold.

Samuel Baker on a hunting expedition to the Balkans saw this seventeen-yea-old girl; felt sorry for her and bought her. He was 38. Whatever his original intentions, the upshot was she was with him in what is now Roumania, and later in Africa, sharing the same tent and overseeing the domestic arrangements dressed in trousers. She shared considerable privations and at one point suffered badly from sunstroke. She justifiably became well known for being the first white woman to have lived for a considerable period in that part of Africa's hostile environment.

They returned to England in 1865 and it was only on arrival that they were secretly married. She became Lady Baker when her husband was knighted in 1866. Later it was hoped she would be presented at court but a whiff of scandal had reached Queen Victoria's ears, so despite her husband's friendship with the Prince of Wales, this never happened.

Florence lived on at Sandford Orleigh as a widow for some 23 years after her husband's death. She was charitable, regularly making gifts to the Gilberd Almshouses. She was demanding of her domestic staff at Sandford Orleigh, putting on white gloves to check the banisters had been properly dusted! Two members of her staff who wished to marry were told to leave. They set up Rundle's, the tobacconist, in Wolborough Street'.[571]

Sir Samuel White Baker 1821–1893

Samuel Baker's father was a wealthy merchant, trading particularly with India, who had interests in banking, shipping and railways and who also had property abroad. Samuel was born in London went to school near Brighton and in Gloucester, and completed his education in Germany.

He married Henrietta Biddulph, and set off with her firstly to Mauritius and then Ceylon. They returned to England in 1855 and Henrietta, the mother of several children, died of typhoid.

Samuel, leaving his family in an aunt's care, went travelling again to the Balkans, where he met his second wife, Florence. From 1859 to 1860 he oversaw the construction of a railway in Romania near the mouth of the Danube.

Taking Florence with him he went to Africa hoping to explore the tributaries of the Blue Nile. Later they set off to seek out Lake Albert. The whole trip took some two and a half years and was beset by dangers and disease.

When he returned to England, he was knighted and his reputation was established. Later he was asked to lead a larger expedition to the same part of Africa. This time the objective was to subdue the slave trade and open the country to commerce.

In 1874 he came to live in Newton at Sandford Orleigh, taking an active interest in local affairs. He lectured widely and wrote a number of books including *The Rifle and the Hound in Ceylon*, *The Nile Tributaries of Abyssinia*, and *Wild Beasts and their ways*. Being, in his time, so famous, he was bothered by unofficial visitors at Sandford Orleigh trying to get a sight of him. To discourage them he put up a notice 'Beware of the Hymenophyllum extremely dangerous, at large in the grounds'. This was a fern. He was a tough specimen even in later life; two years before he died it was recorded he had returned from India where he had shot six or seven tigers.[572]

Miscellaneous

An unusual inquest was held in 1871 on an elephant keeper, John Paton, who had his charge on the mail train at Plymouth in a horsebox. It became restive and killed his keeper. The body being taken off at Newton.[573] According to a report in the *Western Morning News* the animal had been freely plied with rum and beer.[574] Paton is buried in Wolborough churchyard. There was a lucky escape for a girl named Barrow, in 1872, who playing on the steps at Union Bridge, fell into the river and was swept 150 yards through the tunnel. She was rescued by a young man, the miller and his ladder. The paper reported she was sent home 'not much worse for her immersion'.[575] Less fortunate was Mary Jackson found dead at Furzehill Sandpit. She had been trapped by a fall of sand, though the pit was close to a highway it was a lonely spot and she was not found until too late. Her occupation had been digging white sand for scouring.[576] A far cry from our modern cleansers but then a living could be made from digging sand and hawking it. In 1874 one evening a little boy called Beer, about 5 years old, the son of a coach-wheeler, went out to play with his toy wheelbarrow. He was found at 6 a.m. next morning two miles away, still standing up with his barrow in his hands but numb with cold and speechless. He was warmed in a nearby factory, given refreshment and shortly recovered.[577]

There was a remarkable wedding at the Registry Office. The Bridegroom Mr William Wray was 92 and the bride Miss Louisa Curson was 'coming 59'.[578] A fat bullock grazing in Bradley Meadow near Vicary's tanyard was struck by lightning in 1887 and killed on the spot.[579] In February 1892 there was an exceptionally heavy snowfall between three and four feet deep. A snowplough had to be used to clear the roads. It almost approached the severity of the blizzard of the year before but this time it was followed by a rapid thaw.[580] 'A freak of nature' was reported at the market, among sheep brought in for sale was one with five legs, three in the front and two behind.[581] The next year the Newton branch of St John's Ambulance Corps was founded in Wolborough Church Hall.[582] Newton over the years had many encounters with cattle and sheep escaping their herdsmen and dashing into unlikely places, however, 1898 provides something unusual. The newspaper article was entitled 'a strange visitor' when a performing bear, which had been exhibited in Bank Street, entered the shop of a grocer and, after inspection of the Beechwood Hams and Silverbrook Tea, made its exit from the side door.[583]

CHAPTER 8

A LONGER LOOK
1801–1901

Elihu Burritt walked through in 1868, on his way to Land's End and commented that 'One part is now called Newton Bushel another Newton Abbot' he also said 'A kind of new town is growing up around a small park or common near the railway'. *Kelly's* in 1883 stated 'There is a great demand for residences and the town has been, and still is rapidly increasing' the directory added that there was much in the locality to interest the geologist and the botanist.[584] A directory of 1890 offered 'Newton Abbot is the principal market town between Plymouth and Exeter and during the past thirty-five years has increased very considerably in size and population. It may be said to form one town with Newton Bushel in the parish of Highweek'.[585] Finally a description at the end of the period 'Situated in the very heart of the most lovely portion of the loveliest of English counties the town possesses extraordinary advantages both natural and acquired. It is the key to South Devon . . . A considerable trade is also done in timber, culm and slate, and the railway works, iron foundries, saw mills, malt kilns, and breweries combine to make Newton a notable business town'.[586]

There is a particular difficulty with Newton's population figures from the first official census in 1801 until the twentieth century; there were two parishes, Wolborough and Highweek and, not all the population was urban, quite a proportion, particularly, in Highweek was rural. Although considerable efforts have been made to be accurate they are unlikely to be absolutely correct.

Data from the census provides evidence of what was happening in Newton Abbot. It demonstrated the growth, which occupations were burgeoning and where from, and how far people were coming to the prosperous town. However, despite the quantity and quality of this information, by itself it paints an incomplete picture; there is a need to examine the town in relation to its peers. See Appendix 1 for a comparison of growth. Here the main towns are listed showing their populations in 1801, 1901 and the percentage of growth over the period.

Taking England as a whole the total population rose from about 8,893,000 in 1801 to 32,528,000 in 1901 an increase of some 368 %. The county of Devon only achieved 195 %. It was a relatively slow growing area. However, the urban population in Devon was higher than the rest of the county with its 309 % growth, although even then it was lower than the national average. One inference from these figures is obvious, there was in Devon considerable rural depopulation. There was also a considerable movement from other towns and incomers arriving from elsewhere see Appendix 3. This shows the widespread of the geographical locations of the birthplaces of immigrants to Newton.

When comparing individual towns in Devon there is considerable variation. The four towns of, Cullompton, Uffculme, Ashburton and Modbury all grew in the first forty years but shrank over the century. There are another fifteen towns which also grew at the beginning of the century but then declined although they did not fall back below their starting figure. These are Bere Ferrers, Tavistock, Braunton, Torrington, Kingsbridge, Ottery St Mary, Honiton, Broad Clyst, Bampton, Colyton, Crediton, Hartland, South Molton, Chudleigh and Topsham. Some of these even then had better growth overall than say Axminster or Totnes. The important point to gather is that in Devon in the nineteenth century an inland town was more likely to end in a state of decline, very different indeed from what happened at Newton Abbot.

The port towns, with the one exception of Topsham, show significant growth and are all in the top half of the list. The best of them, Plymouth, is a special case because it was also a naval base of national importance as well as being a considerable port. The resort towns are the front runners, though even here there was a wide range of performance from meteoric Torquay to lowlier Sidmouth.

What put the other seven inland towns of Bovey Tracey, Buckfastleigh, Exeter, Holsworthy, Okehampton Plympton, and Plymstock, in the expansion league? These increased over the century. Is there a clue here that can help our understanding of Newton's even greater growth? Some were 'Union' towns, but not all of them, and there were a lot of 'Union' towns amongst those that did worse. This may seem surprising because although 'Union' towns were originally picked with care, to be 'convenient socio-geographical centres' as sites for the new central workhouses, they developed other responsibilities to become minor provincial capitals.

Bovey Tracey and Buckfastleigh were manufacturing centres and Bovey had some spin off from the clay trades. Exeter was both a civil and an ecclesiastical administrative centre, a large market town and a nodal point for road and rail communications. Well-to-do families were attracted by climate, amenities and scenery and this created a building boom, both for private housing and public buildings. Holsworthy and Okehampton are both market towns but so were many other towns that did worse. So it is difficult to pick out special factors for their growth.

Okehampton had its useful strategic position on the route around the North of Dartmoor and was the meeting place of no less than five turnpike roads. Towards the end of the century it began to benefit from military expenditure. The army's first camp at Okehampton was in 1875. Plympton and Plymstock gained from the proximity of Plymouth and the growing dockyard. The construction of the Plymouth Breakwater from 1811 to 1841 gave Plymstock an enormous fillip. Plympton also gained from the proximity of clay.

It is difficult to sum up these disparate towns but they do illustrate several factors that aided growth. There was manufacturing and the clay trades at a time when there was much building and rising living standards. A thriving market and being a communication centre were assets. There was, too, the relatively new prosperity that could be engendered if the well off could be attracted to take up residence. Farsighted local landowners could also be a major player in development – such as the Courtenays at Newton. [587]

Newton in 1891 was a busy community and the scope and spread of the occupations tell us much about the town. See Appendix 2. In 1891 Newton was similar to many other places in Victorian times in having a large number of 'Domestic Servants'. There were over seven hundred. The greater number were unspecified but there were over a hundred 'Cooks' and 'House Maids' but only 21 'Parlour Maids' and just four 'Butlers', the traditional top servant. Further proof, if it were needed, of the demand for servants was the operation of a Servants Agency as early as 1847.

The next most numerous category was that of 'Living on Own Means' at well over four hundred. A substantial total indeed, and the evidence is still there today in the large houses and villas on Wolborough and Knowles Hills.

The railway provided the next largest employment. There are particular problems in trying to establish true figures because terms such as engine-driver or coach-painter might not necessarily have been railwaymen. Adding up obvious railway occupations, but for balance omitting all 'Coach' occupations, gives a total of over three hundred. This total is less than quoted by Rhodes,[588] so thought was given to the possibility of workers commuting by rail or on foot. Peter Kay, the railway writer, expressed the thought that the former was unlikely because of the paucity of early morning trains. [589] A check on surrounding parishes only found 8 railwaymen in Kingsteignton and 3 in the Ogwells. It would seem classification is the basis for any discrepancy.

'Tanners' and 'Fellmongers,' not far short of two hundred, represent the next largest industrial occupation. Adding 'Builders', 'Carpenters', Painters, Plasterers', 'Plumbers' and 'Stonemasons' there is a crude total approaching four hundred for the construction industry. Admittedly not all carpenters, for instance, would have been employed in building, on the other hand a number of 'General Labourers', which are not included, almost certainly would have been.

By 1891, although the population of Devon as a whole had only risen to 111% during that time Newton had forged ahead to 236%. Among the occupations that grew even faster than the town's phenomenal rate were: 'Architect', which is not surprising, 'Bargeman' and 'Clay Cutter' a commentary on the expansion of the local ball clay industry. 'Brickmaker' was an offshoot of the clay trade and 'Shipwright' is another new occupation ancillary to the same trade. Clay initially did not feature at all as rail freight, and some clay was still being water-borne up to 1939. 'Clerk' shows an enormous increase that is, in part, a sign of the times, as well as Newton's flourishing economy; the same might be said of 'Accountant', 'Banker' or even 'Printer'. 'Coach' increase is also high although Newton had coach-making industries of the old fashioned horse sort, much may be due to modern coach making for the railway. The increase in the number of 'Commercial Traveller', might in part be due to Newton's attractiveness as a railhead in the days when such travellers went by train. 'Living on Own Means' maybe proves the success of the aristocratic

(opposite) The church end of Wolborough Hill clearly shows villas that were never built. Maybe when we consider the open field space we still have left besides the churchyard we can be glad of that.

(opposite and following) This is Rowell's development plan for the Courtenay Estate on Wolborough Hill. The main point to grasp is of course that this was very much a planned development and an aspect of Newton's exceptional growth that is sometimes overlooked. Not all the planned roads were cut or villas built. It is possible that this was because the Estate found houses were more popular on the southern aspect of the hill, so that they concentrated on these, and never finished all those on the northern side. The original plan was done as one whole map, unfortunately because of difficulties of reproduction only three sections are shown here.

(opposite) This is the town centre at the time the plan was drawn. Note the earlier Seymour development on Knowles Hill, top right.

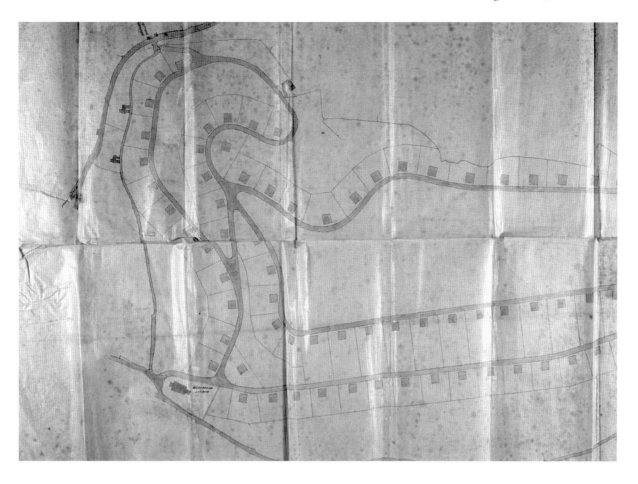

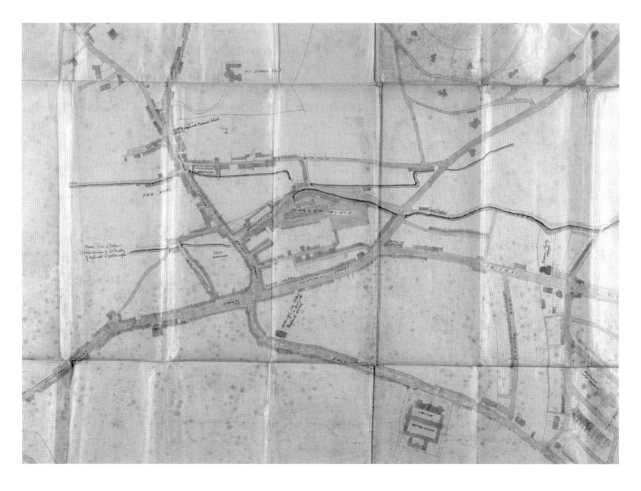

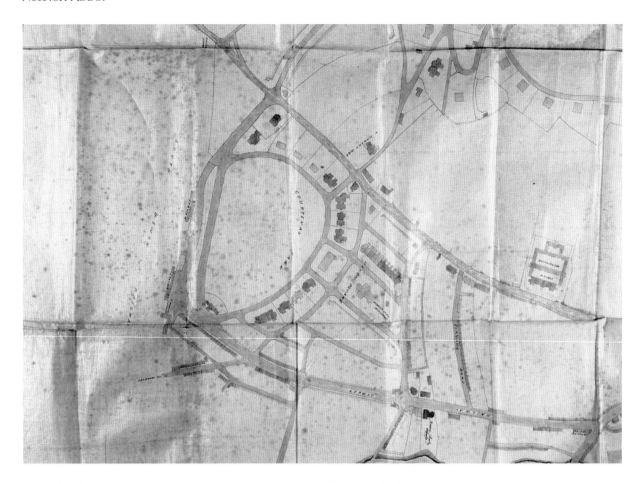

property developers, the Earl of Devon and Duke of Somerset. It also no doubt account for the bigger than expected increase in 'Domestic Servants' and 'Housekeepers', perhaps too for 'Drapers' outdistancing many other retailers because of demand for curtains, bed-covers etc for the new villas. The same villas certainly would have accounted for the large increase in 'Gardeners', though a tendency for some gardeners in 1851 to call themselves labourers may cause some distortion. 'Lodging House Keeper' perhaps proves that building was not keeping up with demand and certainly confirms the influx of workers from elsewhere. 'Post' shows above average growth and as well as confirming a growing population owes something to the multiplicity of late Victorian postal deliveries and the new technology of the telegraph. 'Railway' and 'Tanners/Fellmongers' were mentioned in the big battalions above but would also of course be qualified to be included as showing exceptional growth; the construction trades as a whole would not, possibly because they were already heavily engaged in 1851. Not significant in numbers but interesting as a sign of changing times are the arrival of 'Gas Engineers', a 'Lamplighter', 'Oilman' and 'Photographers'.

There were also losers, trades that had declined or had not kept up with the town's development. Historically the most interesting group were those who had served the Newfoundland trade. This for centuries had been one of Newton's mainstays but with the decline and shift of this trade away from Teignmouth and Dartmouth to larger ports the local demand had diminished. This would account for the large decline in 'Boot & Shoemaker'; Newton had been heavily into the production of sea-boots. Other Newfoundland trade casualties were 'Fish Hook Maker' and 'Cutler'. 'Ropemaker' was another

The areas close to the station Courtenay Park and Devon Square, St Paul's shows up well as does the Workhouse. Queen Street, not yet called that, is a long way off being fully developed.

expected casualty but a diversification to 'Manufacturer of Steam Packing', rope-like material used for insulating hot steam pipes, stemmed the decline. That 'Tanners' so patently overcame their loss of trade of leather for sea-boots, can only be put down to the entrepreneurship of the Vicary family who had built up what was probably the biggest tannery west of Bristol at that time. Other trades that had disappeared between 1851 and 1891 were 'Candle Maker', perhaps not surprising, and 'Glove Maker' and 'Lace Maker' yet these two trades were still present at Torrington and Barnstaple respectively. 'Farmer' was a significant loss, in part due to the general decline in farming since the eighteen seventies, but the very fact that the town was growing so fast meant the area devoted to agriculture was being reduced. Gardeners in 1891 were tending plots that had once been the concern of farmworkers.

Newton could only grow as fast as it did in the nineteenth century because a large number of people moved from elsewhere. Natural growth would not have been sufficient, even though many of the incomers would have been young people and therefore a high natural birth rate would be expected. This is confirmed by a report on the health of the district in 1878 which said "In the locality of Newton, however, the birth-rate is again much higher than in other parts of the district, and in this year exceeded the All England average." [590] See Appendix 3 for the birthplaces of incomers.

It is generally supposed that the nearer the place, the larger will be the number of incomers to a town. However, the vicissitudes of unemployment may often add a push factor that can be as important as the pull of burgeoning Newton. Both these facets are borne out in 1891. The nearest settlement to Newton, Kingsteignton provided a total of 251 immigrants. Other very close villages are the Ogwells at 83, Kingskerswell 70, Ipplepen 64, Torbryan 51, Bickington 59, Abbotskerswell 47 and Broadhempston also 47. A little further away, but also with high numbers, are Ilsington with 148 and Hennock 75. The vagaries of mining employment in those places may have provided the push. Ashburton leads local towns at 115, Chudleigh 80, both these places were known to suffer loss of coaching trade when the railway went via Newton. Bovey Tracey lost 115 and Moretonhampstead 69, contrariwise Buckfastleigh was known to have kept busy in manufacturing in this period and only lost 21. Totnes another local town lost out to the tune of 94. The comparable figure for those in Totnes in 1891, who had been born in Newton, was just 16. It is interesting that even the growing resorts contributed quite substantial numbers to Newton. Devon's premier resort Torquay led with 141 and Teignmouth followed with 112 and Dawlish 64.

Plymouth/Devonport the fast growing port and dockyard complex, supplied no less than 229. Exeter which had been adjusting to a period when it was no longer industrial, provided 172. It is possible to reduce these numbers from the bigger places to a percentage of their total population and claim they are insignificant. It seems unlikely, however, that this was insignificant to the 400 people involved.

In Appendix 3 parishes, which only sent very small numbers, less than five, are excluded. There were no less than 141 parishes in that category. 'Devon' therefore includes all these small numbers as well as those who simply recorded their birthplace as Devon. It is useful to remember how large Devon is in size. Quite a number of those folk born in the county had over fifty miles to travel to reach Newton.

Of those not from Devon a small, but intriguing, number are those who were born in Newfoundland, surely a legacy of a trade once so important to Newton? Another of Newton's specific trades, this time the railway, must have been responsible for some arrivals from comparatively far-flung places. A number of these came from Scotland and the north east of England. From Durham, Northumberland and Scotland in 1851 there were a total of 29 and from the same places of origin in 1891 some 40. It is unlikely all would have been skilled, but some were. There was an 'Engineer' husband whose wife was born in Scotland, eldest child born in Bristol and the next four children in Swindon. There was also a husband 'Engine smith' born in Scotland, his wife came from Durham, the three eldest children born in Newcastle-on-Tyne and the youngest in Swindon. An 'Engine fitter' born in Durham had a wife born in Northallerton, their eldest child was born in Swindon and the next two in Cheltenham. As those examples above will have shown, Swindon, or New Swindon as it was sometimes called, was the equivalent of a transit camp. Its significance was based on being chosen by the GWR as its maintenance depot. There were by 1851, just over four years since the railway arrived at Newton, 8 persons living in Newton who had been born in New Swindon and by 1891 no less than 33. There was for instance a 'Boilersmith' born in Swindon or a 'Fitter' born in Swindon whose wife had come from Devizes though not all worked on the technical side. Not all railway staff from a distance came from the north-east or Swindon; there was for instance 'Locomotive engineer' from Cornwall and an 'Engine driver' born in Bermondsey. Contrariwise not everyone from Swindon was a railway employee.

In 1891 of those not born in the county over 80 were born in the British Empire, the biggest contingent being 37 from India. Some came to Newton just for education. However, all were a sure sign of imperial greatness and a comparison can be made with the 20 born in Europe. There were 31 from Scotland, in 1851 this had been 20, but no less than 70 from Ireland, in 1851 just 18, which must be a reminder of the potato famine. Close but non-contiguous counties were Hampshire with 57, Gloucestershire and Wiltshire have 47 although the former could be supplemented by Bristol's 59, and the latter by Swindon/New Swindon's 33. London provided no less than 224. We often consider migration into London at this period but sometimes forget there was also an alternative flow. There were 34 from Yorkshire, 43 from Lancashire, 37 from Worcestershire, and 45 from Kent, another six counties provided over 20 apiece; these certainly show that quite large numbers did travel long distances to work in the small Devon town of Newton. The totals of contiguous counties are: Dorset with 43, Somerset with 143 and Cornwall in the lead at 347. It would be expected that the general decline in that county's staple occupations would provide the push factor.

It is sometimes asserted that only the more highly skilled travelled long distances and that more humble occupations such as domestic servants were recruited locally. Yet there were local servants born in Devon at Bishop's Nympton, Kingsbridge, North Huish, Totnes, Teigngrace, Teignmouth, Stokeinteignhead and Newton Abbot itself. There were also servants, perhaps some travelling with families, born in Ringwould Kent, Middlesex, London, Cheltenham, Gloucester, Gillingham in Dorset, and St Day in Cornwall. As might be expected there were teachers and French governesses born abroad. Another common assumption is that the Irish are likely to be in lowly jobs as some were. There were also a 'Rear Admirals Wife', a 'Railway Advertising Agent and a 'vet' who intriguingly was married to a Norwegian wife, a reminder that romance as well as economics is a cause of migration.

Reverting to the true urban population of Newton, of the 4,126 Newtonians in 1851 some 49.5% had been born outside the town. In 1891 the population had risen to 10,734 and the percentage born outside the town had increased to 52%. In 1851 2,046 Newtonians had not been born in the town by 1891 it was 5,614. The most interesting change is the increasing percentage of 'incomers', from outside the county, at the later date. In 1851 82.5% had been born in Devon and17.5% outside the county. In 1891 the proportion of Devon births was down to 67% and those from outside the county had risen to 33%. In other words the proportion of non-Devonians had nearly doubled. Better communications would undoubtedly have helped this process but would it ever have happened at all, if it were not for the undoubted pull factor of Newton's success?

<h1 style="text-align:center">CHAPTER 9</h1>

<h1 style="text-align:center">THE TWENTIETH CENTURY
FIRST HALF 1900–1949</h1>

Mate's guidebook of 1903 had the following items written about Newton. 'The special merit of Newton is its high suitability as a tourist's centre, a merit cordially recognised by everyone.' 'The site of the town in a ravine between two lofty hills is singularly beautiful, and the views from the high ground are altogether exceptional in their variety and peculiarity.' A *Devonia* journal of 1905 said this of Newton ' It is no exaggeration to say that it is the centre and key to the whole of South Devon. There is no other place so well situated for enjoying the delights of both the seaside and the moorland as Newton Abbot.[591] It also added it was only four hours and eight minutes from London. A Council member Mr A Sampson described Newton as the 'metropolis of the west'. A guide book suggested that the town had seven popular seaside resorts outside

Rabbits at the railway. Staffing levels were higher then and in pre-myxomatosis days rabbits were much more often on the menu.

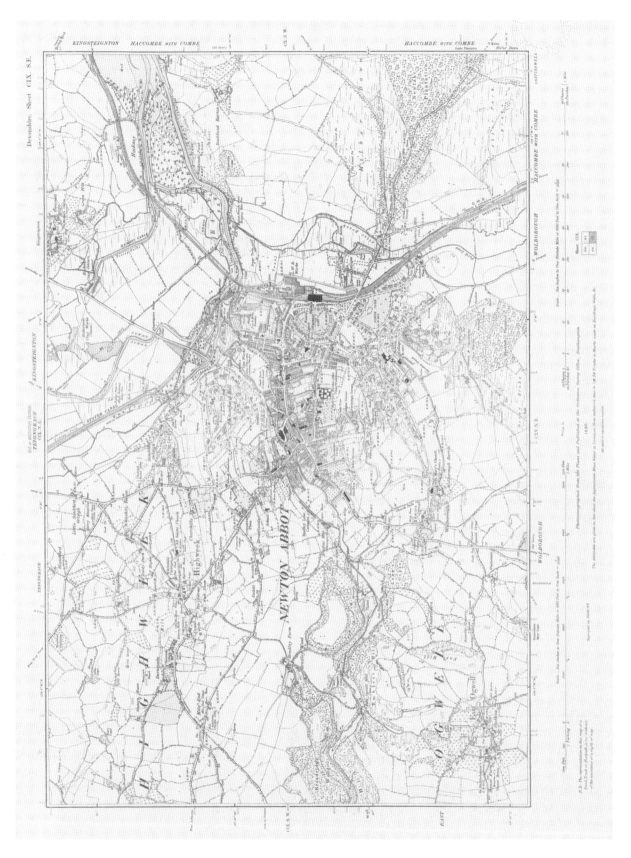

1890 six inch map.

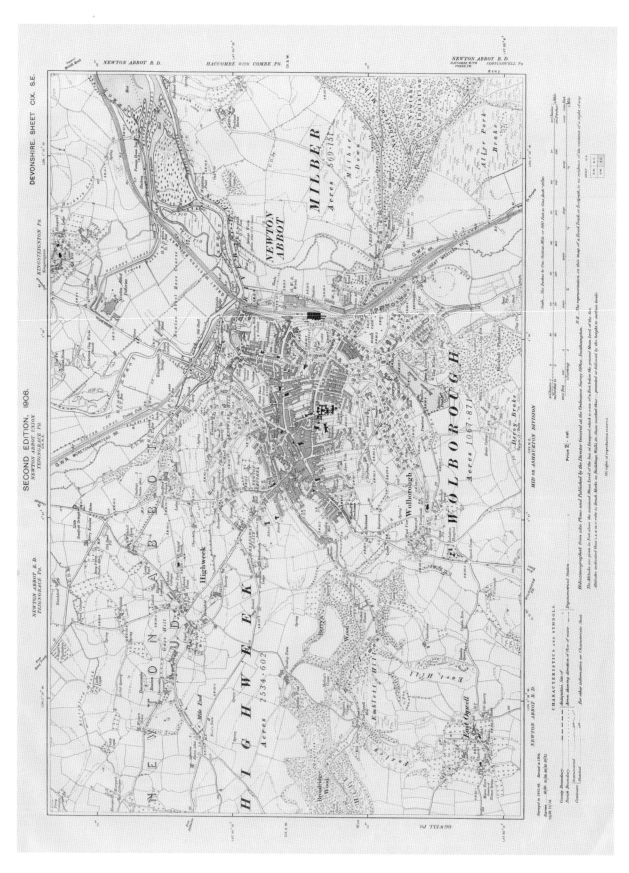

1906 six inch map.

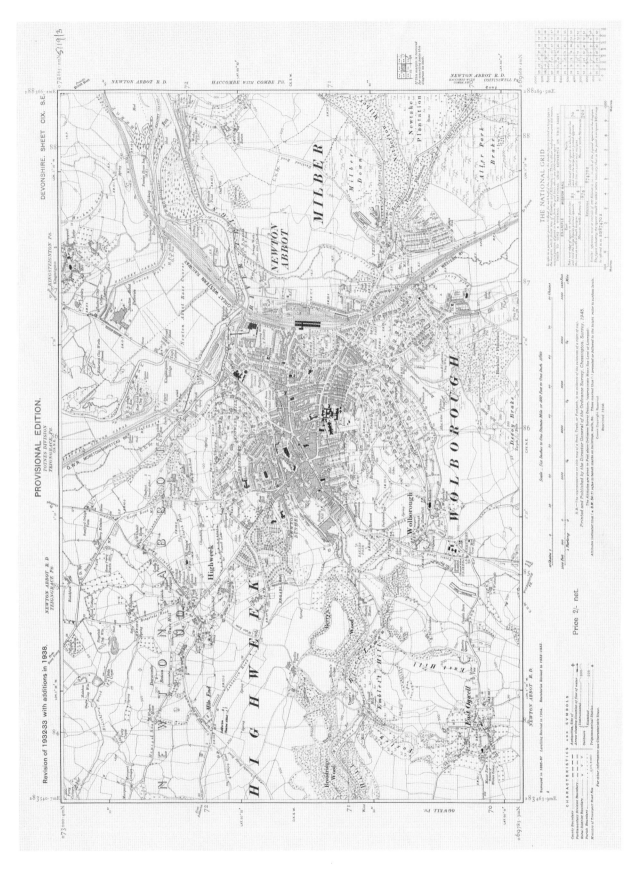

1933 six inch map.

These reproduced Ordnance Survey maps certainly show the growth of the town over the years. This is even though the fastest period of growth had already taken place, and an even wider spread outwards, was yet to come.

It would be impossible to improve on this post cards caption! No doubt the same card was used for many other places but despite the unlikely seashore it does prove that Newton was considered attractive to tourists.

The Newtonian off to the Moor, first decade twentieth century. Coaches were horse drawn then.

its front window, and wild impressive and altogether alluring Dartmoor at the back. However, the most colourful comment of this half century is surely by L du Garde Peach who wrote in his *Unknown Devon* 'I like to sit on the wooded hillside above Netherton and watch the slow tide ebb away from the shining mud banks below, as the red evening light fades from Haldon. Then, in the sweet-scented dusk, one drops down through Wolborough to the pleasant welcome of Newton Abbot.' 'A comfortable little town, this, very proud of its new railway station, and excited at the prospect of acquiring a Mayor and Corporation . . .'

Britain began the century as one of the great powers with the largest empire the world had seen. Although victorious in two world wars, the enormous costs would mean that it did not regain dominance in world affairs. Devon was still a mainly agricultural county and overall farming was a declining industry. The two wars provided fillips but rural population decline continued. The county's saviour was the tourist industry which had a long spell of steady growth. There were motor cars and flying machines arrived as did wireless!

Newton continued to grow, its railway involvement increasing right through the period. There were some changes in its older industries but mostly these prospered and others started. It was of course much affected by war especially the second.

Town Administration

The UDC purchased the Marsh Recreation Ground in 1900. In the next year the long-considered amalgamation of Newton Abbot and Newton Bushel finally came into effect. Milber from Haccombe with Combe was added to make what was, at first called Greater Newton. A comment in verse deserves to be remembered.

On the Amalgamation

By the river Lemon, and the flowing tide,
Stands young Newton Abbot, like a charming bride,
Waiting for her consort–anxious to embrace!
Health and beauty always beaming on her face.

Highweek looks upon her with a longing eye,
Coombe and Haccombe yonder with each other vie;
Ready to embrace her, fold her in their arms;
While in love they chase her, smitten with her charms!

Forth she comes to meet them, standing by the gate;
Lovingly she greets them, and they amalgamate;
Now they are united! Nothing to annoy!
One and all delighted, wish them every joy.[592]

The council was increased to 18 and divided into six wards: Forde, College, Market, St Leonard's, Bradley and Bushel. This last name is the only current usage to remind us of the modern town's twin past. The occasion was celebrated

The Library. Passmore Edwards endowed this fine building in memory of his mother who was born in the town. Sir Redvers Buller opened it in 1904.

with a special dinner in the Alexandra Hall. The Surveyor, Lewis Stevens, designed a new coat of arms for the combined town,[593] the left-hand shield has croziers and a mitre for Newton Abbot and the right-hand shield three barrels for Newton Bushel.

In 1902 Passmore Edwards laid the library foundation stone in memory of his mother who had lived in East Street. He was aged 70 and made a round trip of 240 miles in the day to attend. He caught the 5.30 from Paddington and returned on the 4.52 from Newton Abbot. He joked that if he had come prepared with a speech, the rain would have washed it away. He added he hoped it 'would contribute to the enjoyment, education and elevation of the people of Newton'. Edwards was a man of humble birth but became a journalist and founded a publishing empire. He became a philanthropist founding libraries, art galleries and hospitals. In fact, his first offer to Newton was for a hospital, however, as Newton already had one he settled on a library. The council erected in conjunction the Science, Art and Technical Schools, now the Adult Education Centre. Sir Redvers Buller VC opened the Library in 1904; his equestrian statute is in Exeter. The Mechanic's Institution of the GWR gave the entire stock of over 1,000 books to the new library.[594] Seale Hayne, the local M. P. was sick and unable to attend but sent a second donation of £100.

Kingsteignton changed its oil street lamps for gas in 1904.[596] In Newton, by contrast, the Urban Electric Supply Company opened

An election card of 1892 for Seale Hayne, an MP for many years and local benefactor. As Newton surpassed Ashburton it tried without success to gain the constituency name.

Eleanora N. Stooke

Little is known of this lady, or maybe it would be more honest to say I have failed to find out very much! This is disappointing because Newton is not rich in literary ladies. She was living in the town around the turn of the twentieth century. It was hoped in the local press that her books would feature in the new projected library.

She wrote, at least twelve books: *Angel's Brother, Brown A1: or A stolen holiday, Granfer, and one Christmas Time, Kitty's Enemy, Little Maid Marigold, A Little Sunbeam, Little Town Mouse, Mousey, Polly's Father, Robin of Sun Court, Rose Cottage,* and *While Father was Fighting.*

In *Robin of Sun Court* the setting is Plymouth. However, as the authoress lived in Newton it is tempting to think that her description of the Sun Court may be of the one in Newton. 'Sun Court was generally spoken of as one of the worst slums in Plymouth. The name had been ill-chosen, for the sunlight only peeped into it early in the morning, and then only for an hour or so; during the rest of the day the place was dull and cheerless in the extreme. The houses surrounding the court were squalid and dilapidated for the most part, . . .'[595]

Erecting an electric lamppost in Newton, in 1905, although the first electric street lighting came in 1890. This seemingly mundane task obviously became a great photo opportunity. The children are apparently dressed in their best.

their generating station and the Council opted for electric street lighting.[597] The Electric Company at first offered to light the town for the same price as gas. Gas then offered a considerable reduction to about two-thirds of the current price. Further discussions seem to have brought more reductions on both sides.

In August 1906 the cattle market was moved from the market square to a site between Sherborne and Halcyon Roads.[598] Much later in September 1938 the market area was extended and it was claimed that Newton's market was the most up-to-date in the whole southwest.[599] The Council agreed in 1907 to purchase land from Lord Devon for a cemetery on the Totnes Road.[600] It was opened in 1911 and later consecrated by the Bishop.

The local Labour Party determined in 1905 to become involved in municipal affairs. By 1919 it was decided that a Labour candidate was to stand in every seat. Not one was elected and it was suggested this over ambition had been a bad tactic. However, in 1920 Labour secured two seats on Newton Council. In 1924 the Labour Party adopted Miss Kate Spurrell of Plymouth as Parliamentary candidate for the Totnes Division.[601] Later she spoke at meetings in Newton, some of which were said to be noisy.

In January 1908 there was a by-election in the Mid-Devon constituency of which Newton was an important centre. The Conservatives who had been supported by the Suffragette leader Mrs Pankhurst, surprisingly defeated the Liberals who held the seat. The police quickly escorted the newly elected MP away and advised Mrs Pankhurst to leave promptly. She was not impressed with the advice and, reputedly, laughed at it. She became the target of the angry crowd who were shouting 'those women have done it' and pelted her with eggs. She took refuge in a grocer's shop at the entrance to Hopkins Lane and tried to escape out the back but was roughly handled and hurt an ankle.[602] According to one report, the crowd was all for putting her in a barrel, according to another the plan was to put her in the river. Fortunately for her the police returned and took her back into the shop. Here she had to wait until the police obtained the use of a motor car to get her out of town. Two policemen were

'Suffragettes interfering with voters' is the title showing not a little prejudice, we would have said 'canvassing'.

Suffragettes at Newton Abbot, Mrs Pankhurst was roughly treated here and had to make a dramatic escape from the town with a police escort.

put on each running board. Mr Henry Balls who had recently opened Newton's first garage, drove the car. In the fracas the police superintendent's coat was torn and he was dishevelled, his face smeared with dirt. Several constables had their uniforms torn or helmets knocked off.[603] The mob disappointed at losing their prey then set about breaking the windows of the Constitutional Club in Union Street.[604]

A flag was flown at the Liberal Club on the day in 1909 that Old Age Pensions started.[605] The Council refused an offer of £10 per annum to let a Mr Triggs run his pigs over the Council's ash-heaps.[606] The new drum clock of Lloyds Bank was nearly complete of the site of the old one of Baker, Watts, Alsop & Woolcombe.[607] Keir Hardy spoke at the Alexandra Hall in 1912, and said he would not apologise for holding a meeting on a Sunday. Interestingly the race to build the Dreadnought, a new and much more formidable type of warship was mentioned. This was one of the very few occasions in the local press when

New Liberal Club, 1914, now Porter Black's, the old Liberal club opened by Lord Rosebery had been in Union Street.

increasingly threatening international affairs appeared. In 1913 at the Devon Womens' Liberal Association meeting at Newton, it was stated that there were three professions a woman would not wish to enter, policemen, sailors and railway shunters. Details were published of the proposed Liberal Club in Market Street, now Porter Blacks, heating with hot-water radiators.

When Queen Victoria died in 1901 the Councillors and Guardians met and walked in procession to the Parish Church; the Volunteers went to St Leonard's and the Post Office staff to St Paul's. After the services were over the clerk to the council read the notice of the new king's proclamation at the Tower.[608] The stationmaster issued orders for men to wear black ties but the instructions were not needed because the men had already done so. The Post Office dressed their windows with a black border. Permission was granted to the master of the Workhouse to suspend work for the day of the funeral and the chaplain held a memorial service[609] Coronation Road takes its name from the coronation of Edward VII in 1901, he was to be king for just nine years dying in 1910. The Coronation was held in August 1902 after being postponed from June because of illness. Premises particularly well decorated included the Post Office, the Gentleman's Club, Ballinger's Cycle Depot, *Dartmouth Inn,* and *The Globe.* On the evening previous there had been a Fancy Dress Ball at the Alexandra Hall. The original Coronation day had still been a bank holiday, although decorations were then speedily removed and services of intercession held.[610]

Newton volunteers returning early from the Boer War were welcomed home. Mention was particularly made of the 'khaki' uniforms, still a novelty.[611] In June 1902 came news of peace in South Africa,. There was a special service of thanksgiving at St Leonard's. Schools were closed to celebrate, bells were rung, flags flown and the Newton Abbot Rifles paraded playing patriotic tunes.

Registration of cars started in 1903 with only ten from Newton Abbot. Private owners included Lewis Bearne and Richard St Maur of Stover who had two. Industrial users were the potteries of Hexter Humpherson and the Electricity Works. Just how new cars were is evidenced by the fact that one was made by the Great Horseless Carriage Company another by the Humber Cycle Co! It is intriguing to think that Vallance's, which later became a large haulage contractor

Queen Street, c.1910, the Commercia*l* Hotel *is on the corner on the left, now Pearl Assurance House.*

based at Heathfield, started as farmers who hired out horses and carts to local clay companies.[612] Eggbear's also started as hauliers with a horse and cart in the nineteenth century and were still using heavy horses well into the twentieth century.[613]

There were several other innovations. Balls' Brothers, Queen Street ironmongers, set up Newton's first motor garage.[614] They were later to run a small bus company, operating in the Shaldon, Maidencombe to Newton area,

Battle of the Bouquets

At the beginning of the twentieth century two Newton chemists offered competing brands of perfume. J.H. Bibbings sold 'Bradley Woods Bouquet' and Norman V Stow, their 'Pine Woods Bouquet'. Whether one product was better than the other, or indeed, which was the greater commercial success, is as elusive as their fragrance. A record of their advertising remains to beguile us and, just possibly, make us regret that modern advertising standards would outlaw such outrageous claims!

Bibbing's trademark was a picture of the old mill at Ogwell and claimed their perfume lasted longer than any other scent. They said no expense had been spared in its production and that the whole world had been ransacked for precious and costly odours. It was rich, lasting and refreshing, 'the very souls of flowers pent in walls of glass'. The unanimous opinion after twenty years was that it was 'immeas-urably superior to all other Bouquets'. Handkerchiefs sprinkled with it retained their perfume even after repeated washings. It would also protect clothing against the ravages of moths and was popular amongst all classes of society. Stows promoted their product with a picture of the Milber Pinewoods. Their production was 'Nature's distillation left a liquid prisoner pent in walls of glass'. They were more specific about the ingredients of their product, an extract of the famous Rhine violets with the fragrant principal of Bournemouth pines which formed not only one of the purest, but most lasting scents. They had obtained the services of an undoubted connoisseur so that it equalled perfumes found in Paris but seldom in England. It would act as a stamp of culture and refined taste to the user and had the 'refreshing exhalation of fresh dew laden flowers.'[615]

Ogwell Mill as it once looked. It probably worked up until about 1909 and then later became a popular place for cream teas. Used as a 'logo' for Bradley Woods Bouquet.

and give their name to Balls' Corner at the end of The Avenue. By 1915 they advertised a Rover at £350 but self-starting was £20 more.

The first telephone directory was dated 1899–1900 and covered the whole country. There were just 21 subscribers in Newton. No. 1 was the *Globe Hotel* and No. 3 Rowell & Son, Devon Estate Office. This number passed on to the architects Lock, Son and Land that later became Lock Son and Newcombe. At that time one did not dial a number, but picked up the receiver and asked the operator for the required number. The first telephone exchange was above the old post office, now the Mitre Bookshop. It moved in about 1932 to the corner of The Avenue and Queen Street and then again in the early sixties to Osborne Street.

Manufacturing

Clay pipes were still being made, some two hundred years after their manufacture was first known. E Chapple of East Street even offered them 'stamped with purchaser's name & address if desired'.[616] A report on Henley's Cider stated that the main premises were at Newton, Totnes and London Bridge. Lesser works or depots were at Abbotskerswell, Highweek, Paignton, Blagdon, Ashburton, Kingsbridge and Pinhoe.[617] In 1906 an explosion at the Owlacombe Tin Mine, near Sigford killed John Campiom, a miner.[618] Ben Tillett spoke in the vegetable market in 1909. He was the trade unionist, who first achieved prominence, as leader of the Dockers' Strike of 1889.[619] There was a movement to alter the half-day closing from Thursday to Saturday.[620] This idea rumbled on intermittently from then until 1948 when the traders turned it down.[621] July 1913 saw the start of a strike in the clay pits for better wages it lasted nearly three months until September.[622]

The Poor

Cases reported to the Guardians included a woman in the workhouse who had a husband outside in work. The clerk was instructed to write to the man. The reply they received was; 'I shall require more proof that she is my wife'! This left the Guardians with something of a problem the outcome of which is not recorded. [623] A petty quarrel arose between the Newton Guardians and the Vicar of Shebbear, in North Devon. He had sent to Newton Workhouse a mother and child and the Guardians asked him why. He replied in somewhat unclerical vein that the Guardians were the 'incarnation of incompetence' adding that suffragettes would have been better! Presumably then this was not intended as a compliment.[624] No union would willingly provide for a pauper unless the claimant had residential or other qualification that entitled them to charity in that place. In 1902 the Guardians were able to have a celebration dinner with their friends, when their new boardroom was completed. The old boardroom was converted into a receiving ward.[625]

Health

In 1901 advertisements appeared for old false teeth: 'Many ladies and gentlemen have by them old or disused false teeth which might well be turned into money'. You only had to post them off to Ipswich and money would be back by return. The Isolation Hospital on the Totnes Road, which had recently been finished, now began to admit patients in 1903.[626] In 1911 after an injury in a thrashing machine accident, a man died under the new drug chloroform at the hospital, the first such occurrence in Newton. A new children's' ward was opened at the hospital in 1913. The purchase of the Hawkmoor Estate by DCC for consumptives was recommended in 1912.[627]

Crime & Punishment

A prisoner who had escaped from Exeter Jail in 1903 was recaptured near the *Bradley Hotel* (*Jolly Farmer*) in Newton. He was detained at the police station and then escorted back to the railway in a cab.[628] In 1907 John Lee released from prison after 22 years, caught a cab from the *Commercial Hotel* in Newton Abbot to return to his mother's home in Abbotskerswell. His arrival was quite unexpected.[629] Later he made a trip to Tiverton to see friends and had a rousing reception. Lee had been convicted of a murder in Babbacombe in 1885 and had been sentenced to death. When three attempts to hang him had failed in Exeter Jail the Governor granted a stay of execution and the Home Secretary commuted the sentence to imprisonment.

For the first time, in 1909 magistrates held a separate children's court. The first three offences heard were stealing young trees, damaging a wall and throwing stones.[630] In 1911 Anne Marion Sadler, midwife, was committed to be tried for murder for performing an illegal operation on a Newton girl, a draper's assistant, Daisy Sweetman. An umbrella hawker, George Smith, was charged with being drunk; not only did he claim not to know where he was going, but his donkey was harnessed back to front in his cart![631] Three nougat merchants from London were charged for causing a scene, assaulting a policeman in Queen Street, and cutting the top off a cab driver's hat![632] In 1914 a three-card 'confidence' trick caused a race-day incident.

Country Estates

October 1909 saw the extensive sale of the Ogwell Estate at the *Globe Hotel*. It included Ogwell House, Morley 'a commodious stone & slate farmhouse', Holbeam Mill let to the Loder's, edge-tool makers, Bradley Wood House, later burnt down, Bradley Barton, Bradley Manor an 'exceptionally valuable residential property', Canada Barn 'useful set of farm buildings' and East Ogwell Mill 'water powered corn mill consisting of three floors and fitted with two pairs of stones driven by an overshot wheel'. Present Newtonians will notice two properties that gave their names to primary schools. Ogwell House, often known as the Manor House, the residence of Squire Scratton, became a Church

Hunt meeting at the Manor House, West Ogwell, once the home of Squire Scratton, later a convent, and now Gaia House Trust.

of England convent of the Companions of Jesus the Good Shepherd and later still Gaia House Trust. The sale catalogue is fulsome in its praise of Bradley Manor; 'charming position in a beautiful timbered valley', 'sylvan scenery of almost unrivalled grandeur'. More prosaically it adds 'there is an abundant supply of water from a spring near the house the sanitary fittings are of a modern design and the drains taken to discharge at a point some distance from the house'! The catalogue also mentioned an agreement: the seats along the public footpath near the Mill Leat have been placed there by and under agreement with the NAUDC. The council pay 1d per seat per annum the seats to be removed at one month's notice'.[633] Cecil Frith, the Egyptologist, bought Bradley Manor and restored it. His daughter Diana, who later became Woolner on marriage, inherited it. Shortly afterwards the new owners of Bradley Woods threatened to erect fences, to keep visitors out and asked the council to remove the seats.

Education

The Rt. Hon Charles Seale-Hayne died suddenly in 1903. He had been both an MP and local landowner.[634] It became known shortly afterwards that he had left the then princely sum of £100,000 to found a school that became Seale Hayne College. The foundation stone of Seale Hayne was laid in 1912 and it was to be 'the apex of rural education'.[635] According to Pevsner, work started in 1909 but was not finished until 1916.[636] There was a dispute between contractors and

Nursing auxiliaries at Seale Hayne in 1918. Although the college was built by 1916, because of the war it was only used to train Land Army girls. Part of it also became a hospital specializing in shell shock cases. After the war the first proper students were admitted.

governors of Seale Hayne College about the speed at which work was progressing.[637] Because of the First World War it was not used initially as intended. Instead Land Army girls were trained there, in special four-week courses, and part of it became a hospital specializing in shell shock cases. After the war the first students were admitted and the institution gained a national reputation for its dairying department. During the Second World War it was again used for training the Women's Land Army. It was taken over by the University of Plymouth in 1998.

Education featured in the news of the day. It is recorded in 1905 that for a history lesson, pupils from Newton Abbot walked to Compton Castle. Furthermore they did not go the shortest route but diverted to see Kingskerswell Church on the way![638] Children and quite small ones too, would walk all the way from Newton to Maidencombe in school holiday time to spend a day at the seaside, and then of course, have to walk back at the end of it.

In 1911 Decoy School, which was at first confusingly called Wolborough, was opened.[639] Mr W. Vicary in 1913, with the laudable intent of gaining an increase in teachers' salaries did not endear himself to all listeners by saying that Devon teachers were 'only the refuse' all good teachers went elsewhere for more money.[640] A dispute arose at Teigngrace in 1915 over the school between the new Rector, the Rev. R.A. Cochrane and Major St Maur, the local squire.[641] This was to prove a bitter and long running affair lasting nearly a year. It went to enquiries, to DCC and even the Board of Education. The rector, it was said, was meant to be a man of peace but he had set the parish in flames. He certainly tried to conceal the unfavourable architectural report he had received on the temporary school he had set up. Yet he wanted to have the press at meetings whereas his opponents did not. One miserable piece of bureaucratic meanness was uncovered. The squire, in his generosity provided a cottage for the schoolmistress rent-free but DCC had been quietly deducting £5 from her salary for it. In 1915 Alderman William Vicary JP opened the new Secondary School in Exeter Road.[642] This afterwards became the Grammar School and is today part of Knowles Hill School. There was a girl's school at Huntley, Bishopsteignton established in 1918.[643]

Teigngrace Station in the early 1900s. Evidence of the one-time platform is still there today.

Fire

Darracombe House burnt down in 1909. It had been built for Mrs Ness who had done so much for the Orphan Home for Girls. Afterwards there was contention between Council and fire brigade about the blame for the outdated equipment. A Council committee recommended the purchase of a motor wagon in 1911 as a fire engine. They pointed out that for a recent fire the men had been at the station in 5 minutes but then had to wait another 25 whilst they obtained horses. A motor would also carry twice as much hose. The full Council discussed the idea in February but decided against it.[644]

Religion

In 1902 it became obvious that charity had been variable in the two parts of the new township. It was reported that during the past nine years the Wolborough Feoffees had given £1,486 to their church and £83 to their poor. The Highweek feoffees on the other hand had given £1,000 to the poor and £146 to the church!

In 1903 the daughters of the Holy Spirit, sometimes known as the white nuns, took possession of Ingsdon Manor and named it St Michael's Convent.[645] For a while they supported their community by running a laundry service, washing was collected and delivered by horse and trap. Later they maintained a school that had particular standards. At first only French was spoken no mirrors were permitted and for modesty's sake the boarding girls had to wear a towel in the bath.[646] For a number of years they ran their own private coach, painted in school colours, to bring and take pupils home.[647] The convent closed in 1972, and became an establishment for delinquents. Although their rules were different, they showed their lack of appreciation by setting fire to the building in 1977, badly damaging it. In 1981, permission was granted for its demolition.[648] It is now a housing development.

New St Mary's was built between 1904 and 1908 and the architect was E.H. Sedding. The builder was Hugh Mills, much later his funeral service was held in the church. Some items were moved from the old St Mary's.[649] The church was built on the site of Abbotsbury House, on land given by Mr Vicary. The gate pillars of Abbotsbury House still stand by the cut-off end of Old Exeter Road. There was a demonstration in Market Square in 1914 to protest against 'The Welsh Church Bill'.[650] Despite protests Welsh disestablishment was enacted later in the year. The Rector of Manaton sold a church chalice in 1920 for his own gain; he was deprived of his living.[651]

Headlines in 1911 were given to a monk, aged 24, who had escaped from Buckfast Abbey. He had been there eleven years having joined, from Germany, aged 13! The Abbot in an interview played down the significance. The monk claimed that amongst his penances for a disciplinary offence was flagellation once a week. The new Young Men's Christian Association premises at No 9 Devon Square was opened,[652] now the Town Hall.

Leisure

The pantomime in 1901, at the Alexandra Theatre was *Sinbad the Sailor*; it played to full houses.[653] Sets of Ping-Pong the new society game, now more commonly known, as table tennis were available in the town.[654] In February 1902 there was a performance for two nights only of *A Message from Mars* at the Alexandra Theatre. Times were stated thus: 'Early doors 7 (6d extra all parts) Ordinary doors 7.30 Performance commences at 8.00 Carriages at 10.30'.[655]

In 1903 Buffalo Bill, Col. W.F. Cody, arrived with his 800 performers and staff and 500 horses, in 4 special trains, to give his spectacular Wild West show. There were cowboys and Red Indians and the famous Deadwood coach. There were just two performances on one day but attracted a total gate of 28,000 people. This was a better total than Exeter.[656] A Professor Bounds, the so-called Medicine King, gave an entertainment with competitions in the Vegetable Market. There was a singing competition and the prize was a live large white pig. The man who won was asked to sing an encore with the pig under his arm. The reporter said the pig joined in the occasional chorus.[657] For the first time in 1904 there was a Telegraph Office at the Newton Races.

A number of overseas rugby teams visited Newton. The New Zealand All Blacks spent 8 days practising at the Recreation Ground in 1905.[658] There were various receptions for the players. Later in October, on a return visit, members of the team were each presented with a special Royal Aller Vale Pottery mug with their individual names. The next year the South African Rugby team made Newton their headquarters for their stay in Devon.[659] Two years later the Wallabies from Australia arrived at Newton. The Australian captain said that the 'fame of Newton had reached Australia' and that is why they had come to it. Later they were guests at Newton Abbot Races and at the Constitutional club.[660] After the war in 1924, the New Zealand Team arrived at Newton, thousands 'accorded the colonials a real Devonshire welcome', the visitors much appreciated their reception. Later a grand ball was held in their honour, the visit was concluded with a whist drive.[661]

Newton Choral Society performed Gounod's *Faust* in 1906. In 1908 Newton

Haymaking scene on Wolborough Hill near Newton Abbot. There is a good range of headgear.

Choral Society presented *Freezing a Mother-in-law* or *Frightful Frost* at the Alexandra Hall. Sedgwick's Menagerie visited Newton Recreation Ground. The highlight was a tug-of-war between 30 men and an elephant.[662] On Boxing Day there was rabbit coursing with 40 dogs at Ess Hill, alongside the Ashburton Road.[663]

The news was given in 1908 that a branch of the Boys Brigade would be formed. Respectable boys between 12 and 18 would be accepted. Newton Boy Scouts had a Manoeuvre, it seems to have been an exciting affair, one patrol pretending to have landed by sea and acting as spies to try and blow up Shaldon Bridge.[664] Later in the year the Chief Inspector of Baden-Powell's Scouts came down to inspect them and reminded them of their motto 'Be Prepared'. Next year the Devon County Scouts held their sports on Newton Recreation ground. There was entertainment, they claimed 'at enormous expense', of a troupe of acrobats the youngest being, Master Eugen just 5 years of age.[665]

In 1911 the Devon County Show came to Newton again; this time on the Racecourse, 'an admirable site'. There was a new horticultural section. To coincide with the show *Revel Day,* a play by Jan Stewer (A J Coles) was put on at the Alexandra Hall.[666] The next visit was in 1924 but its success was wrecked by continual rain.[667] A decade later in 1934 the Devon County Show was held in the grounds of Seale Hayne College.[668] This time it had good weather and was a great success. Pictures of the event show a sizeable car park, something not needed in the past. The next visit was in1949 on a site at Stover. Some 55,000 people attended and no less than 2,000 cars were parked. The show was such a success that it was decided the Royal Show should be held there in 1952.

In 1913 Mr R. Hansford Worth gave a lecture, illustrated with lantern-slides, in the Town Hall on 'The archaeology of Dartmoor'. There was a display of tango dancing at the Alexandra Hall as performed at Deller's Café, Paignton. It was said it was an 'immodest and suggestive dance', impossible for any girl of refinement.[669]

Railway

In March 1902 there was an announcement that Newton Motor Car Co. would run their motor bus from Linden Terrace to Railway Station Bridge to meet principal trains, Sunday excepted.[670] The Teign Valley Railway was finally opened in June 1903. Few railways of such a short length had given so much work. Presumably this was why the route had not been used before![671] The GWR in 1904 let it be known they were contemplating a new station for Newton. It was many years before contemplation turned to reality.[672] In 1909 a new goods station was built at Newton and the line between Torquay and Paignton was doubled. Two years later Hackney marshalling yard for heavy mineral traffic was inaugurated. This was in addition to the long-standing goods yard and shunting area adjoining the Kingsteignton Road. It became the busiest yard west of Bristol and continued and increased Newton's railway involvement.[673] The request for a railway halt at Bishopsteignton was turned down by the GWR in 1914.

The GWR ran a summer day excursion from Paddington to Newton Abbot. The train ran non-stop to Newton where the passengers lunched in various hotels. Afterwards they travelled by solid-tyred coaches, called 'observation cars', up on to Dartmoor. Some even went as far as Two Bridges. They returned to Newton for the 7.20 train and were back at Paddington by 10.48. A long day to be sure.[674] A local circular round trip was available in summer. This was rail to Moretonhampstead, coach to Princetown, back to Newton by rail, via Plymouth.[675]

In 1902 a child, Leslie Wotton, aged between 3 and 4 was playing outside his grandfather's Queen Street shop and went missing. He arrived at Exeter on the fast train from Newton! The paper described him as 'so small an atom of humanity who could scarcely utter own name'. The police were surprised he had made the journey unattended but his description tallied with that of the missing boy from Newton so he was duly returned.

Miscellaneous

Newton was one of the last towns in the country to ring a nightly curfew bell. Strangely there does not seem to be any record of when the custom ceased. This was rung at eight except on Sundays but one night the ringer caused surprise by ringing it early at seven.[676]

In 1905 a license to sell alcohol was granted for Decoy although there were already 49 licensed properties in Newton. The next year the clubroom of the Coffee Tavern was converted to a shop and the skittle alley to a dining room.[678] There were four deliveries of post daily in 1906, except Thursday the early closing day, when there were only three. Sundays were even worse; there was just one delivery![679] At Whitsun, a Liberal fete was held at the Recreation Ground, there was a procession with carthorses.[680] The new motor ferry from Shaldon to Teignmouth carried 2,000 passengers on the August Bank Holiday.[681] General Sir Redvers Buller opened a new indoor rifle range opposite the gasworks in Wharf Road. Beatrice Webber, a dressmaker, won a breach of promise action for £20 damages. The young man had bought her a ring, even taken her out the day before the intended wedding day, but then gone off with another![682]

Advertisements from 1902

These advertisements were headed 'Public Notices' The first was from a domestic service agency, and is recorded in full; although it is unlikely that all the positions were in Newton, it certainly says something about the number of servants and their particular hierarchy.

'Wanted matron for girl's training home, cook-matron for institution, cook-housekeepers £40 to £45, experienced cooks, parlourmaids, plain cooks, nurses, housemaids, house-parlourmaids, second and third housemaids, third laundrymaid, head kitchenmaid, kitchen and scullerymaids, general servants; also wanted gardener about 40 (lodge provided), footman under butler, butler-valet (one gentleman), groom-gardener about 20, and other vacancies, at Harris's Agency, Queen Street, Newton Abbot, office closes at 1 on Saturdays'.

The second advertisement was short and humorous from the music business of Charles Heaviside. This is interesting because his brother was the scientist Oliver Heaviside. 'If your piano has been injured. By Bad Tuning or otherwise Send a post card to C. Heaviside The Pianoforte Saloons Torquay who will send round one of his experienced tuners and regulators to put it in good order distance immaterial'.[677]

The *Mid-Devon Advertiser* collected donations for the *Titanic* relief fund. The Empire put on a special matinee performance for the same cause.[684] A party of 25 Newtonians left for overseas.[685] About this time, there were often advertisements encouraging emigration to Australia, Canada and New Zealand, all three countries being keen to increase their populations. An advertisement claimed that 'A gas cooker cooks the dinner without cooking the cook'[686] A Café Chantant was held at the Alexandra Hall in aid of the Senghenydd coal mine disaster in South Wales.[687] No less than 439 miners had been killed at an explosion at the Universal pit in the worst mining disaster in British history.

First World War

During the First World War Newton was further from the scenes of action than it was to be in the Second. None the less, Newtonians paid a heavy toll as the War Memorial attests. There were early casualties and soon rolls of honour were printed of those killed, taken prisoner or wounded. In the local paper A Voluntary Aid Detachment hospital was set up in Newton Hall, a large house in Church Road, now Coach Road, and nearly two and a half thousand patients were treated there. They started coming in November 1914 and continued until April 1919.[688] The first patients were wounded on the retreat from Mons and sailed on hospital ships to Southampton and by train from there.[689] The house was demolished and fresh building took place on the site. Special Tribunals were set up, one in Newton, to hear cases of those who requested exemption from military call-up. A Canadian Forestry Battalion was engaged in the area and felled 700 acres at Stover, setting up a steam sawmill and then moved to Ashcombe. Later there were Portuguese timbermen at Mamhead. Tremendous quantities of timber were used in the trenches and for other wartime construction activities. Rationing was not introduced until late in the war and was not as extensive as in Second World War. There certainly were

Oliver Heaviside 1850–1925

Oliver Heaviside was born in London and unfortunately contracted scarlet fever at an early age that impaired his hearing for life. This hindered normal relations with other pupils at school and may be the reason, despite a good academic record, for him leaving school at sixteen. He continued studying after school; foreign languages, the Morse code and electricity.

He went to work in Denmark in telegraphy in 1868 and later continued in the same occupation at Newcastle on Tyne. While still working he continued his studies and published papers on electricity as early as 1872/3.

Heaviside was in advance of his time working on several scientific problems and made a number of discoveries involving operational calculus and electromagnetic induction. He was not a man who hesitated to point out what he considered to be errors in the work of others. This possibly was the reason he did not receive all the recognition he might have done. He was, though, made a Fellow of the Royal Society and later was the first person to be awarded the Faraday Medal. In 1902 he predicted the existence of the reflective ionosphere, sometimes known as the Heaviside layer. This was the principal means by which long-distance communications were transmitted using radio waves, until the introduction of satellites and fibre-optic cables.

Despite his undoubted achievements; he was an eccentric individual, never married, and in later life lived a hermit-like existence. His brother Charles, set up a music business in Torquay and Paignton and invited Oliver to make his home in Devon, which he did at Paignton, from 1889 to 1897. He later moved to Newton Abbot living for eleven years at Bradley View on Totnes Road. In 1909 he moved to Torquay living in Lower Warberry Road.[683]

shortages of food and for a while in 1918 butchers shops were closed two days a week in Newton. On one occasion the rumour that a grocer had margarine caused a crowd to arrive and he had to call the police![690] In November 1917 there was a scramble for butter in Newton Market. Sellers wanted to keep it for regular customers. The crowd insisted on being served on a first come basis, else they would help themselves!

The war seems to have been unexpected or at least there were more important matters for the local paper. Just three days before the outbreak on August 1st the whole of the front page was devoted to Ulster and the Home Rule Bill. There was a small article on an inside page; 'Will the War spread? Hope not Gone', but there was a much bigger feature on the 600th anniversary of Ashburton Grammar School.[691] Four days after the start over half the front page was on the war. Headlines reported that all Europe was fighting, referred to Mid-Devon and the war and the selfish rush to buy provisions. There was already a recruiting advertisement and the setting up of a Patriotic Fund to raise money for charities such as the Red Cross and St John's Ambulance.[692]

As early as 15th of August came news of Newton's first four casualties, men serving on the cruiser *HMS Amphion* which was sunk by a German mine. Stover House was offered as a hospital, by September it was ready and people were invited to go and see it.[693] By November it had patients. Badcock's the drapers advertised Army blankets, flannel shirts, woollen gloves and knitted socks suitable to send to soldiers and sailors.

A meeting was called to make provision for Belgian refuges. There were some 20 initially at the Highweek Institute and others at Ipplepen and other local places. Newton Sick and Wounded Fund Committee made the arrange-

Courtenay Street early twentieth century, Badcock's big store and Methodist Church, later demolished are on the left.

ments for Newton Hall as a hospital. There were promises of beds and blankets from well-wishers. Newton Abbot Volunteer Defence Force had an inaugural meeting. The tallest man in the army 6ft 9ins Grenadier Guardsman Private H Barter was wounded in action, he had worked for Badcock's in Newton and his parents lived at Littlehempston.[694]

There was a controversy at a Temperance Meeting between ministers and licensed victuallers discussing early closing of public houses because of the war.[695] Devonport Workhouse asked Newton if it could take some of its inmates so it could be turned into a hospital. Newton after discussion agreed to take 50. Newton Workhouse itself later became a military hospital.[696]

In 1916 Newton became an Alien Prohibited Area with other mostly coastal areas nearby.[698] Devonshire Women's War Service Committee discussed women and farm work at the Alexandra Hall.[699] The Girl Guide movement that had started in Newton in 1914,[700] put on a patriotic pageant with proceeds to the Hospital and Newton Egg fund. This fund was to buy eggs for the wounded. The Canadians held a concert at Stover Camp including a Red Indian War Dance. A special meeting of the Council approved planning for a benefactor's offer to replace tents at Newton Hall Hospital with a temporary building.[701] A meeting was held at the Town Hall to popularize War Savings. Advertisements now stated, The Army's Need Every man fit for general service required'. A shop owner asking for exemption told the tribunal 'Women cannot manage a business successfully they want a responsible man over them'. He got a month's exemption but was told not to apply again! The first prosecutions were made in Newton under the new regulations against showing unguarded lights.[702]

There were criticisms of work on a Drewsteignton mansion. Castle Drogo, was not mentioned, but there can be little doubt that it was the target. The response was that work had continued simply because the owner thought it unfair to make those unfit for service unemployed.[703]

War related events continued in 1917. John Dennis of the *Sun Inn* was convicted of illegally buying a tin of army jam.[704] Maidencombe Tea Gardens was fined under food regulations for serving too many cakes. There was a Food Exhibition at the Alexandra Hall with competitions in wartime cookery.[705] At the Roman Catholic Golden Jubilee, Father Vaughan described Protestantism

Florence Farnborough

Florence Farnborough had unusual experiences in the First World War. She was in Moscow when it started, and after training and passing examinations in the Russian language, served as a nurse with the Flying Column of the Russian Army on the Austro-Hungarian front in 1915. She took part in the long retreat from the Carpathian Mountains and then went forward again to enter Rumania with the great Russian offensive under Brusilov in 1916. The Czar, Nicholas II, awarded her two medals of Saint George for her good work.

After the collapse of the Russian monarchy and the coming of the Bolsheviks in 1917 her unit was discharged. The next year she was given permission to return to England but had to return travelling by train right across Russia to the far-eastern port of Vladivostock. She then travelled home via America; coming to live in Waverley Road.[697]

Florence Farnborough served as a nurse on the Russian Front in World War I.

as German made. He could hardly have found a more bitter insult.[706] To celebrate Dominion Day the Canadians held a fete at Stover Park in aid of the Red Cross. Boys of Newton Secondary School went to a farm camp at Bovey Tracey, helping local farmers.[707] Women were wanted for the Women's Army Auxiliary Corps and the Royal Flying Corps needed 500 sail-makers to make and repair aeroplane wings. They wanted good needlewomen who could use a sewing machine for which they received good wages, uniform, quarters, and rations.[708] HRH the Duke of Connaught inspected Newton Abbot VAD hospital.[709]

During 1918 The War Agricultural Committee stated that German prisoners, with guards, may in batches of 4 or 5, do farm work. There was also 'War in the Air' a lantern lecture at the Alexandra Hall.[710] Under the auspices of the National War Aims Council the Motor Cinema, on a tour of Devon, visited the Market Square on a Sunday evening with a splendid display of war pictures.[711] It was announced that Ration Books would be distributed. Henry Warren, tailor advertised 'The new RAF blue shortly in stock'.[712] At the end of October the *Mid-Devon Advertiser* suggested in its headline that Germany was cracking up and longing for peace.[713] Newton rejoiced on Armistice Day and wounded soldiers were driven through the town. There was a meeting at the Tower and services at St Paul's and Abbotsbury. The Seale Hayne Military Orchestra played in the town. Badcock's advertised 'The War Is Won Flags Flags Flags'.[714]

The peacetime Christmas, it was said, put an 'old-time ring in the rejoicings'.[715] The local paper in 1919 had many stories of returning prisoners of war. A cooking demonstration at the Congregational Schoolroom in Queen Street featured; Biscuit Tin Oven, Sawdust Cooker and the Hay Box because

German prisoners of war ploughing a field near Newton during the First World War.

fuel was short.[716] The VAD Hospital closed on 30th of April, there being 23 patients left including one cot case.[717] Peace Day Celebration in July 1919 was marred by incessant rain till midday. Invitations to lunch in the Butter Market had been issued to 1,100 ex-servicemen and there was the usual mix of procession, service, sports, concert and evening dance in Forde House Grounds.[718] On Armistice Day 1919 two minutes silence was observed in the town. Its use then throughout the country was a new departure.

The Highweek War Memorial was unveiled in the churchyard in 1921 and the war orphans of Kingsteignton and Newton were invited to games and tea at the Assembly Rooms.[719] The town's War Memorial was erected in 1922[720] in its central position. The chosen site had been Courtenay Park, but a late decision altered this. Unfortunately, a large oak tree on the site had to be cut down to allow for its erection. The bronze figure at the top of the stone column represents the spirit of freedom. The memorial has the names of just over 230 men who fell in the First World War. Mrs Viola Hamlin, who lost seven sons in the service of her country, laid the town's wreath.[721] The addition for the Second World War was unveiled in 1949.[722]

Despite the war dominating the news there were other headlines from 1914 to 1918. The British Dairy Farmers Association made Newton their centre for a week in 1914, for lectures and visits to places of interest. One of the talks was on the 'Modern cowhouse'. There was a strike at the Trusham Quarry involving some 250 men and some ugly incidents. The confectionery firm of Pollard's was set up in a small shop in Queen Street in 1916. Originally, it was a retail outlet that made its own chocolate items, such as Easter eggs. Later it expanded, moved, and finally settled in Brunel Road. By that time, as well as making confectionery, they had diversified into ice-cream manufacture and the distribution of frozen foods. They had also taken over, amongst others, the old established toffee business of Tucker's of Totnes. Much later still they ran into financial difficulties and had to call in the receivers. The ice cream business continues but is no longer under family control.[724]

The last record of the ancient practice of coppicing in Bradley Woods was of alder trees in 1918 and they were cut for clog making and the shoes were shaped and rough-hewn on the spot.[725] At one time so great was the demand for clogs from the industrial north of England that gangs of men would come south from Lancashire to harvest alders. They would camp out in places such as Lustleigh, on what is now the cricket ground, and it was suggested it was wise to lock up one's daughters when they came south!

A new motor bus service was to be started by Torquay Tramways from their terminus at Torre Station to Newton in September 1914; but the buses they had ordered were commandeered. Messrs. Heaward, of 13 Wolborough Street, gave up their business the West of England Sausage Factory.[726] It was proposed in 1916 that the Surveyor should have a motorcar, it would save his time, especially going to Chipley Quarry. Later there was a suggestion to purchase a steam lorry this would save so much money on horse hire.

In 1917 it was announced that Parliamentary boundaries were to be altered and most of the old Mid-Devon constituency was to become part of Totnes. Newton wanted the constituency to be called Newton Abbot instead of Totnes but this request was turned down. Plans were published for 265 new houses on the Carew Estate beyond Penn Inn. There was argument over whether to use Buckland Brake or Milber, but the latter was eventually chosen, and it was said that it would be a 'Garden City'.[727] This scheme took a while to get started, the first sod was cut in May and the first bricks laid in November 1920. The first ever meeting of women electors was held in the Alexandra Hall.

In 1914 the Newton Amateur Opera Society was formed and although two pieces were chosen for the first performance, it seems *Miss Hook of Holland* was the one put on.[728] There was a whist drive at Phillip's Restaurant for the £2,000 *MDA* Radium Fund. After 33 years the directors of the Newton Coffee Tavern decided to wind up the company, Mr Vicary protested, but the others felt that there were now other facilities such as YMCA, so there was no point in continuing.[729] There was a Grand Ball at the *Globe Hotel* proceeds for an instructional car for the Women's Volunteer Motor Drivers Corps.

Even in wartime breaches of law and order featured. John Pearce, Decoy dairyman, was convicted in 1916 for the fourth time of watering his milk.[730] William Fowler, a railway guard, was charged at Newton Petty Sessions with the theft of a bottle of whisky and a rose tree.[731] Cyril Strudwick died of lockjaw (tetanus) after another boy had thrown a piece of slate at him and cut his head.[732] Laura Penfold, a gypsy, was fined 10s. for allowing a mule to stray on the Kingsteignton Road. When asked if she wanted time, to pay, she said certainly not, she had expected to have to pay £1.

John Galsworthy of Manaton refused a knighthood on democratic principles, his refusal was lost in the post so the honour was published.[733] Gipsy (Rodney) Smith, evangelist and lecturer, spoke in aid of the YMCA funds. The price of post rose; letter rate from 1d. to 1½ d. post cards from ½ to 1d.

Inter-War years, transport

A new garage called Western Garage opened in Wolborough Street.[734] Tractors were coming into their own, they were said not to be a 'rich man's toy' and were six times as fast as a horse. One was exhibited in the Market Square and then next day there was a demonstration at Forches Cross with a charabanc

War Memorial Names

The count of names from the First World War on the War Memorial is 232. The Newton Roll of Honour in Devon Record Office has 204 names, 3 of them with Military Cross against them. No less than 57 were in the Devonshire Regiment 28% well over a quarter. At least 21 in HMS ships so Royal Navy percentage 10%. Deaths were recorded apart from the Western Front in Egypt, Gallipoli, India, Palestine, Salonika, also at the sea battles of Coronel and Jutland. One woman, Olive Maud Rice a nursing sister, is in the Roll of Honour but she is not on the war memorial. The earliest casualty was Thomas Samuel Holwill, 6thAugust 1914 of *H.M.S. Amphion,*

the latest Henry Webber 24th March 1920 presumably a death from wounds received earlier. The count of names on the War Memorial for the Second World War is 137. There is a much smaller proportion in the Devonshire Regiment only about 5%. However the total also includes civilians. It is noticeable that Newton had a higher proportion of Second to First World War casualties than is normal. The usually accepted figure is one to three. Newton's continuing strong increase in population seems to be the most likely cause. There is a separate plaque for the Korean War 1950–1952, with just one name on it.[723]

This picture shows the War Memorial in front of Devon Villa. Until a very late change of plan, the memorial was to have been in Courtenay Park. A large tree had to be demolished to make room for the memorial here.

laid on from the town.[735] The name Forches is derived from the gallows once sited there, later the same area was used for point-to-point races. In 1924 a new bus centre was opened in the Market Square.[736] The Ashburton by-pass opened in 1933.[737]

Near to Newton, was Haldon aerodrome, the first airport in Devon, it opened in 1929.[740] It is interesting in that it was a speculation of the GWR and for a short time, there were air services to Cardiff. A flying exhibition was advertised at Newton racecourse in 1931. Six aeroplanes would demonstrate formation flying, flying upside down, walking the wings and give the opportunity for private flights. About this time the idea was mooted of using the racecourse as an aerodrome.[741] The local airfield was transferred from Haldon to Denbury in 1935 and there was a grand opening ceremony. No less than twenty different machines were flown during the afternoon. A demonstration parachute descent

Free ice cream distribution in a shopping week by Pollard's the local ice-cream manufacturers. They gave away without difficulty 1,500. Picture undated but pre 1962, as there is still two-way traffic in Queen Street.

was made with the intention of landing near the crowd. The parachutist was blown by the wind into a copse and had to be rescued from a tree, fortunately he was unhurt but it was difficult to retrieve the parachute. There were grandiose plans for future services and in a speech Air-Commodore Fellowes said the 'Empire was largely built up by people in the West Country taking to the sea and wandering all over the world. Unless people took to the air they were going to lose that Empire! The airfield went back to Haldon again in 1936. In 1938 there was a proposal for an airport for Torquay at Preston, near Kingsteignton but it was opposed, as it would interfere with clay extraction.[742] Haldon was closed in 1939 but reopened and used in wartime. The airport finally closed in 1945 but occasional aircraft landed there up until 1970.[743]

In 1919 the first railway lorry was in use in Newton. It had solid tyres, no

A heavy boiler on a solid-tyred steam lorry. No prizes for guessing who is in charge!

windscreen and was limited to a speed limit of 12 mph.[744] The railway was still dominant; there was a Railwaymen's Demonstration in 1921, said to be the largest seen in the town. Contingents came from a wide area including Paddington and Bristol. In 1926, Viscount Churchill, the Chairman of the GWR, opened the new red brick station that is familiar today. It was said to incorporate the latest station architecture. In 1928 two hundred men at the GWR works were placed on short time. In the following year the company stated it was putting 23 buses on the Torquay–Newton route.[745]! In 1931 a new railway halt at Hawkmoor opened its name was later changed to Pullabrook Halt because of the considerable distance from the sanatorium.

The Stover Canal continued in use well into the twentieth century. Propulsion by sails using square Viking type rigs was superceded before the First World War by engine driven tugs, first the *Kestrel* and later the *Heron*. Between the wars clay also went to Teignmouth by road so *Kestrel* was scrapped but *Heron* continued. There is a story that she went to the evacuation at Dunkirk in 1940, others suggest she only reached Portsmouth.[746] There is uncertainty when the canal closed down in 1939 of 1943, a reminder that even relatively recent history can be controversial. As late as 1925 NAUDC decided to oppose the Teignmouth and Shaldon Bridge Bill because a low-level bridge would obstruct Newton Abbot access to the sea, and her future industrial development would be seriously menaced![747]

Employment & Industry

In 1920 the railway in Newton employed about 1,000 and Vicary's some 700.[748] but the economy was at a low ebb in Newton and elsewhere. There was a strike in the clay pits when employees, because of the depression, were asked to take a 10% cut in wages.[749]

To raise money for the unemployed there was a flag-day and a concert at the Alexandra Hall by the Triangle Concert Party.[750] The first Ladies' Football match was held at the Recreation Ground with a 3,000–4,000 gate, takings were given to the Urban Council's Unemployed Fund. The teams came from the Plymouth Ladies AFC. The local paper commentated that the 'Majority of mere men came to the conclusion that the game is hopelessly unfitted for ladies'.[751] Holman's Choir from Camborne gave concerts in Newton in aid of the 3,000 out of work Cornish miners.[752] In 1921 street lighting was curtailed and householders had to queue for permits for a half-hundredweight of fuel, because of the coal strike. In 1922 there were at least 200 unemployed in Newton and they appealed to the Guardians of the Poor. In September they broke into a meeting demanding to be heard.[753] Although in January the Guardians protested to the Ministry about delay in unemployment pay, the following February there were further scenes when the unemployed said they wanted work, not relief or loans.[754] Towards the end of the General Strike year there were over 500 unemployed in Newton.[755] In the following year miner's children returned home after a 5-month respite stay in Newton,[756] some had come from the Forest of Dean. By 1929 there were still over 494 on the unemployment register.[757] To alleviate the problem Newton Council discussed the possibility of a seaplane base on the Teign.[758] In 1932 the balance from the Christmas

Barges on the Stover Canal under sail in wintertime. The use of tugboats started in 1914. Note the proximity of the Moretonhampstead railway line that opened in 1866.

fund was used to distribute coal to the unemployed, no less than 724 were recorded. In 1933 a sacred concert was held in the Alexandra Hall in aid of Newton's unemployed.[759] By 1936 unemployment in Newton had fallen to 217.[760]

Torquay acquired in 1922 the generating site of the Urban Electric Supply Company in Newton after having had problems with its electricity power supplies. The Supply Company was operating there since 1899 and held an exhibition in 1905. One early problem was caused by the first cables being laid

Power Station with the cam-ouflage still visible on the cooling tower, the fields in background were to become the Buckland Estate.

A.C. Bulpin & Son

One of Bulpin's early solid-tyred charabancs with a single letter number and a running board. They traded as 'Pride of the Moor'.

This was a business that not only grew and became important in the town, but its development epitomised changing technology. Mr A.C. Bulpin senior came to Newton Abbot in 1900 to work for a firm of ironmongers in Bank Street Warner's which later became Nicholls and Clarke. At first he lived in lodgings in St Paul's Road and cycled by pushbike, back to Taunton each weekend to complete a courtship! Then in October 1909 he started his own ironmonger's business at No 1 Bank Street.

The early ledger shows a good start on the opening day but on the second the takings equivalent was less than 14p. Later there was even one day lower, at the equivalent of 9p. There was overall a steady increase in business from £79 in the first full month November 1909 to £111 by November 1912 and £1170 in November 1919.

During the First World War Mr Bulpin was joined by his son, AC Bulpin junior and they began a business interest in bicycles, motor-cycles and cars. They also set up a taxi service. For the mechanical expansion they took over the former butcher's shop next door in Bank Street. There are extant records of sales of bicycles from May 1917, motorcycles from February 1919 and cars from December of the same year. However, there may have been previous sales. No trade names are recorded for the bicycles but motorcycle sales included Calthorpe, Douglas, a lady's model, Metro-Taylor, Premier, Royal Enfield, Triumph, Wolf, and Zenith. The earliest car sale recorded was a Morgan.

Early car agencies were held for Austin, Clymo, Singer and Ford but at the start it was sales of the Model T Ford which were important. Later agencies continued to be held for Austin and Singer but Morris and Whippet were added and Dennis and Vulcan commercials. The cycle business migrated to separate premises in Wolborough Street, 'Tower Cycles'.

In 1920 a syndicate, including Bulpin's set up the Newton Abbot Touring Company Ltd, a charabanc enterprise running under the name 'The pride of the moors'. For this they started East Street Garage Company at 14 East Street. The first vehicles were made by Dennis, with solid tyres on an ex-war department chassis. The premises were soon outgrown, so additional ones were taken in Kingsteignton Road, at King's Mews, part of the site which later became the old bus station. In 1925 the ownership of the coach business passed wholly to A C Bulpin & Son.

*Bulpin's early garage in East Street, they started as
ironmongers in Bank Street but expanded into cycles and cars.*

There was considerable rivalry with Balls' which ran a similar business. In those days both companies would park unused charabancs in the streets to advertise their services and an argument developed over where they might be parked. Bulpin's originally used a site near the Tower, not surprisingly they were asked to move because even in those days they hindered the traffic. Bulpin's then took to parking nearer their competitor but that evinced protests from Balls'. A special meeting of the Council was held to discuss the parking of charabancs[738] and eventually both companies were allowed to park in the Market Square except on Wednesdays.

In 1922 Bulpin's operated briefly a bus service from Newton Tower to Totnes Plains there were two trips each way, each day via Abbotskerswell and Ipplepen. They also started selling tractors. The garage business was moved to Wolborough Street in 1924. The charabanc and taxi service businesses were sold to 'Grey Cars' in 1929. New showrooms were opened at Wolborough Street in 1967.

In the 1950s the third generation of the family Mr A.C.I. Bulpin joined the business. In 1963 the family sold out their interests in the company but it continued trading under the same name until the late 1990s.[739]

*Bulpin's later premises in Wolborough Street, when they were
one of the biggest garages in town.*

in the gutter where they could be damaged by the wheels of heavy vehicles![762] Newton Council took up an option to buy the undertaking, and then resold to Torquay. In 1924, a new power station was opened at the end of Teign Road: the party from Torquay arrived by charabanc.[763] It was later extended and would no doubt have grown further had it not been for the arrival of the National Grid system in the mid-1930s. Torquay lost control when the industry was nationalized in 1948. The enormous concrete cooling tower built in 1940 was certainly the most obtrusive landmark in the area. An attempt was made to camouflage it during the war. Its demolition provided considerable spectator sport later in the century. Water was drawn from the river and sometimes flatfish fry were drawn in as well. These would develop in the sand filter beds providing fillings for the staff's frying pans!

In 1926 the Trades Union Congress called a nation wide General Strike to support the miners who were already out on strike. There was a large response to the call but was short-lived it started on the 3rd and ended about the 14th of May. Railways were the most important part of economy affected by the strike in Devon, and Newton was greatly involved. The strike was not confined to railwaymen, and comprised a total of 2,500 workers.[764] Volunteers operated the organisation of coal and food supplies and Seale Hayne students were prominent.[765] There were large stocks of coal in Newton so there were no problems with electricity or gas.[766] Large crowds assembled in Queen Street to see the railwaymen march back. Men were only taken back as and when work permitted, and this caused bitterness. Furthermore continuance of the coal strike meant many services were not restored immediately.[767] The shortage of coal caused partial closures of Bovey Pottery and Hexter Humpherson.[768]

Matthew's original shop in Newton, they opened about 1928, at the old junction of Highweek Road to Ashburton and Exeter Road to Bovey Tracey. Their first oven was in the downstairs living room, later the whole of the first floor was devoted to baking.

The Co-op shop in King Street. The Co-op was once the biggest retailer in the town and nationally in the country.

In 1928 Mr and Mrs Ashworth moved from Southport, to open their bakery business, Madge Mellor's, in Queen Street. This firm expanded and continued until 1987.[769] Unfortunately it then failed after a double take-over bid. This was to the regret not only of many Newtonians but numerous other customers who came from miles around to buy their high-quality cream cakes and their pies. They cultivated an old fashioned image and many remember the waitresses in black dresses with white aprons and caps and their cake-boxes in light pink, with the full skirted lady logo. Another baker to come about this time was Robert Matthews. He and his wife Edith took over the cramped corner property at the old fork between Highweek Road that went to Ashburton, and Exeter Road which went to Bovey Tracey. Their first oven was in the downstairs living room, later the whole of the first floor was devoted to baking. Just before the Second World War they moved to Queen Street. Their son Frank ran the business for many more years at one time having a branch shop in the market.[770]

A sub-post office, now gone, was opened at Milber in 1928.[771] Henley's, the local cider firm amalgamated with Whiteway's in 1933 but this firm has also since closed.[772] The Newton Co-op opened a model dairy in 1928[773] and declared a dividend of 1/- in the £ for its members in 1933.[774] Three years later it opened a new grocery warehouse in King Street.[775]

In 1934 Keyberry Mill was acknowledged as one of Devon's 'Old-time survivals'. This water wheel driven, gristmill was a corn mill to grind grain for flour. The mill's efficiency was impaired when the boating lake was formed at Penn Inn but it was still in use until demolished in 1968.[776] Ogwell Mill probably worked until about 1909 and then became popular for cream teas. This finished during the Second World War, afterwards the owner tried to open again, but the council ruled that the property was not suitable.[777]

133

Devon Leathercrafts

Devon Leathercrafts, an early works coach outing, in pre-war days this was an annual event.

When Vicary's leathergoods making up department closed, the Walsall trained manager Douglas set up a new business with Carter to found Carter & Douglas

It started in 1922 in an old stable off Albany Street, behind what was then a small grocery store to day The Albany Veterinary Centre. A horse and trap had to be moved for the five employees and one piece of equipment, a Singer sewing machine. The business succeeded but the partnership did not. Carter bought out Douglas and the name was changed to Devon Leathercrafts.

Just how shaky the business was in its earliest days is illustrated by the story of the Friday morning when it had a good stock of purses but not sufficient money in the bank to pay the wages that afternoon. A buyer had to be found who would take and pay ready cash for the purses that very day.

By 1924 employees had increased to 20 and a move made to larger premises in Sherborne Road. Changing premises was a simpler then, the hands picked up their stools and handtools and just walking with them to their new place of work! The day's order despatch was carried to the post office on foot. Some of the young girls enlivened their afternoon tea break by going into Abbotsbury, banging hard on doorknockers and running away. Needless to say complaints ensued. The first 'clicking press' or

cutting machine was bought at Sherborne Road.

In 1930 the firm moved to Kingsteignton Road to a purpose built factory.

During the war, contract work was carried out making parachute targets for the R.A.F and under the concentration scheme, accommodation had to be given up to other leather goods manufacturers.

In 1956 a much bigger extension was built doubling the manufacturing area. By this time staff had risen to over 100. In 1972 the firm celebrated its Golden Jubilee. At that time Devon Leathercrafts was probably the second largest fancy leathergoods-manufacturing firm in the country. The firm was proud of its reputation in the town as a good place to work and had a number of long-serving employees to confirm its status.

Over the years the range of merchandise varied but was largely based on purses, wallets, key cases and various items of gift merchandise. At the end of the war there was for a short while a big demand for leather wallets for various 'Welcome Home Funds', some of these were sizeable orders. Writing cases too were much in vogue. Thousands of young men were still going away into National Service and girl friends, for obvious reasons, sought them out as presents.

There was a souvenir trade with goods being gold-

*Light-hearted moment at Devon Leathercrafts, c.1950 with a penny-farthing. Not
so much traffic on the Kingsteignton Road then.*

*Queen Mary looks at Devon Leathercrafts stand at 1951 British Industries Fair,
the Festival of Britain year. She once bought a handbag from the firm.*

The Queen Mother visits Devon Leathercrafts stand at the British Industries Fair,
Princess Margaret is on the left.

Devon Leathercrafts before the new extension was built in 1956. Central
machining bench on the left, bench working and button machines on the right.

blocked with the particular crests of resorts. Carter had the notion of a simple way of being able to affix an initial to any leather goods item at the point of sale. He patented his invention that became known as the 'Initial Button'. If any single event must be picked out for the company's success, this invention must surely be it.

The firm built up a considerable export trade claiming to have sent goods to at least 45 different countries. Then came a period of change in retailing, self-service was beginning to spread. Small leather goods, were an obvious candidate for this type of merchandising. Unfortunately this idea of self-service ran directly contrary to the idea of the Initial Button, as the individual packeting meant that

the retailer, to affix an initial, had to unpack the item. Needless to say self-service won and the Initial Button was abandoned.

Problems began to assail the leather goods industry with cheap imports principally from China. It should be added that Devon Leathercrafts was not alone in this predicament of being unable to compete with foreign imports, the vast majority of British leathergoods manufacturing companies ceased to trade.

In the end the business had to shut down and close, it is now Blackler's Garage on the Kingsteignton Road. The firm did finish 'in the black', all creditors being paid.[761]

In the days before it was sold sliced and wrapped in supermarkets, bread was delivered to your door. The Co-op bakery was in King Street.

In the early days of electricity there was incorrect charging caused by inefficient meters. To obviate a series of meter testing centres were set up. One of the first was in Wharf Road. Building started in 1938, and it is still extant.[779] After 90 years trading Fuller's Nursery, opposite the station, closed down.[780] Newton's most memorable 'take-away', was John Valley. He had a hand-propelled mobile chip fryer, no fish, converted with loving care from an old hand cart. It was coal-fired and had four great spiral brass poles going up to the roof. John used to stand opposite the Imperial Cinema where Devon Square meets Queen Street. Unfortunately, he was set on by thieves for his takings one night, and ceased to trade thereafter.

Town affairs

In 1919 the Rural Housing Committee reported the Local Government Board was keen to provide bathrooms. However, it was essential, that if these conveniences were provided, that they should be put to proper use and not utilised for storage space![781] In the same year the Prince of Wales arrived by an early morning train at 6.01. He had said it was too early to expect a formal reception but the Council had gallantly replied that no hour was too early to meet him. The upshot was a very good turn-out, especially of service veterans and school children.[782] In 1920 an idea was floated for a 'Greater Newton' and a conference was held between Bishopsteignton, Kingsteignton and Teignmouth, there was a meeting of the Middle Classes Union at the Town Hall to consider the menace of Bolshevism and a meeting was held of the Newton Branch of Comrades of the Great War.[783]

A request to open the Library on Sundays was refused on the grounds of no proven demand.[784] In 1921 there was annoyance because the Library closed on Thursday afternoon when shop-workers might have used it.[785] In 1933 there were problems at the reading room because readers of the racing news were monopolizing it. It was said 'It is regrettable that Newton Abbot stands alone among the towns of Devonshire in not obliterating the racing news, especially when there is so much unemployment'.[786] The Stover Estate, 2,344 acres, which extended into six parishes (Bovey Tracey, Hennock, Highweek, Ilsington, Kingsteignton, and Teigngrace) and had twelve farms was put up for sale by R. H. St Maur. A road at Milber was named Addison Road after the first Minister of Health, who laid the foundation stone of the inaugural house.[787] J. H. Thomas, member of Parliament and a prominent Trade Unionist, addressed railwaymen in 1921[788] Around the time of the General Strike Labour politicians who spoke in Newton included both George Lansbury, later leader of the Labour Party, and Ramsey Macdonald, twice Labour Prime Minister.[789] In October 1926 Mr Neville Chamberlain, then Conservative Minister of Health, and later Prime Minister, visited Broadlands Estate.[790] In 1927 Mr Tom Mann, described as the world's greatest agitator, addressed a Newton Labour demonstration.[791] In 1929 Miss Margaret Bondfield, who was the first woman cabinet minister, spoke to Newton Labourites,[792] former and future premier Stanley Baldwin passed through Newton, local conservatives gave him a cordial welcome.[793] In 1931 Horatio Bottomley, former MP and editor of *John Bull,* was fined £1 for not paying entertainment tax on a lecture he gave at the *Globe* Assembly Rooms.[794]

In 1922 the idea of imposing a speed limit in Queen Street was turned down. NAUDC decided not to press for the removal of the Tower.[795] The Council declared itself in favour of establishing a Borough of Newton and said it would hold a public meeting in early 1926.[796] Later on application the Privy Council informed NAUDC that they could not be incorporated as a borough because the population was less than 20,000.[797]

Loder's Edge Tool Mill

The Loder family started making edge-tools at Ashprington in 1855 and moved to Holbeam Mill, just outside Newton, in 1877 and continued for three generations until 1943. Loder's supplied tools, mostly locally, but further afield including the South Hams, perhaps from their old connection with Ashprington. A few items were supplied even further away to Plymouth. There was one sale of shovels to the Atlas Tin Mining Co at Camborne in Cornwall. They had a range of customers but many tools were sold through ironmongers in nearby towns and they had a stall in Newton market.

Loder's made a variety of bill hooks, bramble, brouse, furze, grass, half turn, reap, spear, socket, and thatcher's shearing hooks. They made axes, cleavers, hatchets, felling axes, mattocks and knives such as hay, chaff, butchers' and potato. They produced Dutch, double, garden and turnip hoes as well as twobills. Various tools were named thus but these were likely to be a long handled tool with mattock on one side of the head and a narrow vertical blade at right angles on the other side, so when digging they could be turned in the hand and used to cut through small roots. They made milk pans (probably for making Devonshire cream in the traditional way over a very low heat) wedges and shoes (presumably a kind of drag or skid for a wheel). The firm did regrinding, e.g. sheep shears and repair work such as mending chains, gates, ploughs, a tormentor (spiked harrow for rough ground) shafts of waggons, rabbit traps, a water cart, etc and sometimes more domestic items were invoiced in the accounts. Surprisingly perhaps to our modern eyes in a tool specialist's accounts are items for sawing wood, cabbage plants and young ducks!

The Holbeam Mill, or Hobbim, as it was sometimes called, had a lengthy history. It was originally a flourmill for a long while it produced fishhooks and knives principally for the Newfoundland trade. When the mill was taken over by Loder's tilt hammers were installed to produce edge tools. On closure the machinery was acquired by the Science Museum in London. The one-time mill is now a private residence. The National Trust has acquired a similar edge-tool mill, Finch's Foundry at Sticklepath, which well repays a visit.[778]

Holbeam Mill, the Loder Family made edge tools here for three generations from 1877 to 1943. It is now a private house.

Inside the Holbeam Mill, this was originally a flourmill but later fishhooks and knives were made here for the Newfoundland trade. Later still it became an edge tool mill.

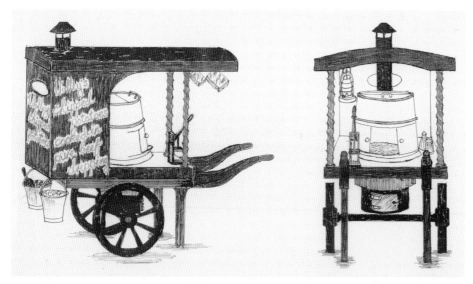

John Valley's hand-built chip cart which used to stand opposite the Imperial Cinema. Paper bags hang from the roof; there is a hand-operated chipper and a fryer on the shelf, buckets of coal and potatoes beneath.

Compulsory weighing of cattle by live weight was introduced in Newton Market in 1927.[798] In the next year the Council closed 40 slum properties and ordered 86 others to improve. A by-pass route through Jetty Marsh was suggested in 1930. It was thought it might be more economical than widening Highweek Street.[799] Later Newton Council turned down the idea although Devon County Council were in favour.[800] Traffic lights first came to Newton Abbot; at the Tower, Drum Clock, and the Avenue.[801] There was a row over the renumbering of Queen Street; traders accused the Council of being high-handed.[802] NAUDC decided to erect 100 concrete houses on the Broadlands estate, 300 applications were received.[803] Later the decision was taken to build 70 more. Over 100 were occupied the following June. Aller Vale Estates planned housing developments in 1931.[804] In 1932 new sewage works opened at Buckland Barton.[805] The Newton Labour party opened a new hall at East Park.[806] The Council rejected in 1934 the idea of pedestrian street crossings but decided to try unilateral parking which was later made permanent.[807]

In 1937 new NARDC offices in Kingsteignton Road were opened by Mrs Whiteway Wilkinson who said: 'I declare these premises open and trust they will prove adequate and convenient for the transaction of your business and serve to remind you occasionally of the poor ratepayers'![808] In February the licence was transferred from the *Turk's Head* (Raj Belash) to *Penn Inn*, but one for Mile End was refused.[809] The bottleneck of Foss's Corner in Bank Street, which faced the Adult Education Centre, was demolished. The press stated it made a striking improvement in the appearance of Highweek Street.[810] It is more than a pity that the rest was later largely destroyed. Sherborne Mill was demolished, the *Western Morning News* noted that 'the town has lost one of its ancient landmarks'. A mill had existed since time immemorial; it originally stood in the midst of a well-wooded vale, deriving its power from the River Lemon.[811] In August 1938, after a night of near tropical rain, streets were flooded and a subsequent relief fund raised over £1,000.[812]

Forde House was sold by the Courtnay's at the *Globe Hotel* in November 1936. Not so well remembered is the accompanying massive sale of Newton properties, triggered by death duties. The sale catalogue noted 'Valuable freehold lands with main road frontages. Ripe for development . . . also garages, warehouses, and stores, factories and factory sites, with wharf frontage, drill

Foss's Corner junction of Bank & Market Streets, c.1936. Note communication masts from old post office, now Mitre Bookshop.

hall, dwelling houses, quarries'. There were sites on the Avenue and along Whitelake, Jetty Marsh and, most of what is now the Brunel Industrial Estate, Aller sandpits and Aller Park.[813] The latter is now the Aller Park Estate. There were suggestions that the council might buy Forde House and that it could be turned into a museum. The council decided against purchase because of possible rate increases.[814]

Bradley Manor, Newton's oldest house, was given to the National Trust. Sadly the agreed opening times are less, than most of their other properties. In the Second World War, the Women's Voluntary Service used the Manor for storing bedding and clothing gifted by Canadians for bombed-out families. Even the chapel held wellington boots![815] In 1968, a wing was leased to the Devon Girl Guides Association.[816]

Women in politics were a new departure in the inter-war years. By 1922 women's votes were becoming increasingly important in parliamentary elections at Newton where 3,410, out of a voters' list of 7,372, were women.[817] In 1921 Miss I. Webster became the first lady Councillor in Newton[818] and much later in 1944 she was the first woman elected as Chairman of the NAUDC.[819] Mrs F. E. Card was welcomed to the Newton Bench in 1924 as the first lady Justice of the Peace. Miss Kate Spurrell, Labour, spoke at a Peace Pledge Movement meeting in 1938.[820]

There were negotiations to transfer Forde Park to the town, as public pleasure grounds, from Queen Anne's Bounty in 1922.[821] These became protracted and there had even been trial borings for clay mining, but the park became town property at the beginning of 1930.[822] The Council later erected a permanent pavilion.[823] Sir Henry Carew put up the Pinewoods Walk, at Milber, for sale in 1924 the Urban Council decided against purchase and it was feared this amenity would be lost. Happily a benefactor, Mr Charles D. Blake, purchased it for the town.[824]

In the late 1920s a considerable area of Milber Woods was felled although the main Pine Walk remained untouched. Public feeling ran high about this and a community effort was made to plant new trees. Thoughtfully, children were engaged to inaugurate the replanting in November 1927.[825] In 1922 the Council discussed whether hard tennis courts should be provided in Baker's Park. In 1931 the UDC turned down a swimming pool site as too costly but the idea of a museum was revived. It was decided in 1933 that a new swimming pool would be placed in Penn Inn. The 5-acre site was largely purchased with donations. The new park was in part a project for the unemployed. To maximize

Penn Inn site before the swimming pool and Penn Inn Park, now MacDonald's and Sainsbury's. The old tollhouse was later demolished.

the benefit of providing work no mechanical equipment was used and the unemployed were given work in 12-week stints. Furthermore as benefactors provided all the funds no costs fell on the rates.[826] The pool opened June 13th 1935.[827] A short-lived paddling and boating-pond opened in July 1937, which unfortunately was silted up by Aller Brook. In 1953 a miniature railway was set up.[828] What started as a project full of altruism finished as quite the antithesis (see Chapter 10).

Health

There was a conference in 1922 on cancer at Darracombe, the beautiful residence of Dr Edgar Haydon, later the women's hostel for Seale Hayne. One type of lip cancer was disappearing as clay pipes with short rough stems went out of use.[829] Dr E. Haydon made an appeal for £1,000 for radium for breast cancer cases in 1929.[830] A children's block was opened at Hawkmoor sanatorium in 1927.[831] The Prince of Wales opened two new wings of the Newton hospital.[832] He was proclaimed King at the Tower in 1936 and reigned briefly as King Edward VIII until his abdication.[833] There was a Ministry of Health inquiry at Newton in 1924 about the provision of a lavatory and baths in the Market Square.[834] In 1929 Court Grange, at Abbotskerswell opened as a Sunshine Home for blind children, although some children were already there.[835] It later became a school for the deaf and is now private housing.

The suggestion was made in 1931 that a maternity hospital should be set up in Newton Abbot[836] and in 1933 a splendid new motor ambulance was presented to the town.[837] In November 1937 schools were closed in Newton, owing to an outbreak of infantile paralysis.[838] In 1938 the Webster Memorial Nurses Home opened in the hospital grounds a long-felt need.[839]

The Prince of Wales, later Edward VIII, on Wolborough Hill driven by Bulpin's.

The Workhouse

The Workhouse was still much in the news during this period starting with an application for a 47-hour week by the Poor Law Worker's Union. The Guardians disagreed. In 1921 Guardians suspended the master of the Workhouse for keeping money that should have been paid as salaries. He went to London and was soon reported as being in an asylum. Two years later thanks to subscriptions two pianos were presented.[840] In 1923 there was a distribution of blankets to the poor of Wolborough.[841] By 1925 the Guardians were worried their casual ward was a 'Sunday school of wickedness', with older members corrupting the younger ones.[842] In March 1927 the Guardians who had been responsible for the workhouse, held their final meeting. The 'union' had been the second largest west of Bristol with nearly 40 parishes and a population latterly of some 100,000.[843] The workhouse did not close but continued under a different aegis. Through the depression the procession of tramps would move from house to house, Newton one day, Totnes the next. Such was the dearth of work that both skilled and unskilled men were among their ranks as well as a few women. In 1933 Dr Ley, who was so well known for his work in improving conditions at the Workhouse died in his 85th year.[844]

Crime

Crime was usually low key but one ex-Newtonian was at the forefront of national news. In 1921 gypsies were involved in battle in the Market Square; hooks, hatchets, and tent pegs were used and one gypsy left for dead.[845] A pensioner, whose pension had been reduced, used his stick to break several windows in the Newton Pensions Office in Union Street.[846] In 1922 Clarence Popham, former Secretary of the Newton Abbot Co-op, pleaded guilty to a £1185 fraud[847] and in 1930 a 90-year old thief was arrested for stealing from a lady's handbag in the Market.[848]

Education

At this period many pupils came by train and a journey from Chudleigh with a change at Heathfield could take as much as an hour and a half. After school these pupils were kept back to do homework and only allowed to go in time to catch their trains. Three brothers, from Haytor area rode on moorland ponies daily and stabled them at the *Seven Stars Inn*. After school they collected their ponies and rode home. They were sometimes used as examples of what could be achieved to latecomers! Later in the 1920s buses started to be used to get to school.[850]

A party of Seale Hayne College students visited Canada in 1927 to take part in harvesting operations.[851] There was in 1932 a mutiny at Dartmoor Jail, Seale Hayne students went to milk the cows and do other urgent farm work.[852] Prince George, later the Duke of Kent, paid a visit in 1932 to the College where he accepted a tin of its Devonshire cream and a cheese. Fog disrupted his plans to fly from Haldon airport and the back-up plan to catch a train also fell through so the Prince arrived quite unexpectedly at Newton Abbot Police station. He was entertained in the charge room and one officer brought in a chair, as the only place to sit was on some lockers. He departed later by car.[853]

Fire

Newton Fire Brigade attended a big fire at Buckfastleigh Paper Mills in 1921. The Chief of Buckfastleigh Fire Brigade said its help was unnecessary, but the directors of the paper mill wrote a public letter thanking Newton, saying in their opinion the mill would have been burnt right down without their help. Five years later another fire completely gutted Bradley Wood House.[854]

Religion

The most exciting church news in these years concerned St Luke's Milber that was begun in 1936, to serve the rapid growth of the town eastwards. The design came from a dream of the vicar W. Keeble Martin. The church is an unusual shape based on St Andrew's cross. Keeble Martin's brother Arthur, an architect, drew up the plans. Building took a very long time and only finished in 1963.[855] The Bishop of Exeter consecrated it and gave the traditional three knocks with his staff on the west door. Keeble Martin then retired, came back for the service and there was a fanfare by the Junior Leaders Regiment Royal Signals.[856] Slater in his *The Churches of Devon* describes it as 'The most exciting church built in Devon since the Reformation'.

Herbert Rowse Armstrong 1870–1922

H. R. Armstrong was well educated, went to Cambridge, and became a solicitor in 1895. He initially practised in Newton, under Hutchings, Armstrong and Hutchings, living with his mother and sisters in Lonsdale Road. He later moved to Hay-on-Wye where he was a partner in a law firm and became clerk to the local court. He married Katerine Mary Friend, a Teignmouth girl he had known in South Devon, in Highweek Church and had three children.

In 1921 he was accused of trying to poison a business rival and murder his wife. He was found guilty, lost an appeal and was hanged in Gloucester Jail on the last day of May 1925. There was much interest in Newton and reports on the trial were in the local press. He set a record in one respect as probably the only solicitor to have ever been executed for murder.[849]

Later the vicar of St Luke's was John Hammond who owned a spaniel called Whisky. This well trained dog would be outside the church each week to greet the congregation. When the bell stopped tolling, he would pad up the aisle to his place beside the prayer desk. Here he stayed until the final blessing was given then, unprompted; he would trot back down the aisle to see the congregation leave.[858]

The Young Women's Christian Association opened premises at No 1 The Avenue in 1919. In 1921 an Indian Village Exhibition was held at the Congregational School in aid of missionary work. There were snake shrines, a bed of nails and a cinematograph display.[859] In 1926 an 'American tea', in which food was individually brought, was held at Highweek Rectory.[860] A Rechabite Centenary demonstration was held in 1934 at Newton, there were 1,500 children and many adults.[861]

Leisure

There was an inaugural meeting of the Operatic Society in 1921. Presumably the earlier venture of 1914 had folded during the war. Children of Newton Scattered Homes were entertained at a Torquay pantomime in 1925 thanks to Mr W.H. Mortimer.[862] After extensive renovations the Alexandra Hall reopened in 1927 as the Alexandra Theatre with a performance of *Iolanthe*.[863]

In 1926 the old St Mary's Chapel was converted into a public hall, with a stage and a balcony, although the west end was kept as a 'wayside chapel'.[865] Newton Abbot & District Musical Comedy Society used it for about 40 years but then had to leave at six months notice when the building was sold.[866] During the Second World War, dances were held and part of it was used as a school.[867] Its future was discussed in 1985 and some Councillors supported demolition; for instance Mrs Nancy Morrison said 'old buildings are a terrible eyesore and preserving them is a waste of money'![868] Fortunately, the majority opinion differed.

Newton Council saw in 1928 a private showing of the banned film *Dawn*.[869]

William Keeble Martin, 1877–1969

W. Keeble Martin was born near Oxford and his family moved to Dartington in 1891. He worked as a curate in the Midlands and Lancashire. In 1909 he married Violet Chaworth, who on receiving his first proposal, protested she did not know him! He became vicar of Wath-upon-Dearne and was offered the benefice of Haccombe and Coffinswell, on the fringes of Newton, which he held from 1921 to 1934. He became much involved with church work on the Milber estate, at that time a fast growing area. A temporary church was built and later the spectacular modern church was started. Keeble Martin's church work took him in 1934 to Torrington but he returned in 1943 to Combeinteignhead. His life long hobbies were botany and painting. He was made a fellow of the Linnean society, edited with Gordon T. Fraser *Flora of Devon* (1939) and produced the *Concise British Flora* in 1965. He also designed a set of floral British postage stamps which were issued in 1967. [857]

In 1931 the Gainsborough Film Company arrived in Newton en route for North Bovey where they made a talking film version of *Hound of the Baskervilles.*[870]

Miscellaneous

Newton Races were revived in 1919,[871] the next year a meeting was called to form a Motor Cycle Club[872] and the Whitpot Mill Tea Gardens, Kingskerswell, advertised dainty teas during the winter months. In 1924 Newton Rugby Chiefs and Newton Juniors won the Devon Cups for the second year running,[873] and in 1925 the South Devon Hounds met in the Market Square.[874] Greyhound racing started at the Recreation Ground in 1929[875] while the first dance was held in the newly erected Forde Hall in 1930.[876] On the 1931 Whitsun holiday 4,500 people left by train for seaside or moorland trips.[877] May 6th 1935 was the Silver Jubilee of King George V, children were given a mug and an illustrated book, old folks a tea. There was a furry dance, beacons on the hills and a torchlight procession.[878] That year the bounds were beaten after a lapse of 40 years: 'Walls scaled and river crossed thrice' was a headline. The 17-mile circuit was walked over two days and a sand barge was used to get walkers across the river.[879] Len Harvey, the boxer appeared in a tournament at Newton.[880] In a 1936I cricket match a hedgehog came to rest between the wickets, the wicket keeper, whose gloves were suitable removed the unusual spectator.[881] 1937 started with the younger generation dancing around the clock tower. The paper said that a 'touch of modernity was given to one of Newton Abbot's oldest New Year's Eve customs'.[882] The first ever-direct broadcast from Newton was of the organist Gordon Brewer.[883]

In 1937 the town was decorated for the coronation of King George VI. Coloured festoons across the streets made it one of the most gaily bedecked in the West Country; people came from some distance to see the decorations. School children chose a treat to the cinema instead of the traditional tea. All three cinemas had to be used to accommodate them. In the morning there

Lawrence du Garde Peach, 1890–1974

Lawrence du Garde Peach was a lecturer in English at the University College of the South West, later Exeter University, from 1922 to 1926. He was sent to lecture on drama in Newton. In 1923 he founded the Newton Abbot Repertory Company, guided it for its first four years, and afterwards became its president. It is as an author and dramatist that he is best known. He began writing for Punch in 1920 and he wrote over 400 radio plays, a number for Children's' Hour, as well as writing Ladybird books and many film scenarios. Among his books were *The Castles of England*, *Famous Men of Britain*, *Famous Women of Britain* and *Unknown Devon*. He also wrote a number of pageants for different places. Newton Repertory gave the first performance of one of his plays *Home Fires* in 1930, an all women cast. He was awarded an OBE. As well as his great interest in drama he also painted for recreation.[864]

was a brief service in the market that finished early, so people could, if they wished, go home and listen to the coronation service broadcast. In the afternoon, there was a furry dance through the streets and a display of folk dancing in Courtenay Park.[884]

There was a mishap: in 1920 the *Western Times* reported that parts of Devon had been turned into a 'Wild West' when a truckload of bullocks at Newton Station ran amok. Some jumped into the Teign and became stuck in the mud. One was so wild it had to be shot on the spot. Another beast went all the way to Exminster where it attacked a man.[885]

Cinemas

Over time Newton had some four cinemas: the *Alexandra* in Market Street, the *Empire Picture House* in Lemon Road, the *Imperial Electric Cinema* in Queen Street and the *Odeon* off Wolborough Street.

There seems little doubt that the *Alexandra* is the oldest. It had been licensed as early as 1890 for theatrical performances and in 1899 the Council was calling the lessee's attention to insurance requirements for cinematograph and biograph exhibitions. There is confirmation it was showing films in 1909, but there were long periods when it did not. Films started to be shown regularly in April 1927. About this time a balcony/circle and projection room were put in. The first films were *Prisoners of the Storm* and *The Cheerful Fraud*. Like the other early cinemas in the town it also offered a live entertainment act each night as well as films. This entertainment was a regular occurrence for a year and continued intermittently for another two years. Towards the end of 1931 it closed for three days to install a 'Sound Reproducer' and afterwards showed the all talking *Charley's Aunt*. It became a two-screen cinema in 1996 with seating for 250 and 140. It still survives as a cinema and stages the occasional theatrical performance.

One very early film in Newton was of the funeral procession of Queen Victoria in February 1901. It was shown at what was called a London Exhibition that had various attractions in the Market Hall. The film itself was projected in a side room at a charge of 3d.

The Poole family were the important entrepreneurial family in the development of the cinema in Newton. They started with a mobile 'Miroma' which they took around the fairgrounds. They then set up successively the *Empire* and the *Imperial*.

The *Empire*, close to the Recreation Ground, opened as a 6,000-sq. ft. indoor roller skating rink in 1909. The newspaper headline announcing this called it 'Rinking'. In January 1911 the *Empire* changed to entertainments and showed pictures. By May 1911 it changed programmes twice weekly, and showed each week the world's animated newspaper. Every important event was faithfully portrayed at *Poole's Empire*. They even showed a 45 minute epic *The Fall of Troy*. By July 1913 it was open six nights a week at 8 p.m. and there were matinees on Tuesday, Wednesday, Thursday and Saturday at 3 p.m. In December 1914 the *Empire* announced it had Kinetophone, the most recent invention, the 8th wonder of the world. They also put on the pantomime *Cinderella*, adding 'This is not a picture'. By January 1915 it claimed to be showing the latest news and pictures from the war front. The pantomime at the end of the year was *Babes in the Wood*. Film programmes at this time often showed an episode each week of a long film, hoping obviously to lure patrons back; providing the origin of the expression cliff-hanger. One such was *Greed*, an insurance swindle, another was *The Shieling Shadow* in 15 episodes.

In 1922 the Newton *Empire*, advertised itself as 'The Popular place where everybody goes', had two performances daily at 2.30 and 7.45. Amongst other films it showed were *The Duke's Son*, and *Blind Husband*. Later the *Empire* brought back skating sessions on certain week-day afternoons to the accompaniment of the *Empire Orchestra*. Arrangements were made for a late train, after the performances, to Moretonhampstead and patrons' bicycles were stored free. In 1923 it was for a short while turned into the *Palais de Danse* which opened each Thursday and Saturday. The *Blue Lagoon Dance Orchestra* and *Non-stop Jazz Joy* were advertised. Special arrangements were made for late buses to Torquay and Teignmouth after the dance. Presumably the venture was not a success because it reopened in September 1924 as a cinema. In 1929 *The Empire Dance Hall* was acquired for billiards and in October 1936 changed into an indoor bowling-green. The hall was used for other activities such as badminton and the name *Empire Badminton Club* survived for some years after transferring to another hall.

The *Imperial* was a little later than the *Empire* and was at the corner of Queen Street with its junction with Lemon Road. This opened on the 20th of September 1913 as the *Imperial Electric*. There were continuous performances from 6 p.m. on Mondays, Tuesdays and Fridays from 2 p.m. on Wednesdays, Thursdays and Saturdays. The 500 seats were all plush tip-ups; there was 'luxury and comfort'. Pictures changed Monday and Thursday. At first two clever lady pianists provided the background music. Later there was a small orchestra and later still an organ. One of the early pictures was *The Man in Black*. For some while, as well as films, it also put on live entertainment acts like the *Empire*. In April 1915 it advertised 'Country Stores Night Friday useful presents given away. Come and see what you will get'. The film at the beginning of 1916 was *The Cricket and the Hearth* in four parts. In 1917 the film *Battle of the Ancre* which showed tanks in action was billed. In October 1918 both the *Imperial* and the *Empire* showed, in aid of the Red Cross, *No Man's Land to Blighty*. In 1921 the *Imperial* had a special show for Warriors' Day, proceeds to the Earl Haig Fund, the *City of Purple Dreams* was one of the films.

The *Imperial* films included the better-known *Little Dorrit*, and *The Hound of the Baskervilles*. News of the *Imperial's* impending closure came in November 1961 when it was learnt it was to be sold to a drapery store, Harvey's. The last films were shown in mid-January 1962. The one time cinema's imposing façade is still very easily picked out at the Queen Street junction with Lemon Road.

The *Odeon* was the last cinema to open in Newton. The idea had been aired as early as 1933 in the old Sun Court off Wolborough Street, it was then called a 'kinema', cinema became the accepted name later. It opened on 17th February 1936 and seated 1,000 of whom 250 were in the balcony. The first main picture was *Anna Karenina* with Greta Garbo and the supporting picture was *Unknown Woman*. The *Odeon* was used for occasions that required a large capacity, such as an election address by the Minister of Food in 1945, and for Grammar School Speech Days and even a fashion show. It closed in July 1972. One of the last pictures was *The Severed Head*.

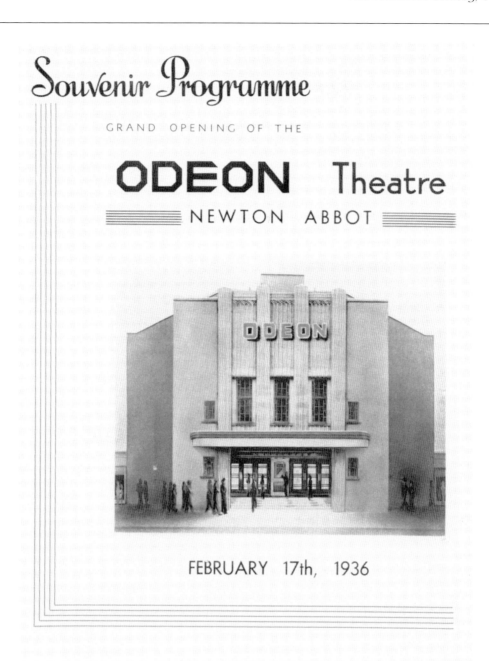

Illustration from the Souvenir Programme of February 1936 produced for the opening of the Newton Abbot Odeon cinema. It was closed in July 1972.

Second World War

In August 1936 there were articles in the *Mid-Devon Times* on the 'Germany of Adolph Hitler'.[887] The next year there was an announcement that the transport of the 5th Devon Territorials would be mechanized. The first Air Raid Precautions organizer for South Devon was appointed in 1938[888] and the first air raid sirens were tested. In the next year an ARP divisional office was set up in the Midland Bank Chambers in Union Street.[889]

With war clouds gathering fast, Britain belatedly adopted conscription.

Denbury's old airfield conversion for militia, later used by army and Junior Leaders, now Channings's Wood Prison.

Camps were urgently required to house these new soldiers, at first called the Militia, and one was established at Denbury on the one time airfield. It was a rush job and a large temporary working force was billeted in the area. Later the American forces used it[890] and it also became the home for the Junior Leaders' Regiment Royal Signals. The last commander of the unit, Colonel Lionel Gregory inaugurated the Ten Tors challenge event on Dartmoor. In 1969, the camp, then known as Rawlinson Barracks, became redundant and despite considerable local opposition, and an alternative application to use it as a holiday village,[891] was opened as Channing's Wood prison five years later.[892]

Some 32,000 gas masks weighing 18 tons arrived in Newton.[893] The first contingent of evacuee children arrived before war was declared on September 3rd. Newton Schools, it was said, would not reopen until the evacuation scheme was complete; later opening was further delayed until air-raid trenches were dug.[894] In early September it was optimistically stated that 'black-out' was nearing perfection. Yet in October came the first prosecutions for infringement.[895] A

Col. Percy Harrison Fawcett was reported killed. Fawcett was educated at Newton College and from 1906 to 1910 he surveyed the borderland between Bolivia and Brazil despite perils such as vampire bats, hostile tribesmen, piranhas and even starvation. His expeditions became source material for Conan Doyle's *The Lost World*, and Peter Fleming's *Brazilian Adventure*. In 1925 he set out on his final expedition with his son Jack, who had also attended Newton College. He disappeared near the River Xingu in Brazil. Despite reports of sightings and several rescue expeditions no trace of him has ever been found.[886]

---

branch of Peace Pledge Union was refused use of local halls for a 'Stop the War' meeting.[896] This caused a heated council debate on the merits of patriotism versus free speech.

Newton was much more fortunate than Teignmouth and Torquay but did suffer two raids with casualties. The first was in August 1940 and had the biggest toll with 16 killed and over 50 injured. The attack came before a full alert was sounded. The station was hit unfortunately a number of people were waiting for a train. Debris from the station was found in Courtenay Park. The Station Cottages by Station Bridge, now David & Charles, were badly damaged.[897] Two bombers dropped some six bombs on the station and its yards; an accompanying fighter machine-gunned the area. Casualties might have been much higher but luckily a long distance train from Crewe to Plymouth had left just a few minutes previously.[898] The local paper reported the raid with headlines 'Casualties in Nazi raid on SW town'. Although the paper showed a picture of the damaged Station Cottages because of censorship Newton was not named. One lucky couple was Mr and Mrs Beardmore who had lived in one cottage for 30 years. They had been out for a walk and returned to find nothing but bare walls.[899]

The second raid was in April 1942 when five were killed and others injured. Houses in Devon Square, Mount Pleasant and Torquay Road were hit as was St Paul's church.[900] A stray bomb landed harmlessly in Wolborough churchyard in May 1941. A large piece of shrapnel is kept in the church.[901] After the severe bombing of Exeter, in 1942, its retail trade dwindled and Newton, already the market town for a large area, gained additional business.[902] This would have been in contrast to the pre-war shopping pattern, when Newtonians would occasionally, especially at Christmas time, combine a visit to the Exeter pantomime and go shopping.

Thousands of children, some accompanied by mothers, some by teachers, were evacuated from London and other large towns to what were then regarded as safe areas. Newton played its part and theoretically could have taken some 8,018 but in practice a lesser figure of some 3,818 places were registered. This was made up of 1,374 unaccompanied children, 170 teachers and helpers and 2,274 others. For these, over 2,000 mattresses and 6,000 blankets had to be provided. In addition, another 1,286 places were covered by private arrangements with householders. Some of the totals planned for individual roads were in Albany Street 6, Courtenay Street 11, Decoy Road 21, Highweek Village 54, Mount Pleasant Road 18, Netley Road 54, Rundle Road 24, and Union Street 15.[903]

A description of one trainload of arrivals puts a much more human face on these bald statistics. A correspondent reported 'there were 320 of them, plus their teachers who came to the town about five o'clock. Each with a (gas) mask slung across their shoulder and bearing the burden of spare clothes and rations etc. in haversacks, bags or brown paper parcels, they looked around in wonderment at their strange surroundings but allowed themselves to be marshalled in perfect order'.[904]

Whole schools were evacuated. The new girl's school just completed and opened by Miss Thelma Gazalek MP was shared with Southwark Central School from southeast London.[905] This school was well known as the Highweek Secondary Modern School for girls but later became part of Coombeshead. The Grammar School for its part had 200 evacuees added to its numbers and needed to introduce a two-shift dinner system.[906] Later as German bombing intensified thousand more evacuees arrived.[907] There was one final late flow of evacuees into the area in July 1944 caused, by pilotless-planes better known as buzz bombs, doodlebugs or more simply V1s

In June 1945 most evacuees left. Some had come down from London as young children in September 1939 and had stayed with the same foster parents. There were some heart-rending farewells with tearful children clinging to their foster mothers and the foster mothers just as moved. Of the few that remained some simply had no home to go to and in a few cases contact with parents had been lost.[908]

151

Landgirls haymaking during the Second World War. There had been tractors in Newton for a decade but horses were still the main motive power on local farms.

Landgirls were billeted in Park House in Courtenay Park; this later became the headquarters of Watts, Blake and Bearne. The Workhouse was taken over in September 1939 by the Royal Navy as a hospital,[909] so that the sight of naval uniforms became commonplace in the town. It continued in this role until March 1946. After a while seven anti-aircraft guns were sighted around the town with a Royal Artillery command post in Wolborough Street.[910] There was an armoured train too, based in Newton which carried anti-aircraft guns. The idea was that it could patrol the line down as far as Brixham and take cover in a tunnel, if the opposition proved too great![911]

Several firms in Newton helped the war effort. Western Garage, from 1942, repaired parts of aircraft such as Spitfire wings. In all they handled over 5,000 parts. H. Beare & Sons Ltd also made aircraft parts. Another factory in Bradley Lane made the so-called self-sealing petrol tanks for fighter aircraft.[912] Devon Leathercrafts made parachute drogue targets. A canteen for service personnel opened, at the YMCA but soon moved to the Congregational Church. The canteen had been planned pre-war for the militia at Denbury but did not open until November 1939. It expanded into a night hostel did sterling work and the canteen closed about February 1946, although the administration organization was based on the Wolborough Parish Rooms until early 1949.

British Restaurants were established in both Kingsteignton and Newton Abbot. The government set them up, during rationing so all could buy a cheap meal away from home. Customers had first to buy plastic tokens; there were different coloured ones for each course. Food was then collected on a cafeteria basis. Kingsteignton was one of the first in the district and opened about August 1942 next to the Wesleyan Chapel in Gestridge Road. However, because of lack of support it closed early in the summer of 1943. The Newton's restaurant inception was a saga and it was surprising it was ever instituted in view of strenuous opposition from some Councillors. The idea had been floated as early as April 1942. By August it was thought the old soup kitchen in the Wolborough Parish Rooms might be suitable. The Ministry of Food turned this down, but thought the Market Square, which the official had seen on a quiet Tuesday

Blockhouses were built at strategic entrance points to the town for the Home Guard in World War II. A few survive, for instance there is this one on the Old Totnes Road and there is another in Rundle Road.

might be satisfactory. The Council opted for a hut on the Cricket Ground that, needless to say, the Cricket Club did not appreciate. By July 1943 it was said the committee was losing heart. In September it was decided by just two votes to proceed with a restaurant to seat 150 in what had been part of the car park for the Recreation Ground in Marsh Road. Though partly rebuilt it is now the Teignbridge 76 Social Club. Even then the battle was not over. By December construction was in progress and it was hoped would be completed by Christmas. The pro-faction sensibly sent a party to see how the successful British Restaurants were run at Brixham and Sidmouth. Those against accused them of wasting money and said they could have travelled less far to Kingsteignton to see how it should not be run! In February 1944 opening was delayed through a lack of equipment. March saw the formal opening. The first meal was leek soup, roast beef and Yorkshire pudding or boiled potatoes, jam tart or rice pudding or biscuits and cheese, cup of tea; the total cost was 1/6 (7.5p). On the first open day they served 195 meals, but time spent queuing was a problem. From June the enterprise ran profitably for some years. It later provided dinners for Bearne's schoolchildren and was sometimes used for other functions. It was latterly sometimes called the Civic Restaurant. Although it closed as a restaurant in April 1950 it continued as a canteen for Bearne's School.

The tank in Baker's park, a memento of the First World War was sold by the NAUDC for scrap metal.[913] To get the tank into the park in 1919, part of the wall was taken down. There were no such problems when it went, it was cut up on site. There were also two field guns, one of which had been captured by the Devonshire Regiment when they broke through the Hindenburg Line in 1918.[914] A party of 28 patients from the Newton Royal Naval Hospital were given a trip on Dartmoor courtesy of Devon General, with a tea at Manaton. Some were unable to walk having contracted frostbite in Norway. One hundred and fifty ARP members had an exercise to see if they would be able to cope with the crash of an enemy bomber on a road junction. The Home Guard, which was first known as the Local Defence Volunteers, and later affectionately as 'Dad's Army' was set up. Britain had been impressed by the effect of German parachute troops and hoped that a country-wide defence force might counter this in case of invasion. The Home Guard carried out regular drills and there are still concrete blockhouses, built for and used by them, in Rundle and Old Totnes Roads. After all fear of invasion had gone there was a standing down parade on the Newton Abbot Recreation Ground at the end of December 1944.[915]

In 1941 a letter came from Lord Beaverbrook congratulating Newton Urban and Rural Councils on collecting enough money to buy a Spitfire. It would be called Newtonia. The Council announced they would apply to allow cinemas to be opened on Sundays. There was opposition but they went ahead. Cinderella was performed at St Mary's Hall, with a cast of 50, a fancy coach and ponies. It was in aid of scouting and local charities. Newton Co-op advertised 'Fire fighting appliances and stirrup pumps' they also announced they still had footwear without Purchase Tax. Purchase Tax was a forerunner of Value added Tax. Devon General had vacancies for female omnibus conductors, who must be physically fit and good at figures. In one week there were two convictions for blackout offences in Newton prosecutions occurred frequently thereafter. The inaugural meeting of the Newton Air Training Corps was held, there were 51 applicants to join in the first batch. The 30 WVS working parties, in the district, which included some men and boys, had used 22 cwt. (1118 kg) of wool and 2,272 yards (2078 m) of material making woollies for servicemen and supplies for hospitals.

Iris Anderson, a four-year-old evacuee, fell into the Lemon near Union Bridge and was swept away underground. Her friends alerted her mother, who ran through the market towards where the Lemon reappears. She shouted for help to a passing soldier, Sergeant Stokes, who dived in and rescued Iris. Owing to a shortage of ingredients Newton Co-op announced 'No Hot Cross Buns will be made this year'. Newton Townswomen's Guild asked for a unit of women police to be formed to look after the moral conduct of young people. NAUDC decided park railings should be scrapped for war industries. A few months later all private railings were requisitioned. A local draper advertised that as clothing was rationed you should spend your coupons wisely with him. A Newton greengrocer was prosecuted for selling blackcurrants in excess of the controlled price. The local WVS received woollies from New Zealand and raspberry jam from Canada. Urban and Rural Councils had a joint Warship's Week to encourage saving. The target was £240,000 for the cost of a destroyer. A savings indicator was set up by the Tower. Over £257,000 was raised and *HMS Beagle,* currently working with North Atlantic convoys was allocated. A letter of thanks was received from the First Sea Lord Admiral Sir Dudley Pound.

In 1942 those without an outside Anderson air-raid shelter were invited to apply for an indoor steel table Morrison shelter. The Russian Ambassador and his wife wrote to thank the Newton WVS for their good work for the 'Knit for Russia's Army' appeal and Harry Pollitt the Communist Party leader, addressed a meeting at the Town Hall. There was a recruiting drive in town for the Navy Army and Air Force Institutes. Soap and washing powder were to be rationed and there was a 24-hour anti-invasion exercise. A Devon & Cornwall Clothing Depot opened in Baker's Park. The establishment of the Girls Training Corps proceeded in Newton.[916] J.F. Rockey's the department store, now *Richard Hopkins,* because of shortage of staff, restricted lunchtime hours. Dried eggs became available and were accompanied by explanatory literature. To the question 'How long do dried eggs keep?' the official answer was 'That is a difficult one . . .'!

A far cry indeed from modern practice of sell/use by dates. The WVS assisted in collecting rose hips. These were made into syrup to replace the vitamin C not available due to the shortage of oranges. The Duke of Kent, the King's brother, who had visited Newton as Prince George in 1932, was killed in an air accident. The first prosecution took place for misuse of petrol, the basic ration having been abolished.

In 1943 the first American contingents for the new large purpose built hospital at Stover arrived. The hospital employed over 600 staff and was designed to deal with the expected casualties from the forthcoming invasion of Europe. Many Newtonians were grateful for their presence because urgent civilian cases were sent there from the overloaded Newton hospital.[917] An American construction unit was stationed near the town and was short of practice. Someone in the town had the bright idea that they might be willing, for the sake of a training exercise, to level the site of what became the Brunel Road trading estate. There were big piles of ash from the power station there as well as other rubbish. The whole job was done swiftly and at no cost to the town. The Americans were given a written address to thank them, and the unconfirmed story is told that the commanding officer was also passed a bottle of whisky, it not being known that he was a teetotaller!

1943 was also busy, at the Newton Hospital Annual Meeting the possible impact of the Beveridge Scheme was discussed. A Denbury girl, Lettice Curtis, 23, was the first member of the Air Transport Auxiliary to fly a British 4-engine bomber. The ATA ferried planes from factory to aerodromes. Post-war as a test-pilot for the Ministry of Supply she was to break the women's speed record in a Spitfire at 313 mph.[918] Evacuees at the Wain Lane School had dwindled to 30 and those that remained had lost their distinctive accents. General Von Arnin, the German commander in North Africa, who had succeeded Rommel, surrendered to J.B. Glennie, a Newtonian, who was an officer in Royal Sussex Regiment. The Newton Abbot Hospitality Committee invited 200 American servicemen to refreshments and a dance at the *Globe Hotel*. A flag-day and collection was made to provide a 'Newton Abbot bed' at the new Stalingrad Hospital. Amongst many contributors were Devon General, Devon Leathercrafts, the *Railway Tavern* and the Tower Bun Shop. 'Holidays at Home' events were held over the August Bank Holiday, which was then at the beginning of the month. There was a fete at Sandford Orleigh to provide comforts for the Free French Forces.[919]

In 1944 there was a nation-wide two week 'Book Drive', in Newton, this produced no less than 43,000 books. The books were used by the forces, to replenish blitzed libraries and as salvage. That year there had been a threat from felling to the woods at Chercombe Bridge and Becky Falls. NARDC sought a preservation order on them and was successful. A 'Salute the Soldier Week' was held to encourage savings. A young Newtonian, James Mason 21, serving as a pilot with an aircraft carrier on Arctic convoy duty, attacked and probably sank a German submarine. For this he was later awarded the DSC. It would have been a day he would have long remembered because the very same evening he underwent an operation to remove his appendix! An American band provided entertainment for a mile of pennies event to raise funds for the hospital. It was said that the playing thrilled Newtonians. Badcock's advertised 'Utility furniture', Utility clothing and furniture were made to government specification, eschewing ornamentation, and were sold at controlled prices. A

This was a Victory in Europe (VE) celebration at the Penn Inn pub then named The Penguin. *Most of the parties were held in streets but some were different.*

Swimming Gala was held at Penn Inn Baths in aid of Red Cross POW fund. Returning prisoners of war later said how grateful they were for Red Cross Parcels. Fire Watching, which had been operational since January 1941 ceased. Possibly a little early, a Council committee was formed to plan peace celebrations. *HMS Beagle* gave up a week's sweet ration for Newton children in hospital, in gratitude for kindnesses they had received from in the town.

In 1945 there was a second burglary within a month on the joint offices of the Ministry of War Transport and Ministry of Food in Devon Square. Coupons for 26,000 gallons of petrol and 3,000 clothing coupons were stolen. A married woman, Mrs Gladys Hole, was charged with concealing an absentee US serviceman. A local man, Gunner Bowden, taken at the siege of Calais nearly five years before was released by advancing Russian forces. A report from Moscow said he would be brought back as soon as possible. A 'Milk Bottle Recovery Week' was held. In May Victory in Europe Day was celebrated. Thousands sang and danced in towns and villages until early morning. Netley Road had a particular mention for brilliant decorations. A Furry Dance was held at Sandygate and children's parties were plentiful. A 'Make Do and Mend Week' was held with sessions that included Home Dyeing and Slipper Making.

Peace now came back to Newton as it did for the whole country. Some things returned to normal quickly but there were years of rationing yet to come and hardships that were caused by shortages of fuel and housing. Election meetings were held for the forthcoming General Election and Sir Stafford Cripps, later Chancellor of the Exchequer, spoke in support of Labour in Newton.[920] Later Brigadier Ralph Rayner, the sitting Conservative, was re-elected with an increased majority, but nation-wide Labour won by a landslide. The Red Cross Penny-a-Week Fund that had raised £10,000 in the district was wound up. It was hoped in July that street lighting would be restored to its pre-war standard by the end of the month. Newton Abbot Athletic Ground Co. Ltd. offered the Recreation Ground to the Council. The Council accepted and discussions followed whether there should be dog-racing and what code of football should be played. Rugby won the first round but the second round went to soccer. Victory over Japan was celebrated in August and there were street parties, bonfires, fireworks, and a floral dance through the streets. Forde Park School held a torchlight procession through the town. Newton and district held 'Thanksgiving Week', the theme was 'save for peace as you did for war'. Air raid sirens were heard again, they had been adapted in use to summon firemen. The 'all-clear' was used, but even then some that had been bombed disliked the noise. There was a road fatality when a motorcyclist ran into the back of an ambulance on the Newton–Bovey road. A German POW gave evidence at the inquest. There was a proposal to close Bearne's School. The peacetime Christmas was said to be a relief, without blackout.

The Council's Thanksgiving Committee decided against gifts to returning servicemen, which was quite unusual in the area. It planned to have a Memorial Hall instead but later the idea was dropped. Later a meeting to start a new Welcome Home Fund was held in the Town Hall. In 1948 this fund presented National Savings tokens and a scroll to over 1,000 men who had served. The Second World War addition to the War Memorial was unveiled in 1949 by Earl Fortescute Lord Lieutenant of the county.

The impact of the Second World War on the town was much greater than the earlier war but other events did take place. The Council in 1943 considered whether valuable items given to the town, including Chelsea China, should be given to Torquay Museum.[921] The disused Stover Canal was discussed by Council, which stated it would like to retain the facility of the towpath. The town was relieved in 1944 to learn that Torquay had decided not to try and purchase Osborne Park which they had used as an overflow coal dump for the power station.[922]

In 1940 Newton College closed after 79 years existence. It reached its zenith in numbers in 1893 when it had 170 pupils. In 1924 it had 146 but by 1937 had sunk to 47. There was then a slight upturn with wartime evacuees but not enough to make it viable. The most famous pupil had perhaps been Sir Arthur Quiller-Couch. The school itself later became Forde Park, an approved School that closed in 1985. In 1986, Teignbridge purchased the playing fields and part of the college site was sold in 1987 for housing.[923]

In 1945 two nursery schools were proposed. Then in December at the *Commercial Hotel* was held the sale of the Churchill's Estate. The sale catalogue detailed; 'residence with garages, stabling, kennels, gardens and lawns', and rooms included: 'telephone room, billiard room, servants' hall, butler's pantry, and scullery, dairy (or larder), chambermaid's pantry.'[924] The house later became Knowles Hill School, the title no less with over 130 pupils, It was for both boys and girls with a nursery department; the headmistress was Miss Rainford. The area is now the Churchill's Estate.

The end of January 1945 saw the heaviest snowfall since 1940. The suggestion was made that the bus station should be moved near to the GWR railway station. Paulo's Circus came for one day; there were ponderous elephants, and daredevil riders. Anderton and Rowland's Fair came to the Rugby Field at Marsh Road. Marionette Follies 'Dolls that dance' was an attraction at St Mary's Hall.

In 1949 Balls' buses were permitted to increase fares for the first time in 23 years on their Newton – Shaldon – Maidencombe services. Apart from the large Devon General organization two other small bus operators were then in being. These were Gourd's of Bishopsteignton who worked from Newton via

Bishopsteignton to Teignmouth and Potters who went from Newton to Liverton, Haytor and Widecombe. The Tor Bus closed in 1963.

Rationing continued after the war and three Newton grocers in Fairfield Terrace, Buller Road and at Decoy were charged with an offence in relation to points rationing. For the general public points allocations were increased. Points were a system of rationing for a large number of goods in short supply that enabled purchasers some choice. More dried fruit was available but the fat ration was reduced. Newton Abbot Dairies was fined for distributing too much milk, they said it was the fault of kind-hearted roundsmen. In 1948 Bovey Tracey Co-op amalgamated with Newton Abbot.[925] Older Newtonians may remember Mark's pitch outside the market after the Second World War. He was one of those superb brand of salesmen who could collect a crowd just for the sheer entertainment value of his cheerful patter. He usually wore a crownless straw hat and no doubt did a lot of business. Sadly he was later mugged and retired.[926]

Post-war industry

There were fears in 1947 of a labour shortage when German POW's returned; most would be gone by Christmas. There was a petition against Osborne Park being a coal dump as it created coal dust that got into people's houses and children had no open space to play. Later a party was held to celebrate the Park being freed from its coal. Cull's, the timber merchants, established in 1800, was taken over by Reeves and Fox Elliot of Plymouth. At one time Cull's imported timber by ship to Teignmouth and floated it up the Teign in rafts landing it on a slipway near the junction of Marsh and Lemon Roads. They then employed 15 to 20 horses to haul it to their sawpits. J.H. Pollard's Ltd., the electrical suppliers, were advertising as 'New Lines' 2ft and 3ft fluorescent light fittings. A sign of changing technology was the sale of the prize-winning stud of pedigree shire horses from Teignharvey Farm who were 'giving up horsekeeping'.

The Bovey Basin is probably the largest source of brown soft coal, lignite, in Britain. It has never been popular as a fuel because of low calorific value and burning with a most unpleasant odour. Originally poor cottagers used it; this ceased with the arrival of the railway in 1866. There were later attempts to fire pottery kilns and to make gas from it. In 1913 a German company established exploratory workings, some dozen Germans were employed, but these ended at the outbreak of the First World War.[927] In the early 1920s another attempt at exploitation was made with the idea of extracting montan wax used in polishes, carbon paper, lubricants, and fruit coating.[928] At the end of the Second World War there was a great fuel shortage so a serious attempt was made to use it. Open cast working for lignite was carried on day and night. In 1948 permission was given to build a briquette making plant. However, as coal became more readily available the attempted exploitation ceased.[929] The last commercial venture was to sell it, under the trade name Acta Bacta, as a long acting fertilizer for gardens.

Post-war administration

In January 1947 the first post-war houses opened on the Buckland Housing Estate. The total cost of each house, was £1,400 which some thought expensive. The first prefabricated houses were erected in Manor Road; four went up in nine days. Three railway carriages were brought to Forde Road and converted into comfortable homes, the external GWR decorations were retained.

In 1948 Newton had a quieter start to the year than usual because the bells of St Leonard's Tower were out of order. NAUDC was against letting the County take over the Library because it felt it had been given to Newton. In 1949 gas companies were nationalized. In 1954 production ceased at Newton and supplies were brought from Torquay. Later as natural gas became available countrywide Torquay too ceased production. To-day much of the old gas works site is the smart D'arcy Court residential development. Few would care to remember the site's many rats who feasted at the nearby slaughter house but lived in the warmth of the gas works! It seems a world away rather than just 50 years since local women would arrive with their battered old prams to collect half a hundredweight of coke for household heating and cooking.[930]

By February 1949 all electric street lamps were fitted with time switches. The lamplighters, usually with a cycle and always with a long pole, no longer had to go laboriously, morning and evening to each lamp, switching them individually off or on.[931] How many today would know the old time expression 'to go like a lamplighter'? as a metaphor for speed? How inappropriate it would now seem!

There had been a long-felt need for a maternity home in the area and it was decided that part of the Institution (formerly the Workhouse), would be used, this opened in April 1948. It was said this would be temporary but like so many other measures, it continued a very long time. There was also a proposal that the Isolation Hospital should be closed. The Government's plans to take over voluntary hospitals were criticized locally. A party of 15 Dutch children came to Newton, for respite and when they left in June they were given a farewell party in the British Restaurant. Newton was given 1,000 bulbs for its public parks. The Newton Institution reopened as a hospital in 1947 and local patients were the first to return. The hospital fete was washed out by weather, a rare occurrence despite English summer weather. There were fears that this fete, one of the great social events of the Newton calendar would no longer be held because the Government was setting up the NHS. Should the fete continue to provide a welfare fund to provide extra comforts? The new nurse's home, The Laurels in Powderham Road was opened. In 1948 the Naval Hospital Comforts Fund was wound up and the balance went to the benevolent fund of the British Legion. Court Grange at Abbotskerswell reopened as the Sunshine Home for the Blind in 1949. A new Home Helps scheme was launched in the town.

The Polish Camp

The Council were informed that the former hospital at Stover was surplus to requirements and the first idea was to turn it into 120 flats. Instead it became a home for Polish people displaced by war. Because of boundary changes in

Eastern Europe many could not return unless they became Soviet citizens. Some of those who could return and still be Polish preferred not to do so because of the communist regime in Poland. Originally there were no less than 46 'camps' across the country. The Stover camp officially opened in the summer of 1948 but some Poles almost certainly were there before. Originally there were probably 800 residents many with families. However, as some returned home, emigrated to America or became absorbed into the English community numbers shrank and 'camps' were progressively closed. The one at Newton Abbot, sometimes referred to as 'Little Poland', is the only one left. In 1948 there was an exhibition of handicrafts by Polish women at Stover. Some women had travelled via India, Australia, New Zealand, and East Africa before coming to England and there was evidence of designs from all those places on view. In 1964 Stover was renamed Ilford Park, and it was rebuilt 1990/2. By the end of the century numbers had stabilized to about 100. In the post war years it was customary in the Newton area to find young Poles at school and older ones working in all sorts of local jobs, as builders, in factories and in market gardens. The Polish ladies were also well known as prominent purchasers at any local jumble sale. Perhaps the saddest aspect of this influx is the Polish sector of the Wolborough Cemetery, where so many came to rest, so far from their original homes.

Post-war leisure

A golf course at Milber was mooted but nothing came of it. Point-to-point races were held at Forches Cross. There was a Hawaiian Ball at the *Globe* with Lelanie, the sensational hula-hula dancer, tickets were 6s. but other ranks in uniform were half price. The Devonshire Association came to Newton after a fifty year gap. The blind children at Court Grange Abbotskerswell gave a concert. There was a selection for Miss Newton in conjunction with a swimming gala. Mr F.W. Baker of Watcombe Film Studios, Torquay, was the judge. There was controversy over letting the Market Hall in the evenings for badminton, was this wasting light? In 1947 a service was broadcast from Newton Congregational Church; there was clear reception as far away as Yorkshire. The town had been mentioned in an Itma programme. ('Its that man again') featuring the comedian Tommy Handley. A Youth Week was held with several events including tableaux on lorries and six-a-side football.

A 'Carroll Lewis, Search for Stars' talent contest for radio, screen and stage and a Silver Lining Savings Week were held. The Newton rugby team, the All Whites, secured a long lease of Rackerhayes and needed practical help from volunteers to get the ground fit for use. Forde Park School held their annual sports and a silver collection was held for the Waifs and Strays Society. More importantly the Olympiad torch passed through Newton in 1948 en route to Torre Abbey for the Olympic yachting regatta in Torbay. Large crowds waited to see the local Newton runner come along the Kingsteignton Road to turn into Queen Street to pass on the torch at the War Memorial. Unfortunately the leading motor cycle marshal turned down the Avenue, the runner following. The crowds in Queen Street, learning they were going to be by-passed, surged towards the Memorial blocking the road. It took some time for the runner to get through and eventually find the next torchbearer! Even then that was not the end of the chaos as the next runner started, the lead motorcycle braked hard to avoid a pedestrian. The runner ran into the motorcycle, injuring his leg so that he had to retire and a substitute had to be found to continue the journey![932]

The footpath to Flow Point from the Newton to Teignmouth road was obstructed with a locked gate and High Court action was taken to reopen it. The judgement mentioned it was the landing place for the village before the railway. On the 1st of January 1948 the railways were nationalized and the GWR became part of British Rail.

Miscellaneous

Sometimes the small headlines provide interesting evidence of the way we used to live. Bananas arrived for the first time for five years in 1946; they were ripened in a specially heated store at Gibbon's, the grocers, in Market Street. They were sold only to those under 18 and some smaller children had never seen them. An advertisement announced that post war radios were in stock. Bread rationing was introduced. Badcock's advertised 'The curtain problem solved by plastic, coupon free; it can be made into raincoats, handbags, swimsuits, and tablecloths'. Newton Food Committee licensed two 7-day cafes in Newton; it was felt they would meet a public need. The Townswomen's Guild had a casket presented from Gisborne NZ and cakes from Queensland Australia. There were complaints of low gas pressures particularly on Sundays when many people could not cook their dinners. New gas mains were to be installed to rectify the problem. The WI started a stall in Newton Market to sell flowers, vegetables and cakes. A market trader was fined for selling nylon stockings without coupons. He said he bought them for his aunts in Petticoat Lane but they did not want them because they were not fully-fashioned! The Meals on Wheels scheme was adopted for two days a week for OAP, blind and infirm not able to get to the Civic (British) Restaurant.

In early 1947 a very heavy snowfall ushered in a particularly hard spell of weather. All buses were discontinued for a day and some routes, such as to Totnes and Ashburton, took several days to restart. Later freak conditions produced a heavy rainfall that froze on landing. This produced a scenic effect on trees and bushes but devastation to telegraph wires and poles which were then all above ground.

The Round House at Haccombe was totally destroyed by fire. The surprising thing, considering the location today, is that it took someone half an hour to reach a telephone, to summon the fire brigade.

CHAPTER 10

THE LATER TWENTIETH CENTURY
1950–1999

'Plymouth and Exeter rarely come into contact, . . . their shopping and entertainment hinterlands are separated by the 'buffer-town' of Newton Abbot'.[934] 'Newton Abbot is a town with a great historic past . . . always a bustling market town'.[935]

This half-century has seen more change than any other in both Newton and elsewhere. Television has become dominant and cinemas declined. Pounds, shillings and pence have been replaced with decimalized currency. There has been enormous alteration in shopping habits from grocers to supermarkets. Standards of living have vastly improved but brought standardization in dress and other things. In Devon agriculture has further declined; tourism has changed but is still a very important prop of the local economy. The rural exodus has at last been halted as the county has become an attractive area for retirement dwellings, and commuting by car has increased. The proportion of those living in Devon who were actually born in the county has shrunk

During this period the town expanded over nearby fields in nearly all directions. Prosperity was maintained by opening numerous trading estates for manufacturers and later, wholesalers and large retailers. The rail peak came and went; followed by a period of great decline, steam departed and inter-city arrived. Newton never solved its increasing traffic problems and ruined much of the town in the process. Pevsner called it 'one of the worst examples in the county of callous road engineering'.[933]

Following the Town and Country Planning Act of 1947, a survey was made of Newton in 1950 and a Development Plan issued in 1952, which included Kingskerswell and Kingsteignton. The plan highlighted the fact that the Newton area produced in greater or lesser degrees almost all the planning problems likely to be found in the urban areas of the county. To its traditional function

162

Shapley Court in 1962, a typical court. The courts came into being as infilling when the town's population increased. Over time they became notorious for squalor.

as a market centre of a large agricultural area, it added a small centre of manufacturing industry, based on ball clay and the servicing of road and rail traffic. The centre of the town was old and–under the circumstances of the trade and traffic of the mid-twentieth century–congested.

The Development Plan stated the Torquay to Newton Abbot was the most densely trafficked road in South Devon. It made several proposals; dual carriageways from Drum Bridges to Whitehill and Jetty Marsh by-pass road, from there, again dual, continuing along the first part of the Avenue and taking off at the corner to come out by the railway station. It also recommended realignment of the Newton–Torquay road with a Kingskerswell by-pass! It was suggested this might take some while but land should be earmarked and kept for the route, which ran roughly parallel and on the north east side of the railway. The report also advocated, as a matter of urgency clearance of cottage properties grouped in courts and alleyways and the need for a new police station, civic building with courts, post office and telephone exchange. It discussed the pros and cons of a market on a new site but did not advocate it, owing to the complexity of the problem and the diversity of public opinion. It suggested providing industrial estates for existing businesses and to attract new ones, to make the town the 'industrial centre for Torbay'.

Holiday traffic, passing through Newton in August 1954 caused such intense jams that the traffic lights had to be turned off, and resort made to manual

Traffic in the Avenue mid-1950s, before the Kingsteignton – Newton by-pass was built, all the main road traffic from Exeter to Torquay went through the town.

An accident at Aller in the 1950s. Notice the main road telegraph poles and wires, then commonplace.

control. A scooter travelling at 45 mph on the Newton–Torquay road, in 1961 was the first speeding offence to be captured by radar. Kingsteignton celebrated 1250 years. There was a half-hour delay to the start of a parade caused by Newton race traffic. Maybe considering the time span celebrated, that was not important! Traders in Queen Street were against the trial one-way system in 1962 because it was eastbound. They were presumably right because it was later altered to westbound and has stayed that way. In 1963 plans were announced to by-pass Ideford Arch, then part of the A380. It was decided to charge for the Newfoundland Way car park. The first set of pedestrian-controlled traffic lights was installed in Courtenay Street in 1967. In 1972 Newton's traffic situation was described as dangerous, ludicrous and chaotic by the town's chamber of trade.

There was a snowy start to the year in 1963. The very cold spell delayed the widening of the Station Bridge to a dual carriageway and several other measures were taken to try to solve Newton's traffic problems. Still at this time the main flow of traffic for Torquay passed through both Kingsteignton and Newton Abbot. It was hoped an extensive one-way system and extending car parks would alleviate the problem. However, as the *Western Morning News* so rightly foresaw,

St Leonard's Tower, c. 1962; traffic can still pass either side of the Tower. Note Martins Bank back right and the sign for the Odeon cinema on the left of picture.

Station Bridge, a single car-riageway in less busy days before the Second World War, Mellor's Garage later Acton Tool, precision engineers, is on the right.

further improvement would be essential.[936] In 1964 a ball and chain demolished the old arch at Kingskerswell that was thought to be 150–200 years old. It had been due to be demolished before the war, some material even being on site but the work was aborted because of the outbreak of war so it was only delayed for a quarter of a century! In 1966 the Board of Trade civil aviation department suggested closing Exeter Airport and building a new one between Exeter and Plymouth. Heathfield was suggested as a possible site but later was said to be unsuitable so Exeter kept its airfield.

The new fire and ambulance station opened at Balls' Corner, on what was once partly the site of Matthew's the blacksmith. It was the first place in the country to be able to control the traffic lights, from inside, when a fire-engine or ambulance wished to leave the station.[937] Later a large roundabout succeeded the traffic lights. The ambulance staff had grown from 8 to 20 by 1991, so the station needed a revamp and a second storey was added.[938]

The *Western Morning News* wrote in 1977 'after surviving many road improvement schemes on the approach road to Newton Abbot from Torquay the old toll house at Penn Inn is being demolished'.[939] This was to make way for the Kingsteignton and Newton Abbot By Pass for Exeter to Torquay traffic. The by-pass was desperately needed although it did nothing to solve the problems of Dartmoor to Torquay traffic. It seems a pity that such an attractive old building was not saved. The contractors who did most of the work on the by-pass, Peter Lind, over-reached themselves and went into liquidation.[940] Many remember their hutted working 'village' alongside the by-pass next to the Teignmouth road roundabout. The new Penn Inn roundabout opened in 1975, although the pedestrian under pass was completed later.[941] The new by-pass itself, well behind time and way over budget, principally because of problems with the foundations of the viaduct section, opened in May 1976.[942] Interestingly it was claimed the idea for it had first been aired as early as 1919.

In the spring of 1988 it was announced that Halcyon Road would be widened to take two way traffic so traffic should cease going through the centre of the town.[943] Others thought a loop road at Jetty Marsh would be better. By January

1993, the *Dawlish Post* was reporting problems with traffic tailbacks caused by the widened Halcyon Road and in late summer 1995, the go ahead for Jetty Marsh was reported, it opened in 1998,[944] some 68 years after it had first been mooted![945] Even though the distances on the memorial milestone were put the wrong way round, the new road at Jetty Marsh rapidly proved the better option. By the time it was built the original continuation scheme to take traffic on towards Penn Inn was blocked by new housing. There had also been a scheme to improve Coach Road but later traffic calming humps were installed instead.

In December 1995 the footbridge over the A380 dual carriageway was built. There had been three fatal road accidents with people taking short cuts across the dual carriageway road,[946] a fence had been erected to prevent these accidents but it had been vandalized. It was discussed whether the bridge should be so built to prevent objects being dropped on traffic below but this was not done and incidents have since occurred.

In 1950 a scheme to turn all the main thoroughfares in town into one-way streets was announced. A scheme for moving the fountain from the middle of the road in Kingsteignton was approved at a parish meeting in 1951. In 1952 Queensway Buckland, was named in honour of forthcoming visit of the Queen. In 1954 Marlborough House was demolished for the new bus station on the Kingsteignton Road. There was belated but considerable opposition wanting it moved back to the Market Square. Later the site was expanded and covered facilities provided with the demolition of Frank Halse's warehouse and old blacksmith's premises.

Incredible as it may seem now, there was a proposal to put a petrol filling station in front of Forde House near Penn Inn. Mr Shobbrook, a great champion of Newton, opposed the idea saying it would be a tragedy if Forde House became completely cased in by modern development. The new Teignbridge offices behind the house were started in 1984 and finished in 1987.[947]

In 1960 a poll in Abbotskerswell and Kingskerswell rejected joining Torquay County Borough. The licence of the *Newfoundland Inn* was transferred to the new *Drive Inn* (now *The Plough*) at Buckland. Later in the year the *Newfoundland,*

The Fair used to be held in the Market Square; the old bus station was there too. Market Street was closed for many years every Good Friday to maintain its status as a private road.

This was the first bus station on the Kingsteignton Road begun in 1954. It moved here from the Market Square.

one of Newton's oldest inns, which had been on the site for some 300 years and was one of the focal points of the town's longstanding involvement in the Newfoundland trade, was demolished. So much history wiped out for the extension of a modern store premises.[948] For road improvement it was reported early in 1961 that a Georgian house in Wolborough Street was being demolished. The first documentary evidence of it went back to a Richard Ford, a lawyer, who practiced there in 1748. It had Adam style fireplaces and fine ceilings. The Ministry of Works scheduled it as a building of importance and special permission had to be obtained to demolish it. A council official was non-committal when asked about the fittings![949] The final drink was drawn at the *Commercial Hotel* in 1960 and it was demolished three years later. Work started to make the Station Bridge a dual carriageway in 1962. Part of Courtlands Garden was cut back and traffic lights were installed at Penn Inn. One night in May of 1969 the *Queen's Hotel* caught fire. Fortunately a rail inspector saw smoke pouring from the building at 3.25 a.m. and raised the alarm. The 50 guests escaped unharmed and were accommodated for the night at the *Globe Hotel*.[950]

The Tax office moved in 1964 from the *Queen's Hotel* to Pearl Assurance House. The *Week House Inn* opened at Highweek in 1966 despite fears it would spoil the amenities of the village. In the same year the *Globe Hotel* opened a new restaurant called the Dickens Room. In 1966 the council decided to turn the Recreation Ground into a car park. Interestingly in the following election all those who had voted for the car park lost. In 1967 demolition work started in Victoria Place and Albany Street for a car park. The Esso Service station opened in East Street, one of the most modern in the West Country. Work started on the Community Centre, now Courtenay Centre, on the Kingsteignton Road that was to become a dual carriageway![951] The RDC and UDC once again discussed merging. An exhibition of three different ways to develop Newton was shown at the Methodist Church Hall. A final graduation parade of Junior Leaders was held at Denbury1967, they had been there since 1955. It was announced that the army would arrange the building of 130 houses in the

Newtake area for families of servicemen but later this number was reduced.

In 1967 the local council were asked to repair the steep footpath, once known as the Donkey Steps, that led up from King's Mews to the end of Rundle Road but they decided instead to close them. The residents of the Knowles Hill area forced a public enquiry and won the day. The inspector considered the path was useful and gave access to vantage points where countryside views might be enjoyed'.[952] The council then, instead of making minor repairs, that had been asked for, was forced into making an expensive refurbishment. The Donkey Steps were so called because, early in the century, a Mr O'Shaughnessy used to graze a donkey in the field at the top. This hill used to be known as Break Neck and was popular on race days as an unofficial grandstand.[953]

In 1970 a major colony of 500 rats was discovered in a storm water culvert near the centre of the town. Work started on a new sorting office in Highweek Street to replace those in Bradley Lane. The new office was strangely built askew as could be seen for many years. In the same year plans to remodel the town centre were announced including a new home for the General Post Office. This had moved precipitously out of its old building, now the Mitre Bookshop, and had for years been in unsatisfactory temporary accommodation in Bearne's Lane. There was to be a new market hall, a landscaped open market complex, Market Walk, and a multi-store car park with an improved sheep market beneath.[954] The multi-store car park started operating in December 1971 and formally opened the following February. The pedestrian bridge was added in October 1978.[955] Amongst other places demolished were the old town centre fire station and public baths.[956] These baths were a public amenity when few homes would have baths, or showers. The fee at one time was six old pence, 2.5 p, for which you were issued with a towel and a piece of soap. An attendant ran the water with a special key and there was no way of adjusting temperature or adding more water.[957] The shopping project began by 1977 and was operational in 1979.[958] There were critics of the proposals, one said they would 'destroy the identity of the town'. There were further protests at the opening and there were complaints about who had, and who had not, been asked to the opening. The name Market Walk was derived from a newspaper competition. By 1999 there was talk of the development needing a face-lift.[959]

St Leonard's Tower was legally conveyed from Wolborough Parochial Church Council to the Urban District Council in December 1971. There had been two schools of thought; Councillor Prouse had suggested selling the Tower to America! Councillor Shobbrook had been for retention and refurbishment and luckily, he won the argument. There was a protest march in 1972 against the suggestion of moving the supplementary benefits office to Torquay. In 1973, the Tower bells were returned after renovation and re-tuning. The celebration included a procession and mummers, dancers, acrobats, a ram roast, ducking-stool, puppet show, maypole dancing, handbell ringing, medieval jousting and country sports.[960]

NAUDC that had started in 1901 ended in 1974 with the Local Government Act. Although the position of mayor was retained, the Newton council became in effect just a parish council. For a while there were doubts if this status would be allowed to Newton although Ashburton, Buckfastleigh, Dawlish and Teignmouth had all obtained it. However, some intense lobbying over most of 1973 secured that status. Newton was now part of the much larger Teignbridge authority. Newton Abbot, that one can roughly say had taken 700 years to form had lasted only just over 70! The new authority began in April 1974 at what had been the old RDC Offices on Kingsteignton road.

In 1975 the Council sought to demolish the fourteenth century Priest's House in Highweek Street because it was becoming unsafe. It was Newton Abbot's oldest extant building and Mrs Lamb, a local stalwart fought hard to retain it.[961] However, the council did agree to take down, store and re-erect the facade. Nine years later they were reminded of this, but claimed there was a lack of money.[962] They were later used for another purpose and thus urban Newton's oldest building was lost forever. Archaeological work was not able to prove that the building had once had a religious connection but it had certainly belonged to someone with means.[963]

In 1965 the Devon & Courtenay Clay company closed its pits at Decoy.[964] The area was later bought by the Council and turned into a Countryside Park with a boating lake, paddling pool, and children's swings, very different from its working life. There was considerable opposition, at first, to the idea of a lake, because local house owners were worried about possible subsidence. The decorative gates at Decoy are from the old Penn Inn Park.[965] Close by, the council set up a nursery for plants in Coach Road.

The idea of a museum in the library was rejected in 1962 because of lack of space, the Head Librarian said 'I think the word 'museum' tends to frighten people away'. However, the library did hope to devote space to local history. Finally in July 1978 Newton opened a museum in the Town Council Offices. Newton, despite its long and varied history had never had a museum, although a number of potential exhibits had been housed in the library[966] and in 1991, it was announced it was combining with a Railway Museum. In 1998, the Museum was stated to be off centre and a difficult place for visitors to find. There were continued ructions over whether the County Council of local council should own the Library. The County Council had taken over the building in 1974. Newton Town council had threatened to sue the County Council, to regain ownership, but it could have cost the ratepayers £10,000 and they might have lost. Many did not care who owned it as long as it continued as a library[967] In November 1993 the Railway Studies section at the library was opened.[968]

In 1975 the Council again considered roofing Penn Inn outdoor swimming pool but costs had increased. Forde House passed through various hands; at one time being involved in the antique business and was offered to the National Trust. Teignbridge District Council which had previously decided not to buy it finally bought it in 1978.[969] Thus Newtonians could be glad at its preservation but disappointed at their paucity of access. In 1980, after its refurbishment Queen Elizabeth II visited Forde House.[970]

Local authorities continued what was thought of as their vandalizing approach to Newton's past by demolishing 13–29 Highweek Street, five of the properties were listed as buildings of historic and architectural interest. Application was made to the Secretary of State to secure permission and objections by the Ancient Monument Society were ignored. This was the demise of Newton Bushel's best know hostelry the old *Seven Stars Inn*, nearly opposite St Mary's Chapel.[971] Early in 1988 it was announced that the *Globe Hotel* one of Newton's two major hotels, and one-time coaching inn, was to close with the loss of 30 jobs. As a listed building, it was hoped that some forms of development would be prohibited.[972] It is now part of Austins department store.

Ever since the chanelling of the River Lemon, Newton had been subject to floods. The principal ones had been in 1851, 1894, 1929, 1938, and 1974. At the end of 1979 came another, a five-foot wave swept through the town. Bank, Courtenay, Queen and Wolborough streets were flooded as well as the new Market Walk shopping precinct and some premises had two to three feet of water in them. Much damage was caused to stock because the flood came on Boxing Day when so many shops were shut.[973] Coastguards and Royal Marines came with boats to rescue people. An emergency centre was set up at Coombeshead School and gave shelter to over 100 people. A massive clean up, hindered by lack of electricity, ensued. There are descriptions of bedraggled Christmas trees, broken toys, soaked upholstery and carpets, heaps of assorted merchandise piled up along the streets.[974] A team of Royal Marine divers was used to carry out an underground survey along the 400 yards of the River Lemon tunnel after the flood.[975] Floods finally ended with the building of the Holbeam Dam across the Lemon above Bradley Woods in 1982.[976] South West Water spent some £500,000 to provide a dam and radial gate, so floodwater could be stored and released gradually. There had been discussions for fifty years but the River Lemon was finally tamed.[977]

The destruction of Newton's past continued in 1981 with an application to demolish three more ancient buildings in Wolborough Street. The Ancient Monument Society said that the limited relief provided for town centre traffic did not justify the loss of these buildings but this did not save them.[978]

In May plans were announced to turn the defunct British Rail Parcels Sorting Office, later National Carriers Depot, into a youth leisure centre to house a commando assault course, roller skating and a five aside football area. Mr Gorman the scrap-metal merchant was the promoter.[979] It opened as Olympus in December 1981. Closure was announced in the spring of 1983, although it drew 2,000 youngsters a week it was not paying. It was robbed at least a couple of times but the police were pleased with the venture because there was less vandalization when it was open. The one place that was sure to have welcomed the closure was the local fracture clinic. The indoor roller skating rink had kept them busy! In August the first betting shop opened in a main street in Newton when William Hill moved from Albany Street to 23 Queen Street. Betting shops then were a new departure; they had come about thanks to new legislation.

In 1984 the Town Council bought the old YMCA building for use as a town hall. It opened the following year as Great Western House.[980] Some older men will remember long hours spent there. Happy ones when playing snooker and not so happy ones when it was a dance and the girls had mostly departed to Denbury Camp lured by army lads in uniform! Later part of the building was used for the Town Museum and its Railway Room.

In 1985 and despite opposition, Penn Inn Park was sold; so depriving the town of one of its open spaces. As the press put it, 'a piece of land which rightfully belonged to children was shamefully sold off for a superstore which few wanted and nobody needed'.[981] A plaque has been erected in Keyberry Road in memory of what was lost.

Opposite this spot was
Penn Inn Park
1935–1985
Created by public generosity
Destroyed by corporate intrigue

170

An unusual 1990s aerial view of the town. Wolborough Street car park is present, but so is the now vanished bus station.

It was altogether contentious. The council claimed the purchase money would assist the building of an indoor pool but apparently they accepted a low price for the land. Trago Mills offered twice the price obtained.[982] Some suggested that as the sale was for a Co-op store, it was not the same as selling to an ordinary commercial concern. At the time, and later, it was stated that the main Co-op store in Newton would not close, but it did.[983] Furthermore the Co-op sold the Penn Inn site to Sainsbury's only a few years later in 1996, when Sainsbury's also bought their Paignton store. The Newton store shut in October and re-opened two weeks later as Sainsbury's.[984] The one-time park was turned further from its original state in 1997 with the arrival of Macdonald's. Again there was opposition, with an overwhelming majority of local inhabitants being against it.[985]

The old Town Quay, on the Teign just after its juncture with the Lemon, was re-opened in 1988 as an amenity.[986] The circular base of the former crane remains as evidence of what a work-a-day place it was less than half a century before. Plans were announced in 1990 for the development of the Wolborough Street area. In 1992, it was said that the scheme faced delay [987] and this hiatus continued for a number of years. An archaeological dig was carried out on part of the site but little of interest was found.

Crown Buildings, on the site of the former bus station were completed in 1992. They were to house the Inland Revenue, employment services, and DSS.[988] They officially opened the following March. The building was to incorporate one of the new 'one-stop job shops' enabling people not only to look for jobs, but to seek career advice and 'sign on' all in the same place.[989] The old market gates were erected at the ends of pedestrianized Courtenay Street.

Sandford Orleigh was put up for sale in 1992; it dated from 1830 and had belonged to both George Templer and Sir Samuel Baker. After the Second World War, the house had been an hotel and the old kitchen gardens were a market garden. Run by a former prisoner of war of the Japanese. He gained some advantage from the original garden stock, being able, for instance, to sell mulberries to the *Imperial Hotel* at Torquay. Latterly the house had been Lupton House School, a specialist establishment for boys with behavioural problems and learning difficulties. Later still part became a commercial gym and finally it has been developed for housing.

In March 1994 the heads of cattle and sheep, surrounded by a farm waggon wheel, appeared on the northern wall of the *Swan Inn*. They were made of steel and were the result of a joint effort by Teignbridge and Newton councils to 'highlight the community's character'.[990] In July 1995 a ceramic tile mural of cows and sheep was unveiled on the wall of the multi-store car park. The Japanese born artist arrived at the wrong time for the opening and went away before the official party arrived.[991]

Finally in 1998 Radio 4 on its 'You and Yours' programme invited nominations for the ugliest town in Britain. Newton was among those put forward. In support, it was stated that the multi-storey car park was a monstrosity and that the idea of turning a public park like Penn Inn into a supermarket, and not a prepossessing store at that, underlined the point. The Mayor came to the town's defence saying it was an 'unfair blow'.[992] Plans to turn part of Jetty Marsh, a habitat of kingfishers, into a nature reserve were announced and later implemented.[993]

Housing

There had been a desperate shortage of housing post-war. Much property was destroyed in air raids and others through lack of repair had grown practically uninhabitable. Two examples may set the scene. In Kingsteignton the conversion of a 25-year old wooden hut into two cottages was quoted as a satisfactory example of what could be done. Secondly, an ex-soldier and two children, 9 and 8, took to living in a one-time Home Guard blockhouse. It was just 8 feet by 10 feet, near Forde House the family collected water from Penn Inn Park. Two solutions to try and solve the serious housing problem are set out below.

When pre-fabricated houses were first discussed in the town, in the autumn of 1944, it was stated they were undesirable and unnecessary! The Council however, later applied for 100 and was allocated 40. These were built in a one-time aircraft factory at Weston-Super-Mare, were delivered on lorries in sections and then put together on a prepared site. The first were erected in Manor Road in April 1947 and nine were completed in just four days. Little furniture was needed because they had built in cupboards, wardrobes and drawers, a rarity in those days. They were supposed to have a life of 5/10 years but many lived happily in them for much longer. In fact, in 1970, the Council was anxious to evict the last pre-fabricated house dwellers in Manor Road.

A second means of overcoming the shortage were housing associations to enable people of various skills to build their own houses. The Newton Pioneer Housing Association set up in 1950 had, engine drivers and postmen among their members. They laboured in evenings and at weekends and largely did all the construction themselves, and it was cheaper than having to buy a house. The houses were of what was then a revolutionary modern but simple style. The designer afterwards emigrated to Canada. The houses were built in the Laurie Avenue area and can still be seen there. When the first two houses were finished in 1953 they were open for public inspection and the occupants were decided by ballot.[994] The snag with the scheme was, that though at the start there was every incentive to work, as time progressed more members obtained their houses and progress on the remainder became much slower. It was a mild January in Newton in 1956, but then February came in with 18 degrees of frost. No less than 125 council houses had their water systems frozen. In 1962 the Beverley Sisters, so-called 'blonde bombshells of song', opened a Gas Board show house. New 3-bedroomed houses at Highweek, with garages and central heating were on sale at just under £4,000. In 1966 Newton considered inviting an overspill from a heavily populated area; this would have meant an influx of 10,000 to add to the existing 18,000 population. A council sub-committee was appointed to examine the idea.[995] Plans were announced in 1966 for a development of 300 houses at Bradley Barton, eventually there was to be a church and a public house! Shock was reported, in 1969, when it became public knowledge that NARDC still owned several houses with only outside lavatories. In August 1982, the go ahead was given for a housing estate at Heath Park, Newtake.[996] The prestigious sheltered housing Bradley Court opened in 1990. It was hoped the new Chapel Hill/St Mary's complex would be finished by August of 1991.[997] Plans were published in 1999 for large new housing developments, perhaps as many as 400 houses for Newton Abbot. The biggest block would be beyond Mile End Road alongside the Ashburton Road. House building started alongside the Jetty Marsh by-pass.

Retailing

The joint Food Control Committee of the NAUDC and NARDC were only wound up in 1950. For Newton's 1952 Shopping Week a special contest that caused much interest was 'The Nigger in the Woodpile'.[999] This would not be politically correct today, another significant change in half a century. Co-op shareholders were against amalgamation with Buckfastleigh, Paignton and Torquay in 1960 but in 1969 agreed to merge with the Plymouth and South Devon Co-op. In 1966 the Fashion floor, of Newton Co-op placed an

Shopping

We know markets in Newton go back many centuries, but not how long there have been shops in the town. Newton's level site has helped its retailers. In the days when many folk came by train Newton, which had its station on the level, would have the advantage of places such as Ilfracombe or Okehampton where any laden shopper would have a massive climb back to regain the station. As Hoskins shrewdly remarked; level streets were an 'important consideration for Devon country people who climb enough hills at home and like to give their legs a rest on the day off in town'.

At first all shopkeepers would have been independent. The first multiple retailer to arrive was the Star Tea Company in 1853. It was an isolated event because it was about another half century before others arrived. Star Stores were still in Newton until at least the 1920s. By 1902 Singers, the sewing machine firm, had a presence in the town. W.H. Smith's arrived in 1905 in Queen Street and later moved to other sites.

Marks and Spencer's came to Devon in 1912 and opened at Exeter, Plymouth, Torquay and Newton. At this stage, they were still only a penny bazaar, a far cry from their present status. Cecil Putt, a later manager at Newton, established something of a record for the numbers of branches at which he had worked. He started at Manchester then moved in turn to Shrewsbury, York, Leeds, Bristol, Hereford, Wolverhampton, Bradford, Luton, Leicester, Marble Arch, Nottingham, Bournemouth, Portsmouth, Middlesborough, Derby, Poole, Taunton, Torquay, Southampton, Weston-Super-Mare, Rugby and finally 21 branches later, Newton Abbot!

Before the First World War there were two department stores in Newton, these were Rockey's and Badcock's. Rockey's was in Queen Street and was a branch of a Torquay store that was taken over by Harrods in the early part of the twentieth century. Badcock's was a Newton based firm and had a very large store in Courtenay Street. Later Badcock's was taken over, and for a few years was renamed, Dingle's, part of the House of Fraser group. Austins, the present large department store, opened at the beginning of March 1924, at 6–8 Courtenay Street in what were very small ground floor premises. Mr Robert Austin had come from Romford in Essex and had taken over the long established drapery business

of W.T. White. In 1945 they held a memorable sale, there was a queue of 700 people when the doors opened and 5,000 customers were served during the day. The attraction was goods in short supply such as sheets, blankets, linoleum squares, carpets, rugs, mats and half-coupon rate clothing. There have been a number of extensions over the years; one in 1955 enabled an entrance to be made in East Street. There was a new shop front in 1961 and in 1970 they opened a Scandinavian type restaurant 'The Pine room'.

By the 1940s, multiple grocery stores had proliferated: Home & Colonial, International, and Lipton's were later joined by Maypole. There were still plenty of independent stores in town, grocers and others. Some of the bigger independent retailers, such as Gibbon's and Halse's, had, as well as their retail businesses, wholesale departments supplying other shops and outlets in country districts. The biggest food retailer, surprising as it may seem now, would have been the Newton Co-op. As well as a department store in Queen Street and a town branch in Bank Street, it had country branches in Abbotskerswell, Bovey Tracey, Chudleigh Knighton, Denbury, Ipplepen, Kingskerswell, Kingsteignton, Lustleigh, and Moretonhampstead.

Undoubtedly the second half of the twentieth century saw the fastest period of change ever, with a big decline in independent shopkeepers and the Co-op. The transformation has been to self-service and supermarkets. An early self-service shop was C & F Watts at 133 Queen Street; in 1971 Ford and Lock which took over the old Ball's Garage premises next to Bearne's School, would have seemed a step nearer the supermarket of today. Tesco, at first a 'cut-price' grocer, although even then, with a chain of 500 shops, announced their coming by buying three shops in Wolborough Street in January 1966. This was Tesco's second shop in Devon. They opened at the end of November 1967; the shop had been just 38 weeks in construction. It was called a supermarket although it only had 4,000 square feet of space and 40 staff. There was a grand opening ceremony and double Green Shield stamps were an incentive on opening day. They moved out of town to the Kingsteignton Road site in 1981. It has grown since then to 43,000 square feet and has a staff of 550. There is a plan for a further expansion. Since Tesco first came it has moved upmarket and in the process become the biggest grocer in the country. Sainsbury's did not arrive until 1996.

The changes have not only been to grocers. Of the former three big ironmongers, Bidgood's, Mid-Devon Stores, popularly known as the 'dustbin' because it stocked everything, and Chappell's, only the latter remains. Out of town, B & Q and Home-base have taken their place. Every independent chemist has been taken over. Another change has been the growth of take-away food shops; many now grouped at the station end of Queen Street. In November 1993 Marks and Spencer's opened at the Willows outside Torquay. This aroused fears of closure at the Torquay and Newton branches, Torquay did subsequently close but Newton happily survives.

Newton was the centre for a while of some multiple operations though in one case many Newtonians were probably unaware of the fact. This was G. Widger & Sons Ltd., Queen Street glass, paint & wallpaper merchants. Although it did not look like it, this was the headquarters of an extensive West-country chain of similar shops. They had branches at Barnstaple, Bridgwater, Exeter, Newton Abbot, three in Plymouth, Plympton, St Austell, Torquay,

and Truro. There was also Tapper's which had furniture shops at Dawlish, Exeter, Teignmouth, Southampton, Portsmouth, as well as Newton. In addition they were early into the travel agent business and grew to have branches at Exeter, Exmouth, Newton and Paignton. Torbay Mill had their central location at Lemon Mills and had shops at Brixham, Dartmouth, Dawlish, Kingsbridge Paignton, Teignmouth, Torquay, Totnes and Newton.

There have been enormous changes in retailers themselves and indeed in the way that we shop. So much so, that the young may find it hard to comprehend, or appreciate, how different shopping is now from just 50 years ago. The small urban mostly grocery shops were the first to go such as the stores in Church Road and Albany Street. Next followed the chain store provision merchants. More recently there has been the demise of suburban shops, even post offices, such as Milber and Highweek. This has been paralleled by the closure of more rural shops in places like Combeinteignhead, East Ogwell, Ponsworthy and Poundsgate. Yet Newton, despite problems, has remained an important shopping town with the third largest catchment area in the county.[998]

advertisement 'Does your fur need renovating?' In 1972 they opened their new store in Queen Street. Ernie Matthews, who was totally blind, opened his kiosk shop in Broadlands Avenue in 1962. In 1964 Elliot's of Wolborough Street were fined for selling pork pies unfit for human consumption. Many older Newtonians will remember this old fashioned baker's shop and café, which was then open for long hours that few others matched. Mrs Underhill won a prize for a holiday in a competition run by Church Road stores. It was billed as the small grocer's answer to trading stamps. Barclays refurbished bank reopened and three former managers attended.

Trago Mills came to the Newton area in 1968, then described as 'a group of huts on a boggy lowland site'. It was perhaps the first of the plethora of out of town shops that were to come.[1000] Traders in town correctly foresaw this as a threat. The following year Rev. Stokes of Wolborough deplored those few shops that opened on Good Friday. One market day in 1970 was unusually quiet when farmers staged a one-day boycott of Newton Market because of the Farm Price Review. Six-day trading for shops arrived, in 1974, some had already anticipated this but others continued for years to half-day close on Thursdays. Next year a shop in town followed the example of an out of town store by opening on Sunday. Teignbridge decision was to turn a blind eye to Sunday trading.

The second D-Day was February 15th 1971 when old pounds, shillings, and pence were scrapped in favour of the new decimal system. Possibly because it was a nation-wide event little news featured afterwards in the local press. A sidelight was thrown on the fact that some banks were already computerized whereas others were not. An elderly woman in Kingsteignton, who could not grasp it, was other than a one-day wonder provided the lighter side. She said she would not do any shopping on Monday but wait until Tuesday when everything would be normal again![1001] Sadder was the old stallholder in the market who had a sign 'No new money taken here'!

Newton's last cycling milkman Charles Stow retired in 1970. He carried 40 pints on his bike and had averaged 20 miles a day for 45 years. His round for Milber Dairies covered Mile End, Broadlands, Milber and Buckland. Newton's oldest grocer Balster & Son, founded 1891, closed in April 1979. It had been started by Edward Balster, who moved to Newton after managing the grocery section of Harrods in London. His son Cyril took the business over but Edward was still doing accounts for the business aged 91.[1002] Cyril and his wife had kept up with the times meeting the fierce competition from the multiples by operating a delicatessen. In 1980 Lipton's in Courtenay Street closed; they had a staff of ten, three of whom moved to Torquay. They originally had two shops in Newton but the Queen Street branch had shut a few years before.[1003] Tesco had fought a long battle for an out of town site, at first unsuccessfully, at Heathfield. The argument against was that other businesses would suffer. Tesco's counter argument was that the town would be worse off if they built a large store at, say, Torquay. The store opened with parking spaces for 560 cars. A new roundabout was made on the Kingsteignton Road to improve access.[1004]

In 1982 a gas leak one night caused a massive explosion in the New Market Walk precinct, luckily, only one woman was slightly hurt. Police declared an emergency and sealed off the town centre. The Post Office closed and sightseers were asked to keep away. In the following year Newton's oldest outfitters J.S. Pethybridge, at 86 Queen Street, closed, they had been trading since 1907. The site was sold to the Newton Abbot Kitchen Centre.[1005] In April 1984 Woolworth's announced the sale of their store after over 50 years in the town. They had opened in Courtenay Street in 1929 and moved in 1971.

In June 1987 the Mole Valley Farmers set up a new depot in the former Cadburys/Schweppes building on the Brunel Road Industrial Estate. They stated

Pethybridge's men's outfitters, 1907–1983. The array of caps and hats remind us of a time when most men went about with their heads 'covered'. Queen Street Post Office can just be seen next door.

'Newton Abbot is the natural centre for the agricultural community in South Devon'.[1006] DIY came in August that year in substantial form with the arrival of B & Q at Jetty Marsh. The opening was a colourful affair with a New Orleans Marching Jazz Band, Mardi Gras dancers and a massive fairground organ.[1007] This enabled the first part of the Jetty Marsh by-pass to be built but it remained a dead-end for some years. The store was a shade of vibrant reddish-orange and protests were successful in having it repainted in a less strong colour.[1008]

In December security cameras were installed in the town centre, it had taken three years to get them. These were a joint venture between the council and shopkeepers; it was hoped they would make the town a safer place to shop. The consumption of alcohol in the town centre had previously been banned in 1997.[1009] One notable shop owner Mr Charles Austin of Austins of Newton Abbot, who had won the military cross in the First World War, celebrated his 100th birthday in 1998.

Industry

Torrential rain caused the Stover Canal to burst its banks and flood North Quarry of Newton Abbot Clays Ltd in 1950 and there were frequent complaints about power-cuts in the area. The headlines at the end of 1954 were that Newton was entering the jet age, because Centrax were coming. The firm emanated from the London area and tried at first to purchase the Royal Show site at Stover. This fell through but in December they were given planning permission to build a factory on the Shaldon Road.[1010] Much of the site had been woodland felled during the First World War. They also set up factories at Heathfield and Exeter and originally manufactured gas turbines but later produced blades for jet-engines, gears and axles. From the end of 1969, until March 1970, they had a prolonged strike that was reputed to have been the longest ever in South Devon.[1011] By 1985, then employing 750 people, Centrax announced their biggest order to-date of six million pounds for gas turbine generators for off shore oil-rigs in the North Sea.[1012] Centrax's plant at Heathfield was sold in a management buy out in 1989. Its new name was the Heathfield Construction Company and it would build and rebuild dump trucks mainly for quarrying.[1013]

The year 1957 was difficult. At the beginning there was petrol rationing and reduced bus services in the aftermath of the Suez Crisis. Later there was an eight-day Devon General bus strike and an outbreak of foot and mouth disease at South Brent which affected trade. Bovey Pottery, that had been operating for 200, years closed down. The firm ran into financial trouble at the end of the previous year some of the 130 operatives accepted a reduction in wages and others went on strike. Even if there had been no strike, survival would have been problematical, because modernization was overdue. Part of the pottery is now the House of Marbles and a few old small brick-built bottle kilns have been preserved.

The Rope Walk in East Street closed in 1959. The Co-op opened a bakery on the Brunel Estate; it was later taken over by Spiller's French and then closed when employing 33 workers.[1015] Later Hill Palmer and Edwards became bakers on the estate and fancy cake production from Plymouth in 1982 increased the workload. In 1985 the bakery closed with 250 workers.[1016] Those who worked elsewhere on the estate would simply miss their morning waft of the wonderful

New Devon Pottery

This business started in a small way in a private house and garage at Beaver Lodge, Rundle Road, in 1957. This was a good time to start because Bovey Pottery was closing down and therefore a skilled nucleus of workers was available. In early 1958 the firm moved to small factory on the bank of the River Teign on the Brunel Road Trading Estate. Because the pottery started at Beaver Lodge a beaver design with a jug was adopted as the firm's registered trade-mark and appeared as a bottom stamp on the bases of most of the articles manufactured. Some wit once queried why a 'potty otter' was used.

There was a very early setback because of a fire. By an incredible chance circumstance one director was on a social club visit to the Torquay Fire Station and she took some convincing that the fire call was real. This was because, having a young family, she was often late and thought her friends had inveigled the firemen into pretending they had a call to 'pull her leg'. Despite the fire and severe technical problems the business grew and space was rented from Halse's in Brunel Road for an office, mould making shop and carton storage. The factory doubled in size and later the rented accommodation was given up when a second larger extension was built.

Consultants later substantially improved the efficiency of production and suggested following Hornsea Pottery's example by inviting visitors to look around the pottery and thereby sell seconds at an enhanced margin. A small wooden shop and visitors' area was erected; gardens made and extra part-time staff taken on to act as guides. This annoyed the landlords, the Urban Council, who tried to hinder and thwart the venture. With hindsight their approach seems ludicrous, but then manufacturing was seen as having a bigger employment ratio than retailing. Despite the opposition the operation did prove a success and later the shop was doubled in size. Coach parties brought business to the town and boat trips of visitors came up the river from Teignmouth.

A good potential market was identified initially for a particular type of pottery. This was known as 'Devon Blue', inscribed with souvenir place names in white. This had the drawback that sales were seasonal and

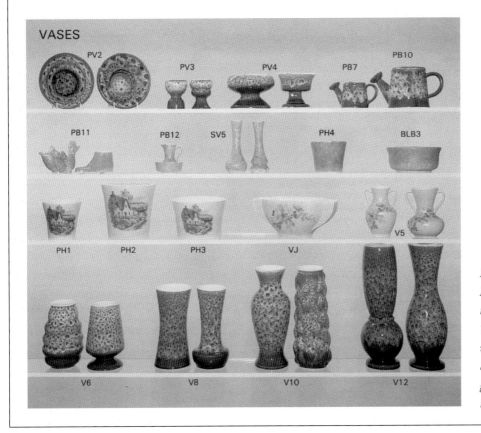

Range of New Devon Pottery items made for the florist trade in 1981. The top and bottom rows were finished in brown and white reactive glazes sold under the trade name 'Dartmoor'.

orders had to be taken before it could be manufactured. It had been hoped that the ware would sell in reasonable quantities with mottoes but this largely proved not to be the case. Another cream coloured souvenir line 'Named Decorated' was developed; this could be made for stock and simply souvenir place named and decorated to order at a later stage. This was a tremendous advance but there were still problems of finance through the winter. Three different designs, generally floral, were chosen by market research each year.

Later fancy and reactive glazes were produced the most successful range being a brown and white effect that was marketed as 'Dartmoor'. Articles were made specifically for the florist trade such as vases, jardinieres, and pot covers and these finally proved to be the solution of seasonal selling by producing reasonable sales all through the year. The pottery had grown big enough to commission transfer designs for its exclusive use. It was in the forefront of mug designs later taken up by other potteries. These for instance, included ranges of ponies, working horses, English wild animals and birds. Souvenir items, such as mugs, were also produced for royal occasions such as jubilees and weddings.

The other big change was a move more towards tableware. This area was where the weight of pottery sales was to be found. There was a steep learning curve but eventually ware for tea and dinner-sets were produced. The permanent personnel rose to 35 with additional part time staff in the summer season. The output from the pottery was sold to shops all over the United Kingdom, literally from the Scilly Islands to the Shetlands. There was also a useful export business, notably Canada. Special lines were also made for sales promotions and such things as eggcups in the shape of a train for an Easter-egg manufacturer, beehive shape containers for honey producers and storage jars for fudge makers.

Cheap imported pottery did not directly affect New Devon Pottery because it did not greatly compete with their lines. However, the fortunes of many larger potteries in Stoke-on-Trent were hit badly. They began to seek out the smaller niche markets making such items as florists' vases. This increased competition and brought about the decision to close down in 1984. The site on the Brunel Industrial Estate is still known as Pottery Units.[1014]

smell of newly-baked 'Mother's Pride' bread.

David & Charles started up as publishers in Newton Abbot in 1960, and moved to premises on the old Station Cottages site. They took over the Readers Union Book Club and later were themselves taken over by Readers Digest in 1984. Since then there has been further changes of ownership. In 1961 the Milber Service Station opened. A special foam-washing machine was installed so the public could wash their own cars. Geest set up in 1961 a new banana-ripening centre at Heathfield they aimed to process a million bananas a week. In 1964 shoemakers, Clarks of Street considered opening a factory for 400 at Newton, but went to Barnstaple, however that factory has now closed. Newton was a little unusual in moving direct from a manual exchange to Standard Trunk Dialling in 1965. Until then one had to ask a telephone operator to connect you to a caller in another area. Newton was declared a black spot for telephone kiosk vandalization. Standard Telephones acquired the old mill at Bovey Tracey to open a factory making capacitors. It had an erratic start, having by extensive advertising built up its personnel to 68, it closed in May 1967. Then, after three months closure, it reopened in September with 30 staff.

In 1967 the Central Electricity Generating Board was accused of making a million-pound mistake at Newton Power Station. A complicated system for tipping railway trucks laden with coal was installed but presumably because of snags it was abandoned after a very short time, and reverted to bringing lorry loads of coal from Plymouth which caused considerable dust in the vicinity.

The Cooling Tower was erected in 1940 and despite its early camouflage paint certainly dominated the area.

Newton Abbot Power Station, now only a sub-generating station, became less used, and closed in March 1974.[1017] Forty jobs were lost on Newton's closure and the one full-time resident was found a new home. Sooty, the power station cat, the mother of no less than sixty kittens.[1018] The cooling tower was 250-ft tall and its demolition on a Sunday morning in September 1974 created great spectator sport. One lady on Knowles Hill asked her friends to 'coffee and an explosion'. Holes were drilled for explosives and the operation was planned so masonry would fall at an angle into an open space. Debris from the demolition was free to takers and used, among other things for driveways at East Ogwell, hard-standing for caravan sites, and building up the banks of the River Teign by the racecourse.[1019] The main building was removed in 1977 and the site has since been redeveloped for housing.[1020]

The 160 foot high, 80-year-old pottery chimney of Hexter Humpherson on the Kingsteignton Road was demolished in 1968 to make way for new warehouses. It proved as stubborn in its demise as it had been steadfast in its working days. Some 24 hours after it was scheduled to collapse it was still standing. Explosives were ruled out and the steel hawser meant to pull it down snapped. As the base had already been drilled to weaken the tower it was thought too dangerous to try to attach another hawser.[1021] The Pottery Cottages opposite the site remain; they were made of the firm's yellow brick so prevalent in much of Newton. It can hardly be said to look attractive but is of a remarkably good quality, as anyone who has ever tried to drill it will concur! In 1980, the site was developed for industrial purposes.[1022]

Lyons Maid opened a large frozen food and ice-cream warehouse at Heathfield in 1969 and three years later one of the oldest, and at one time, by

On a Sunday morning in 1974 its demolition created an enormous spectator sport. The two photographs were taken less than a minute apart.

far the most important business, in Newton ended in 1972 when Vicary's finally closed.[1023] Only 20 years before 300 men and women had been employed but the staff had dwindled to 50. In its last stages enormous lorry loads of raw material were delivered to be combed at Bradley Mills and then taken to Bradford in Yorkshire for final processing. It cannot have been viable. Sanderson, Murray and Elders, the owners, were cutting back elsewhere as well. Not only was this the end of a business it was the end of a trade that had continued in the town for some six hundred years!

The coal miners strike in 1972 resulted in power cuts and plunged the area into darkness. In December 1982 it was announced that Cull's, the former timber-yard, would be turned into town centre flats which it was hoped would be complete by December 1983.[1024] Older townsfolk may well remember the screech of the working saws and the dramatic sight of the 'saw doctor' with sparks flying, machine-sharpening, a large band saw blade. 'Saw doctor' was the name given to the man whose job was to keep all the saws sharpened. Alvan Blanch in Salisbury Road was closed with the loss of 30 jobs they had taken over four years earlier; the old established engineering firm of Beare's.[1025].

Mod-Dec Windows opened a new factory near its headquarters at Milber in 1984.[1027] Nashua Photo Products Limited stated they would move to Newton. They hoped to create 40 new jobs in film processing. They were so successful that when badly affected by the postal strike in 1988 they were employing 400 people.[1028] In 1998 they sold out to another American firm District Photo of Maryland.[1029]

In June 1986 Daks Simpson, clothing manufacturers said it would close the factory in Brunel Road with the loss of 150 local jobs. They had been in

H. Beare & Sons

This firm was established *c.*1850 at Liverton moving to Newton in the late 1870s or very early 1880s. The assumption is that this was to be nearer the railhead and to a centre of growing importance. There is though no direct evidence to prove this. An important part of its early work was the manufacture and repair of waterwheels for local mills, an example is at Cockington. In advertised in *Kelly's Directory 1873* as implement makers, iron and brass founders, makers of steam engines, water wheels, apple mills, cider presses, bone mills, saw benches and barn machinery.

Beare's was hard hit by the depression after the First World War and taken over by Willcocks & Sons, Dial Foundry of Buckfastleigh in 1932. It continued to trade as Beare's. There were two main sides to the business: ordinary agricultural engineering and the specialist manufacture of fruit processing machinery.

The agricultural side had agencies for large manufacturers, such as International Harvester, but also made adaptations and specialist machinery.

Output from the other side of the business was used both in the cider trade and soft drinks industries. Fruit presses were the mainstay of this business but they also made apple elevators, apple mills, pomace disintegrators and similar equipment. Work was done for individual farm cider makers and large firms such as Carter's of Coleford (Ribena), Coate's of Nailsea, Showering's of Shepton Mallet (Babycham) and Whiteway's of Whimple. They also produced items outside this trade; for instance shredding machines for the clay extraction industry and saw-benches for the timber trade.

During the Second World War Beare's made aircraft parts but afterwards, this section of the business was sold to Wallington Weston and left Newton. In the 1950s the agricultural engineering side developed outlying branches at Stoke Canon near Exeter and at Kelly Bray near Liskeard in Cornwall.

In 1963 F.J. Reeves and Fox Elliott Ltd of Totnes absorbed Beare's. Further agricultural branches were established at Kingsbridge and Umberleigh in Devon and Norton Fitzwarren in Somerset. Reeves disposed of the two parts of the company separately. The engineering side at the Avenue was acquired by Alvan Blanch in 1979 and closed in 1983. The agricultural core, based at Rixy Park, was acquired by Ken Holmes in 1987 and went into receivership in 1991, although the original branches at Stoke Canon and Kelly Bray survived.

The Willcock's family resigned from Reeves in 1966 but one of them went on to found C.R. Willcocks at Kingsteignton. Part of the site behind the Avenue has now become the Hometeign housing complex.[1026]

Advertising leaflet for a Beare's Cider Press. The firm specialized in fruit processing machinery and were also agricultural engineers.

Cheese building for apple juice production, on plant made by Beare's.

the town since the 1950s and had originally made sheepskin coats and gloves.[1030] There was a connection still visible in the town that was much older. There had been in Courtenay Street a bespoke tailor called Parkin. He had been another ingenious Newtonian who had invented something and patented it. This was a reversible coat that he called 'Invertere'. He sold the patent to Daks Simpson. The tiled plaque that commemorates his invention is still high on the wall above his one-time shop, opposite Pearl Assurance House. In August, there was compensating news that another clothing manufacturer, although smaller, was doing better. Vander, which made waterproof clothing, started as a one-man business, had grown to 20 and had received a 3,500-coat contract for workers on the new Falkland Islands airport.[1031]

In 1988 Newton Abbot's short-lived revival of manufacturing the 'Triumph' motorcycle ceased. Production was to be concentrated, at Decoy, on the cheaper 'Matchless' model. Mrs Thatcher had praised this machine on her visit the previous year.[1032] By 1989 the steady increase in the use of double glazed windows brought the news of another firm coming to Newton, this was Europlas. Devon Desserts, moved from Dawlish, and opened one of the most advanced chilled food-processing plants in the country in Brunel Road.[1033] It made chilled

In Courtenay Street high on the wall opposite Pearl Assurance House. A reminder of another Newton inventor, Parkin the tailor, who patented a reversible raincoat.

and frozen desserts, such as trifles and cheesecakes, and hot ones, such as spotted dick and bread & butter pudding.[1034] They expanded in both 1992 and 1994 and opened a new factory in 1999.[1035]

In May 1983 the British Legion moved into Manor House in Wolborough Street but by 1988 it was announced that they would leave. There were mounting debts as the membership had fallen from 600 to 300.[1036] The *Mid-Devon Advertiser* took it over in 1990.[1037] The Manor was originally built in 1534 before the Dissolution and it became known as the Great House of 'Ullborough' and civil courts were held. In 1835 it was a school run by a Mr Philip. It had also been a lodging house, private residence, head quarters of a car dealership, offices and latterly the British Legion Club. At one time, it had housed Truscott's, the plaster ornament manufacturers, who took their trade name 'Manorware' from the building. Later Truscott's moved to the Brunel Road trading estate but after some years ceased trading.

In April the naturalist Andrew Cooper opened the Devon Orchid Exhibition Centre at Forches Cross.[1038] He was the son of a former director of Truscott's 'Manorware'. The Orchid Centre was set up by, brother and sister, Wilma and Brian Ritteshausen. Their business had been started by their father after the Second World War and moved from Kingsteignton to Forches Cross. They had shown at the Chelsea Flower Show for over 40 years and had created a number of new varieties of orchid.[1039] In 1992 a new set of five British postage stamps with orchid designs was launched in Newton.

In 1991 it was announced that the long established Tucker's Maltings would open to visitors. In 1994 they added a brewery;[1040] and announced they would hold, what was then Britain's only beer festival.[1041] The event was repeated later but on the first occasion numbers and thirsts were misjudged, so that the event ran 'dry'! In 1998 Carlton Benbow the shopfitters had a prestigious order for work at the National Maritime Museum at Greenwich.[1042] In 1999 discussions took place between the National Farmers Union and Teignbridge whether a farmer's market could be set up.[1043]

Watts Blake & Bearne which became a public company in 1966, announced plans to extend their Southern Quarry by diverting the rivers Teign and Bovey. They applied to DCC for planning permission. In the first place they seem to have done their homework and set out to try and meet local objections.[1044] Incredibly, considered that the application was costing over half a million pounds, they had the wrong figures worked out for the rivers' water flow. They therefore withdrew from the subsequent public enquiry in 1998.[1045] The opposition had genuine concerns, but it also seemed likely that green environmental excuses cloaked some 'not in my backyard' factor. In 1997 Sibelco the Belgian sand quarry business took over Watts Blake and Bearne. It was the largest ball clay firm in the world, with 600 employees in Devon and 600 overseas. Until then, it had been one of the last large firms in the West Country to be locally owned.[1046] There was the usual announcement that the take over would not make any significant difference!

Railway

Railway news continued in the headlines but the period was mostly one of decline. In 1950 the General Secretary of the National Union of Railwaymen missed a civic reception at the National Conference in Newton because his train was late. Dainton Bank, the long rise from Aller on the Plymouth line, designed when atmospheric power was envisaged, had long been a problem for heavily loaded engines. In days of steam, 'banker' engines, waiting at the bottom to assist trains up the slope were a familiar sight, It was a natural test hill therefore when experiments were carried out with British built turbine-engines. In fact in March 1952 the first locomotive towing no less than 17 carriages cleared the gradient at 90 mph![1047] The turbine idea was dropped and diesel-engines supplanted steam. In 1954 Newton hit the national headlines for an unofficial railway strike that started there and spread elsewhere in the country. The strike was unpopular with much of the public. In 1956 a railway crane fell across the line at Bishopsteignton; for 24 hours all trains were diverted by the Teign Valley line.

Steam up at the station, probably in the 1950s when Newton reached its rail peak. The garden right foreground once belonged to The High School for Girls then the offices of the local driving examiners and is now an accountant.

A steam train leaving New-
ton for the west, one of the
old wooden signal boxes is
on the left and a tall tele-
graph post to the right.

The year 1958 saw the closure of regular passenger traffic on the Moretonhampstead line in June and the Ashburton line in November. Many older Newtonians will remember the half-length platform No 9 at the station where the 'Moreton Flier' began its run. In truth, it was anything but a flier, and stories abound of the friendly way in which it operated. For instance, the drivers whistled when leaving Brimley Halt, if they wished to pick up a can of tea from the Station Café at Bovey. It was then the job of the junior cafe assistant to dash across the road to the station with the can. However, in 1958 there was a harbinger of things to come, when a 2,000-hp diesel hydraulic locomotive passed through Newton station on a trial run on the main line. In 1960 the last steam-engine was repaired at Newton. Only a couple of years later all locomotives based in the town became diesels, although the occasional 'steamer' could still be seen on a freight train or on a passenger train from some other depot. In 1969 passenger trains were run for one day only to Bovey Tracey the first time since 1959. Some 500 people used the service and BR said it was a success, but had no plans to repeat the event.

Replica of 'The Rocket' at the belated 150th celebration in 1997 of the railway's arrival at Newton in 1846. Picture taken in the one-time goods yard.

The proposal to close Kingskerswell Station was announced in 1964. Newton RDC refused to oppose closure but Torquay said it would. Moves have recently been made to see if a station could again be opened at Kingskerswell. The Golden Hind super express fast train service to London, was launched, it took just about 3 hours leaving Newton at 7.51 a.m. Warning came of the closure of the Rail Goods yard; work was to be concentrated on Paignton and Exeter. There was considerable local opposition; partly alleviated by the idea it might become an area coal distribution depot. All senior Newtonians, whether railwaymen or not, will remember the railway hooter which sounded across the town for the last time in 1965. Although latterly, in the charge of British Rail, its origins went back to when there were few clocks. It used to sound no less than six times a day; 'Three times between 7 and 7.30 am, twice at lunchtime and again at the end of the working day at 5 p.m.' [1048] In contrast to this, the first clay liner trains left Newton in November of the same year. [1049] In 1977 the main railway bridge on the road to Torquay was doubled. The railway lines had to be closed for two days to enable the work to be done. [1050] Before the Second World War Mellor's Garage was beside the road going to Torquay just beyond the railway bridge. Later this garage became Acton Tool, precision engineers, but when preliminary work on the widening started they moved to smaller premises in Hopkins Lane. Early in 1978, it was announced that locomotive servicing and carriage cleaning was to be moved to the Laira depot at Plymouth [1051] thus Newton's involvement in train maintenance ended after 130 years.

'Tiny' the sole surviving broad-gauge engine built at Plymouth in 1868 left Newton Station for Buckfastleigh. Taken out of service in 1876 she was due to be scrapped, but was used instead until 1927 as a stationary engine at Newton Abbot. Having reached the end of her second working life the scrap-yard again loomed. Happily her uniqueness was realized, so she was put on display on a platform at Newton, staying there until sent to Buckfastleigh Railway Museum. [1052] In 1996 plans were aired for a large railway museum in Newton using some of the old redundant rail property. [1053] It was suggested it would be a major tourist attraction and might make a rail museum second only to the national collection at York. Later the *Western Morning News* predicted the idea would fail for lack of cash, which indeed it did. However, the town would still have liked a smaller scheme because the Railway Room at the Museum was insufficient. In June 1997 Newton marked the arrival of the railway 150 years previously. Technically this was a little late because the first train had come on the last day of 1846. However, the summer was the best time for the celebrations. There was an exhibition including a replica 'Rocket' at the one time Goods Yard. To help mark the occasion a 6ft high floral statue of Isambard Kingdom Brunel was placed outside the Town Hall. The figure was made using carpet bedding plants Brunel's jacket was purple leafed, his waistcoat yellowy-green, his top hat purple and his eyes were made from houseleeks.[1054]

Health/welfare

Lady Mountbatten the Chief of St John's Ambulance visited the town in 1951. In 1952 the WVS staffed a 'Lynmouth Relief Depot', for the victims of the flood disaster, in the former American camp at Heathfield. Newton Abbot Round Table raised £35 for the East Coast Flood Relief fund in 1953 by guessing the weight of a pig. It was in 1952 that Broadlands, the house, was obtained by DCC to be turned into an old people's home. In 1966 Mapleton, on the Ashburton Road, was opened as an old people's complex of 7 bungalows and 10 flatlets. It was named after Dr Mapleton, a former officer of health.

A protest by Newton Labour Party against charges in the NHS in 1961 was aborted because the organisers had flu! In 1966 a new children's' ward opened at Newton hospital. The Casualty Department was re-opened in 1973 after 21 months closure brought about by shortage of casualty officers. It was announced in 1994 that major operations would no longer be performed in Newton Hospital, they would be moved to the new £3.5 million state-of-the-art surgical block at Torquay.[1055] In 1998 Newton Hospital celebrated its centenary.[1056] Later it was in need of modernization. Rather than rebuild on the present site other locations were considered. This would have the obvious advantage that the old hospital could go on working until the new one was built. The first option considered was near to Teignbridge offices on the Brunel Road estate.[1057] The next almost unbelievable idea was the cricket ground; the third option was at Jetty Marsh.

The Family Planning Association opened a birth control clinic in 1964; the first in the Newton area. In October 1983 a home for mentally handicapped people opened in the former county council's boys' home in Highweek Road.[1058] In December the Town Clinic, first mooted in 1969 opened in Albany Street. It was a joint venture between the Torbay District Health Authority and a group of local general practitioners. In 1984 work started on Hometeign House, which was to be a warden-assisted sheltered housing scheme in Salisbury Road.[1059] New health offices opened in 1990 on the old Torflex site in Brunel Road with a food department, a housing section and an environmental control section. A doctor's surgery opened, after pressure for a number of years, on the Buckland Estate to supply the needs of the 3,000 inhabitants in 1992. Greenhill Farm, at Kingsteignton was converted into a day centre for the elderly.

To aid recycling an experiment was tried, in 1994, of having two wheelie bins for rubbish emptied alternate weeks. This initially caused protests over worries there would be problems with smells particularly in summer.[1060] Over time those with the system seem to have adjusted, though strangers always marvelled that in Teignbridge black, not green, was the bin for recyclable rubbish!

Workhouse

In 1963 the old workhouse, the 'House of Dread', in East Street came down.[1061] It had been there over a century and a quarter and had been at the centre of the Newton Union. It had truly been feared and the centre of a national disgrace, so there cannot be the regret at its departure as there is over so much of old Newton. Yet, at Totnes the workhouse has been modernized for fine living accommodation and at Southwell the National Trust have reopened the workhouse as a visitor attraction. During the First World War Newton workhouse served in part as a hospital and to house German POW's who had volunteered to work on local farms. During the Second World War the workhouse served as a naval hospital and on closure part was converted to geriatric use.[1062]

Education

To cope with the big post-war increase of population in this area Milber County Primary School was opened in June 1955.[1063] In 1957 there was an epidemic of Asian flu that mostly affected young people, a number of schools had only half their pupils attending and some classes had to close. In 1966 some children from Newton went on the school cruise ship *Devonia* for a two-week educational voyage to Stockholm, Leningrad and Copenhagen.

In 1962 Seale Hayne celebrated its existence for 50 years. The students, to raise money for charity, made the world's largest trifle in 1989. It contained some 1,000 kg, not quite a ton, of cream and 350 litres, about 77 gallons, of custard but only 100 litres, about 22 gallons, of sherry, not forgetting the jelly and sponge! The headline was 'No Trifling Achievement'.[1064] It was sold off in platefuls to students and others in the town centre. The Minister of Agriculture, Mr D. Heathcoat Amory, opened, in 1993, the new Great Hall at Seale Hayne. Three years later the college had a visit from Russian teachers.

Dyrons, the former Vicary family home, became a study and social centre for the sixth formers of Newton Abbot Grammar School in 1971. Later the adjoining site was developed into rooms for teaching, music, art, drama, a sports hall and youth centre. These were officially opened in 1975, the year that comprehensive education came to Newton.[1065] The new Knowles Hill Comprehensive School opened, short of six classrooms, because temporary ones had not arrived. Pupils had to use dining and other non-teaching rooms. Later it was stated that the classrooms would be at least six months late. The new comprehensives were hailed as the great educational movement for the future. They did certainly produce the two-way movement, of the present time, when a number of young Newtonians go to the Torquay Grammar schools and several young Torquinians come to Newton for the comprehensives! In late summer 1990 a plan to merge the two comprehensives, Coombeshead and Knowles Hill, was floated, it would have had some 1,750 pupils and been the second largest comprehensive in Devon, after Exmouth.[1066] Opinion was divided on the matter. One educational expert said the plan was 'an intelligent one'. Others deemed it 'a botch up' having a school on five different sites. However, the `big is not necessary beautiful view' so far has won the day.

By 1980 the surge of building westwards alongside the Ashburton Road caused Highweek Primary to be overwhelmed with pupils, so that in 1980 a new school was built at Bradley Barton.[1067] (Barton originally a 'barley farm' i.e. one good for corn. The best land was likely to be retained by the manor so it usually later became the lord's own farm.) A new computing course was announced for the Dyrons Sixth Form Centre in 1985 this was A Level Computing Science and Technology; quite a stride, for a science just 40 years old.[1068]

Religion

Roman Catholic mass, in Newton, was heard in English, for the first time in 1964. The Mormons announced their intention to build a church on part of the site of Milber Nurseries. It was reported that two of Newton's churches, built a century ago, were to disappear: the Methodist Church in Courtenay Street, built in 1869 for a congregation of a thousand, and the United Reform in Queen Street that had been begun in 1865 and held some 500.[1069] The last service to be held in Queen Street was a harvest festival. The building is now solicitors' offices. The church in Courtenay Street was demolished and became Woolworth's for a while. The modern replacement church for the older ones was built at the end of the Avenue and opened in 1966.[1070] The Salem Chapel, off Wolborough Street, was originally built in 1876 and had seating for 600. In 1982 it had a congregation of 60 so it was decided to sell. It became part of a car showroom.[1071] In 1991 the new Pentecostal Church opened on Exeter Road. They had been in Newton for over 50 years but their previous site off Sherborne Road had been the subject of a compulsory purchase order.[1072]

In 1982 the Salvation Army celebrated 100 years in Newton. They had originally arrived to hold a public meeting at the market and appealed for instruments to form a band. It may seem strange today but when they first made their appearance there was much opposition. Mud, eggs and flour were thrown; a drum was punctured and attempts made to steal their flag. Their first hall was in Wolborough Street, later they moved to the Gospel Hall in Union Street.[1073]

In 1983 St Augustine's Priory at Abbotskerswell closed after 120 years. The community had dwindled, from fifty to just two; deaths had outnumbered those seeking the vocation. When they came from Spettisbury in Dorset, they had hired a special train to come to Newton. The architect Joseph Hansom had drawn the main outlines of their church and he had also designed the Roman Catholic Church at Teignmouth. His name entered English dictionaries as the inventor of the Hansom Cab.[1074] The Priory's high altar was sold and placed on the lawn of the Moorland Hotel at Haytor, now a Holiday Fellowship Guest House. The priory buildings were converted into flats 1986/7; what remains nearby is the evocative cemetery with the simple crosses of the canonesses, the ornate ones of the clergy.[1075]

The vicar of St Paul's in 1997 took a sledgehammer to his own church! This was all in a good cause being the start of a plan to build a meeting room, kitchen and other facilities.[1076] The so-called new St Leonard's was sold and turned into a furniture warehouse. One idea had been to turn it into a gymnastics club but church officials rejected this,[1077] the new St Leonard's had certainly not had the working life of its predecessor.

Crime and punishment

Newton in 1951, unfortunately, gained national headlines as 'a town of fear' after six attacks on women after dark. During March 1959 the foundation stone of new Newton Police Station off Newfoundland Way was laid. Customs men swooped on a motor launch, carrying a cargo of spirits and cigarettes, in the Teign estuary in 1964; two men were caught unloading. Heavitree Brewery tried to secure repossession of *The Jolly Sailor* in 1975, the landlord had achieved notoriety by putting on lunchtime displays of exotic dancing and then disappeared.

Two burglaries at Devon Leathercrafts are worth recording. On one occasion when the roof was being repaired, a slim man wriggled his way through a small hole only to let his identity card get left behind in the aperture. The thief was unaware of his loss and was surprised to be arrested within hours. Another time a serious attack was made on an old but very heavy safe. It was taken down from its position, manoeuvred into an open space, turned over and obviously some hours spent cutting open the back. After all this work the thieves left the entire contents, it was a bag of dog biscuits, for a guide-dog, put there to safeguard them from the mice!

In 1964 Major Simmonds of Denbury Camp who lived on the Aller Estate took his wife shopping to Plymouth. Simmonds, came home alone, saying his wife had failed to return to the car. In 1971, seven years later the police charged him with murder and he came up at the Devon Assizes. Perhaps not surprisingly, with no tangible evidence he was found 'not guilty' and went off to live out the rest of his life in North Devon.

In 1967 the only policewoman in Newton married but said she would continue her career. A team of bell-ringers from Newton police station featured on Radio Four in 1969. Dr Edith Summerskill officially opened in 1974 the as yet unfinished Channing's Wood Prison. There was opposition in Newton to the possible establishment of a bail hostel at Lake View, South Road. In 1975 a traffic warden who had gained notoriety in the national press as the 'iron warden' was transferred from Dawlish to Newton Abbot.

In the early part of 1976 it was decided to build a new courthouse. The Town Hall in Courtenay Street, which was then used, admittedly had its faults, it leaked and the acoustics were poor. It was though a symbol of Newton's great period of nineteenth century growth, so maybe though better treatment could have been found, than brutal demolition. The courts had to be held at Teignmouth from 1976 until 1978 when the new courthouse was opened in Newfoundland Way.[1078] The Liberal Club in Market Street lost its licence to serve alcohol in 1980. Its running was termed 'shambolic'.[1079]

Cameras to watch and control the traffic were installed at Penn Inn, within four months 500 drivers had been prosecuted for going through the lights at red.[1080]

Leisure

As average working hours decreased the amount of time spent on leisure increased. Newton Abbot Athletic club organized their first cross-country Championship for Women in 1950, Jill Warren, a Newtonian, won. Ralph Whiteman, the famous agricultural broadcaster, spoke to local Newton Young Farmers. Wilfred Pickles' radio show 'Have a Go' was broadcast from St Mary's Hall. 1951 was Festival of Britain year; celebrations were inaugurated in the Butter Market and an historical pageant of William of Orange was staged. Dr Charles Hill MP, the 'Radio Doctor' attended a Conservative Rally at Ingsdon Convent.

In 1952 there were special remembrance services for the death of King George VI, Queen Elizabeth II was proclaimed at the Tower. In 1954 four mayors and six council chairmen attended Newton's first civic Ball at the *Globe*. Ray Mawby succeeded Brigadier Rayner as the local MP; he was the first manual trade unionist to sit on the Conservative benches.

Newton Abbot was the first provincial town to which the new Queen paid a visit; the *Devon & Cornwall Journal* wrote 'the honour was well merited'. It continued that most guidebooks said it was 'a place for reaching somewhere else and a visitor's first impression, whether he arrive by road, rail or air is never very favourable. Few landscapes are so completely dominated and dammed by a votive monument to industrialism like Newton's notorious condenser (cooling tower). Yet on the other side of that eyesore lies a variety of achievements and a memory of history which few towns of the size can claim.'[1081] The first reigning monarch to visit the town for 300 years came by train to a station well decorated mostly in blue and was welcomed in Courtenay Park by 6,000 children. The Queen drove out to see the Royal Show that had been nine months in preparation at Stover. Unfortunately, owing to outbreaks of foot and mouth disease, cattle, sheep and pigs were all absent so the numbers attending were less than average at 93,000. Special entrances were made through the walls on the Bovey road, and for years afterwards they could be picked out by the replaced stonework. A number of Newtonians, who chose the show week as a holiday, secured a paid working one as waitresses and other temporary staff.

The opening of the Wenvoe Television transmitter in South Wales brought some viewing to Newton in 1952, although it was still officially outside the national viewing area. It was in 1961 that Westward, commercial television, reached Newton and eight years later its mascot, Gus Honeybun, the toy rabbit, 'turned on' the Newton Christmas lights.

The Coronation coincided with wet weather and local celebrations were put on hold during the television transmission of the ceremony. In 1959 Newton College of Art held a jazz ball at the *Bradley Hotel*. The South Devon Hunt's point-to-point at Forches Cross was memorable for 500 cars becoming stuck in the mud. Newton Abbot Repertory Company gave their hundredth production

'*The Holly and the Ivy*'. Miss E Wheeler retired as secretary of Newton Repertory Company in 1963.[1082] She was a keen local historian and wrote a number of articles about the town. Newton repertory company ceased operations in 1974. The Community Centre had become so expensive that their final production *The Secret Tent* was staged in Bovey Tracey. Three local men entered Billy Butlin's mass walk from John O'Groats to Lands End in 1960. The comedian Ken Dodd opened the Hackney Sea Scouts Regatta.

Buckfastleigh Races was abandoned, in 1961, after 78 years; Newton applied for the Whitsun Bank Holiday fixture date. A horse called Dry Paint was flown from Ireland to Exeter airport, in 1964, to enter a Newton race. By 1967 a new grandstand to accommodate 1,600 was completed at Newton racecourse.[1083] Later a trade fair was staged there; just under 10,000 people attended. The third trade fair was opened by Sir Alec Rose who arrived by motor launch; he was the Portsmouth greengrocer who had sailed solo around the world. A racing highlight was achieved in 1969 when, Queen Elizabeth the Queen Mother, opened the new grandstand at the racecourse. It replaced an old wooden one that had frequently caught fire, usually started by cigarette ends.[1084] The comic actor, Jack Train, best known for his role as Colonel Chinstrap in Itma, came to Newton by train in 1969.

Newton cricketer Len Coldwell played for England against Pakistan in 1962. Newton All Whites played Cardiff. The Milk Race cycling event passed through Newton, on its way to Bournemouth. The Black and White Minstrels opened the Rotary Fete in Courtenay Park in 1967. The Recreational Trust came into being; there was beside the Cricket Field Road car park, a cricket pitch, football field, tennis courts and pavilion/clubhouse. Newton Council agreed to twinning with Vitre, a small town in Brittany in 1967.

In 1970 the Royal Naval Association opened new headquarters in Rundle Road. An action committee was formed to try and acquire the Stover Canal from BR and restore it as an amenity. The grandstand at the old recreation ground was demolished, it was by no means an attractive building, but it had witnessed much exciting rugby and some soccer over the years. Newton entered the Britain in Bloom contest for the first time and won a certificate of exceptional merit. A traction engine rally was held at Newton Racecourse in 1975.

Perhaps surprisingly, in 1973 the coastal footpath was news in Newton Abbot. Because of local enthusiasm the preliminary meetings and the inauguration of the South West Way, which later became the South West Coast Path Association, were held in Newton Abbot. This body was formed to promote the interests of coast path users on Britain's longest official footpath, which stretches for 630 miles, from Minehead in Somerset, right around the Southwest peninsula to Poole Harbour in Dorset.

In June 1977 the Queen's Silver Jubilee was celebrated and the Queen passed through Kingskerswell, Newton and Kingsteignton in August. Unfortunately, the royal party was behind schedule so the visit was brief.[1085] The carnival was revived after a gap of some 20 years with 61 vehicles and over 100 pedestrians taking part. One float from Park Café and Queen's Fish Bar acted as Danes from Denbury, they pillaged their way across the park grabbing the odd damsel![1086] A later carnival in 1980 started with a great splash of colour on the racecourse when 1,700 girls competed in the Great Britain Majorette Championship.[1087] The town twinned itself with Besigheim in southern Germany in 1979, not far from Stuttgart.[1088] The German name was given to the Newton by-pass that became Besigheim Way. Later Newton was also to twin itself now with Ay in northern France. In March 1980 came news that a site at Dyrons was being considered for a covered swimming pool.[1089] It opened in the summer of 1989, a six lane 25-metre pool.[1090]

There was an American reunion in Newton in 1983 when veterans of the US Army 316 Station Hospital, at Stover returned on the 40th anniversary. The American GIs, so called because everything given to them was a 'general issue', paraded in Second World War vehicles and had a reception at Forde House.[1091] At the end of September it was announced that the Newton Abbot Silver Band would close. They had been in existence for 50 years but now were suffering a shortage of musicians.[1092]

In June 1988 came news that an Indoor Bowling Centre would be built at Kingsteignton alongside the racecourse.[1093] The Devon Football Association decided in 1992 to have a floodlit football ground with facilities for spectators, changing rooms, a meeting room and offices at Coach Road.[1094] There was opposition based on limited road access and possible disturbance to nearby residents but the scheme went ahead. East Park Social Club in Kingsteignton Road, which had opened in 1926 closed, and was put up for sale to pay its debts. The Royal and Ancient Order of Buffaloes in Teign Road closed, it had been established in 1929 in Halcyon Road. At the end of 1994, it was announced that stock car racing would finish, after 27 years at Newton Racecourse.[1095]

Miscellaneous

Christmas in 1950 had the largest mail in Newton Post Office since the war; 2 million items were handled. Mr Arthur Shobbrook led beating the bounds over two days in 1954. The death was announced next year, in Newton Hospital, of Miss Olive Katharine Parr, better known by her pen name of Beatrice Chase. An Air Commodore flew from Bristol to open the new ATC headquarters in 1956; this was the first time a helicopter landed in the Newton urban area. In 1964 the Beatles stopped in Newton station, in a special train, but few knew they were there. Postcodes that had been tested in the 1960s were fully implemented in 1974.[1096] Newton Abbot's correct postal address was now TQ12. This indicated that the bulk of Newton's mail was sorted at Torquay but that did not last long because sorting was moved to Exeter. The TQ nomenclature though, has been retained. Fears were expressed in 1973 that Dutch elm disease was infecting the area. Two years later thousands of trees were affected. It is already easy to forget how commonplace the elm once was. The King of Tonga was met at Newton station in 1975 by a Rolls Royce and taken to Dartmouth Naval College to see his son, who was on a short course there. There was a severe water shortage that year and hosepipes were banned. Smokey Joe, the well-known tramp who camped out near top of Telegraph Hill, was taken into hospital. He was later released to a hostel in Exeter but did not long survive. In 1975 the arrival of a Lesser Yellow-legged Wader, from North America, at Hackney Marshes caused an influx of bird-watchers. The landlord of the *Passage House Inn* reported three coach loads from Liverpool but one bird-watcher arrived in a chauffeur-driven Rolls Royce. The year 1996 saw the first wedding at Forde House. Legislation having come in that buildings apart from the traditional churches and registry offices could apply for a licence to hold weddings. The bride, Deborah Agate, worked for Teignbridge and was asked why she wanted to get married at work. Her answer was not only is it a lovely place but it will be the first ever wedding there. The groom was Tony Hart, a master thatcher.

Fire at the Passage House Inn. *Firemen are working on the roof to tackle the burning thatch. Newton in common with many other places, once had thatch in abundance.*

CHAPTER 11

CONCLUSION

In Newton structural factors undoubtedly played a part in the town's development. As stated in the Introduction it was both a 'bridge' town and in a natural corridor. The early history of the area is undocumented and indeed even the origins of the town leave scope for speculation. What we do know is that the area has for millennia been a rich agricultural one, with a more favourable climate than most areas of the country. This surely would have been an attraction to early peoples and indeed the fact that there is such a large iron-age camp at Milber bears this out.

In medieval times the two towns, of Abbot and Bushel, were unremarkable except for their proximity. They were like so many towns in Devon, market and communication centres and involved industrially, in the wool trade. Later Newton's entry in to the Newfoundland trade gave it an advantage over most other inland towns, because few of them were engaged in that trade. At this distance in time it is difficult to appreciate just how important this factor was, but there is no doubt it was substantial. The seventeenth century in Newton was both turbulent and exciting.

It is, however, the nineteenth century that was the most important period in the town's development. It had industry, it became a 'Union' and a railway town, there was clay nearby, and it was on the fringe of tourist areas. Lastly, and often underrated in importance, was the planned development of upmarket housing. Maybe no other town had an exact replication of Newton's assets but there were a number that had several and some had plus points, that Newton did not have. The problem is to decide why Newton was so outstandingly successful.

Two railway decisions were critical. Firstly it was decided that the main line would, after all, go through Newton and it had Brunel's appreciation of Newton's geographical position to thank for that. Secondly there was the decision made, possibly by Brunel but we do not know for sure by whom or why, to site the original Atmospheric railway workshops in Newton. The importance of this siting was the fact that it later led to the much bigger and important railway works.

The 'topsy' factor has already been referred to, because undoubtedly nothing succeeds like success. Once the town started to expand swiftly, not only did firms move there from elsewhere, but also people came to work both from nearby, and some very long distances indeed. The influx of people needing accommodation, schools, places to worship and to shop caused a surge in building. As the town grew, and attracted more affluent residents moving up-market, it became an ever better shopping centre so luring shoppers from increasing distances.

The people themselves undoubtedly made a difference to what happened in Newton. The townsfolk wanted their railway station close by and arranged roads for access. They applied for Local Board status and improved the health of the town through new sewers. The entrepreneurial Templers digging their Stover Canal enhanced Newton's prosperity over a long period. The shrewd Vicarys built up their industrial enterprise and helped the town progress. It was however, the major landlords the Seymours and, particularly, the Courtenays who played a key role. Not only did the latter own a lot of the land used for the railway in Newton but they also owned by far the greater part of all Wolborough. Thus when they had decided to develop, they could do it on a grand and cohesive scale that a series of small landowners could not have matched. Furthermore they expanded in a gracious style, employing more than competent architects and did not hesitate about providing roads, a reservoir and a church. They funded the reconstruction of the *Globe Inn* to turn it into a hotel, opened clay works at Decoy and took a paternal interest in the town's affairs.

History is mentally challenging because it is full of 'ifs'. What if a key decision had gone the other way? Having admitted that, however, from consideration of all the factors above it seems that in the last resort it was the farsighted, go-ahead people who turned the promising site into a boomtown. As already stated other towns had similar assets to those of Newton but on the whole they largely failed to exploit them.

The twentieth century has seen the demise of so many things that were once important to the town yet it has continued to prosper. The canals have closed, but the clay industry still flourishes. The railway workshops and goods yards have shut, but the station remains as a junction and brings business to the town. The traditional industries of wool and leather have all gone, but the modern trading estates help sustain the town. The changes in retailing have been even more dramatic than those in manufacturing. Shopping has contracted in the old town centre area and a new wave of out-of-town stores has come into being. The town's oldest institution, the market, still continues when so many other towns have lost their's. Housing development is no longer mainly the prerogative of large landowners but has continued apace. Newton ceased to be a 'Union' town but became instead the administrative centre of the Teignbridge district.

Traffic has caused the biggest problem to the town. It is true that the Victorians changed Newton nearly out of all recognition but they at least thought they were building bigger and better. In the twentieth century much that was good and of interest was needlessly destroyed to try and solve, without success, the problem of increased traffic. Some towns such as Barnstaple and Teignmouth have done just as badly, but others such as Ashburton and Totnes have saved their ancient centres by efficient bypasses. If the same had been done at Newton could it have been just as prosperous a town with exterior trading estates, but with an interesting historic core; perhaps with a big railway museum to give the town another focus in what remains very much a holiday county?

There are parts of Newton's history difficult to interpret because evidence can be seen as contradictory. Whilst it is always easy to pick holes in the efforts of others there is certainly no claim to infallibility in this work. There will inevitably be mistakes or misinterpretations that will be shown up by subsequent work or more evidence being found. However, it is hoped that what is offered is a fair and reasonable exposition of the current state of knowledge of the town. Furthermore it is also hoped there is more about Newton's past here than is gathered in any other book to-date.

There was a great deal of pleasure in collecting and collating the data. If it provides interest and enjoyment for some readers the time will have been usefully spent.

APPENDICES

These three appendices give those who like figures a diagrammatic and more detailed view of the information in Chapter 8 'A Longer Look'. They show in No. 1 how Newton's growth compared to other towns in Devon. No. 2 is about occupations and No. 3 gives the places of birth of incomers.

Appendix 1 – Devon Towns Compared

Newton Abbot was the fastest growing inland town in Devon in the 19th century. The populations of towns are given at 1801, 1841 and 1901 in the first three columns and the percentage growth in the last column. The results have been sorted so the fastest growing towns are at the top. An attempt has been made to show towns in categories; Resorts and Ports predominate at the top but significantly Newton was neither of these.

Town				1801	1841	1901	% of 1801
Torquay			R	1,933	7,853	33,890	1753
Exmouth			R	2,601	5,119	20,968	806
Paignton			R	1,575	2,501	8,385	532
Newton	U			2,126	3,456	10,738	505
Ilfracombe			R	1,838	3,679	8,557	466
Plymouth		P		44,879	95,942	201,926	450
Teignmouth		P	R	2,579	5,634	9,809	380
Exeter				20,553	42,062	66,872	325
Dawlish			R	1,424	3,132	4,584	322
Bideford	U	P		2,987	5,211	8,754	293
Barnstaple	U	P		3,748	7,902	9,698	259
Plympton	U			2,166	3,690	4,954	229
Brixham		P		3,671	5,684	8,092	220
Okehampton	U			1,500	2,194	3,223	215
Sidmouth			R	2,485	5,080	5,109	206
Holsworthy	U			1,045	1,859	2,076	199
Plymstock				1,633	2,966	3,195	196
Dartmouth		P		3,412	4,595	6,428	188
Bovey Tracey				1,431	1,823	2,658	186
Buckfastleigh				1,525	2,576	2,781	182
Bere Ferrers				1,110	2,142	1,955	176
Tavistock	U			3,420	6,272	5,841	171
Braunton				1,296	2,274	2,135	165
Tiverton	U			6,505	10,040	10,382	160
Torrington	U			2,044	3,419	3,241	159
Kingsbridge	U			1,779	2,793	2,596	146
Ottery St Mary				2,415	4,194	3,495	145
Honiton	U			2,377	3,895	3,271	138
Axminster	U			2,154	2,860	2,933	136
Totnes	U			2,503	3,049	3,116	124
Broad Clyst				1,540	2,401	1,900	123
Bampton				1,364	2,049	1,657	121

Town			1801	1841	1901	% of 1801
Colyton			1,641	2.451	1,982	121
Crediton	U		4,929	5,947	5,266	107
Hartland			1,546	2,223	1,634	106
South Molton	U		2,753	4,274	2,892	105
Chudleigh			1,786	2,415	1,820	102
Topsham		P	2,748	3,733	2,790	102
Cullompton			3,138	3,909	2,922	93
Uffculme			1,837	2,011	1,704	93
Ashburton			3,080	3,841	2,628	85
Modbury			1,813	2,048	1,330	73
Total Urban			158,889	288,749	490,187	309
Devon			340,308	532,959	662,196	195
Resort 'R' totals			14,435	32,998	91,302	633

U = *'Union' town of a*
　　group of parishes
P = *Port*
R = *Resort*

Appendix 2 – Occupations Compared

This table shows the occupation of Newtonians in 1851 and 1891. There are always difficulties with this kind of data because of varying classification and 'unknowns' such as General Labourers. Having said that, the table does provide an overall view of the work being done in the town at the two different dates. Not all callings burgeon, some even decline or cease.

Occupation	Newton 5	Newton 91	Occupation	Newton 5	Newton 91
Accountant	3	11	Dairymaid/man	7	22
Architect	1	9	Dealers	2	13
Auctioneer	3	2	Domestic servant	236	732
Baker	29	65	Draper	37	119
Banker	3	15	Dressmaker	104	247
Bargeman	4	17	Druggist	10	9
Basket maker	6	11	Dyer	2	
Blacksmith	36	61	Edge tool maker	2	3
Boot & Shoemaker	83	50	Engine cleaner	4	59
Brewer	19	15	Engine driver	4	20
Brickmaker		20	Engineer	3	6
Brushmaker	1	1	Errand boy/girl	17	100
Builder	14	35	Factory hand	2	7
Butcher	18	33	Farmer	130	37
Cabinet maker	15	19	Fellmonger	2	44
Candle maker	5		Fish dealer	5	10
Caretaker		8	Fisherman		2
Carpenter	51	122	Fish hook maker	2	
Carter	3	10	Gamekeeper		2
Cattle dealer		4	Gardener	20	92
Chimney sweep	2	5	Gas engineer		7
China & earthenware	4	6	General labourer	13	236
Ciderman		1	Glove maker	4	
Clay cutter	7	36	Grocer	40	82
Cleaner	18	37	Gunmaker	2	4
Clerk	3	29	Hairdresser	4	9
Coach	7	66	Hatter	3	1
Coal merchant	4	13	Haulier	1	11
Coffee house	3	8	Hawker	11	20
Commercial travell	3	27	Hotel	8	20
Cooper	11	4	Housekeepers	15	65
Corn/Forage		10	Illegible	10	29
Corset maker	5		Inland revenue	3	
Cutler	3		Iron founders	10	11

Occupation	Newton 5	Newton 91	Occupation	Newton 5	Newton 91
Ironmonger	10	20	Quarryman	2	6
Jockey			Rail administration	11	62
Lacemaker	5		Rail carriage side	1	23
Lamplighter		1	Rail labourers	8	54
Laundress	43	66	Rail platform staff	11	36
Lawyer	12	32	Rail track maintenance		16
Lime-burner	2	1	Rail train staff	1	31
Living on own means	80	424	Rail workshops	1	18
Lodging house keeper	2	47	Road contractor	1	4
Malster	6	9	Ropemaker	9	6
Man. Steam Packing	1		Saddler	12	14
Merchant	1	3	Sailor	5	14
Miller	4	10	Sand dealer	3	2
Milliner	30	30	Servicemen	6	24
Millwright	6	1	Shipwright		8
Miner	2	1	Shopkeeper	4	36
Mineral water		4	Stevedore		2
Minister	4	25	Stonemason	63	91
Miscellaneous	1	12	Straw bonnet makers	1	
Musician	6	7	Surgeons	2	12
Nurse	11	61	Tailors	32	58
Oilman		6	Tanners	60	143
Organ builder		2	Teachers	31	115
Ostler	11	39	Thatcher		2
Painter	23	56	Timber merchant	21	31
Photographer	2	8	Tinplate worker	12	6
Pipemaker	7	3	Turnpike gatekeeper	2	1
Plasterer	35	32	Upholsterers	3	5
Plumber	2	38	Vet	2	3
Police	2	6	Watchmaker	5	15
Porters	1	13	Wheelwright	20	17
Post	8	48	Wine & Spirit	4	1
Printer	12	38			
Publican	28	31	**Total**	**1766**	**4700**

Appendix 3 – Birthplaces 1851 and 1891

An exceedingly prosperous town such as Newton attracted incomers in considerable numbers. The birthplacees are shown from the Censuses of 1851 and 1891. The classic migration theory is the nearer the places the larger the movement. This is largely true in Newton's case but there are variations. Where Newton departs from the expected norms is that it did attract substantial number from far away.

Devon	1851	1891	Devon	1851	1891
Abbotskerswell	35	47	Combeinteignhead	18	40
Alphington	2	11	Cornworthy	2	8
Ashburton	72	115	Crediton	8	27
Ashcombe		5	Cullompton	10	5
Ashprington	4	7	Dartington	3	23
Ashton	7	9	Dartmouth	17	39
Axminster	4	6	Dawlish	33	64
Barnstaple	3	16	Dean Prior	1	7
Berry Pomeroy	15	18	Devon	92	231
Bickington	35	59	Devonport	20	43
Bideford	2	12	Dittisham	4	5
Bishopsteignton	15	30	Doddiscombeleigh	7	11
Blackawton	4	10	Drewsteignton	5	20
Bovey Tracey	72	115	Dunsford	2	8
Bow		13	Ermington	2	7
Bridford	4	6	Exbourne	2	6
Brixham	12	38	Exeter	93	172
Brixton	2	7	Exminster	2	8
Broadclyst	3	8	Exmouth	3	22
Broadhempston	23	47	Halwell	1	7
Buckfastleigh	11	21	Harberton	11	27
Buckland in the Moor	1	8	Hatherleigh	1	7
Burrington	1	8	Hemyock	3	6
Chagford	16	15	Hennock	35	75
Cheriton Bishop	7	7	High Bickington	2	5
Chittlehampton		9	Holne	5	4
Christow	5	17	Holsworthy	1	10
Chudleigh	55	80	Honiton	6	9
Chulmleigh	1	7	Ide	5	1
Churston Ferrers	5	14	Ideford	17	34
Coffinswell	9	14	Ilsington	75	148
Colyton	1	8	Ipplepen	37	64

Devon	1851	1891
Ivybridge	4	10
Kenn	8	8
Kenton	6	14
Kingsbridge	20	26
Kingskerswell	32	70
Kingsteignton	90	251
Kingswear		7
Littlehempston	1	12
Loddiswell		7
Lustleigh	9	26
Lydford	4	15
Lympstone	6	3
Mamhead	2	9
Manaton	14	22
Marldon	6	8
Modbury	7	10
Monk Okehampton		5
Morchard Bishop	2	6
Moretonhampstead	38	69
North Bovey	8	14
North Huish	1	5
North Molton	5	
North Tawton	9	13
Ogwell	35	83
Okehampton	3	10
Otterton	2	7
Ottery St Mary	5	19
Paignton	11	41
Plymouth	39	186
Plympton	3	21
Rattery	3	8
Salcombe	1	7
Sampford Courtenay	10	10
Sandford	4	15

Devon	1851	1891
Shaldon	8	48
Shobrooke	2	6
Sidmouth	2	24
Silverton	2	7
Slapton	4	7
South Brent	11	15
South Molton	9	10
South Tawton	7	26
St Marychurch	10	27
Starcross		8
Staverton	12	47
Stoke Fleming	1	5
Stoke Gabriel	2	15
Stokeinteignhead	8	27
Stokenham	2	7
Tavistock	2	24
Tedburn St Mary	1	12
Teigngrace	28	25
Teignmouth	70	112
Thorverton	5	1
Throwleigh	1	6
Tiverton	9	23
Topsham	9	9
Torbryan	46	51
Torquay	35	141
Torrington	5	13
Totnes	33	94
Trusham	3	10
Ugborough	2	8
Widecombe	16	33
Winkleigh	1	9
Woodlands	5	7
Total Devon	**1696**	**3827**

Outside Devon	1851	1891
Argentine	1	
Ascension	1	
At sea	1	
Australia	9	
Bedfordshire		4
Berkshire	5	16
Bermuda		4
Brecon	1	
Bristol	13	59
British Guiana		5

Outside Devon	1851	1891
Buckinghamshire	1	17
Caernarvonshire		2
Cambridge		8
Canada	1	6
Cardigan	1	
Carmarthenshire		3
Ceylon	2	
Channel Isles	6	19
Cheshire	1	18
Chile	3	

Outside Devon	1851	1891	Outside Devon	1851	1891
Cornwall	35	347	Newfoundland	3	5
Cumberland	2	2	Norfolk	5	13
Derbyshire	5		Northampton		16
Dorset	15	43	Northumberland	5	4
Durham	4	5	Nottinghamshire		11
East Indies		3	Oxfordshire	1	21
Essex	4	20	Pembrokeshire	1	11
Europe	5	20	Peru	2	
Gibraltar	2		Rutland	1	
Glamorganshire	1	12	Scotland	20	31
Gloucestershire	14	47	Shropshire	2	6
Hampshire	12	57	Singapore	1	
Herefordshire	4	13	Somerset	52	143
Hertfordshire	3	9	South Africa		12
Huntingdonshire	1	5	St Helena	1	
Illegible	2	12	Staffordshire	1	22
India	2	37	Suffolk	1	21
Ireland	18	70	Surrey	5	18
Isle of Man	2		Sussex	4	16
Kent	3	45	USA	10	
Labrador	4		Wales	11	
Lancashire	5	43	Warwickshire	4	25
Leicestershire	2	17	West Indies	3	1
Lincolnshire	2	14	Westmoreland		2
London	45	224	Wiltshire	9	47
Middlesex	12	21	Worcestershire	3	37
Monmouth	2	20	Yorkshire	3	34
Not known	5	7			
New Swindon	8	33	**Total outside Devon**	**357**	**1842**

NOTES

i. Stirling (1830) 63
ii. Stirling (1830) 173
iii. Hoskins (1954) 567
iv. Rhodes (c.1904) 18
v. *Morris's 1870* 527
vi. Jones (1986) 8
vii. EFP, 19 March 1873, 3C
viii. Hoskins, *Devon*, 101

1. John Allan & Simon Timms, *Treasures of Ancient Devon* (Tiverton, 1994) 5
2. *The Times* 4 July 2002 3
3. Robin Stanes, *A History of Devon* (Chichester, 1986) 18
4. Edward J. Bath, *Newton Abbot Roundabout* (1954) unpaginated ch. 2
5. *TDA* 15 376/7
6. *Archaeology of the Devon Landscape* (ADL) (DCC, 1980) 52
7. *PDAS* Silvester No 38 17
8. Roger Kain & William Ravenhill (eds), *Historical Atlas of South-West England* (Exeter, 1999) 70
9. *PDAS* Hearne & Seager-Smith No 53 109
10. *ADL* 53
11. *PDAS* Grant No 53 112
12. Bridget Cherry & Nikolaus Pevsner, *The Buildings of England*, 2nd Edition (1997) 465
13. *ADL*, 53
14. Allan & Timms, *Treasures*, 20
15. NAHR Milber
16. Allan & Timms, *Treasures*, 18–19, 16.
17. *PDAS* Miles No 35 44
18. W.G. Hoskins, *Two Thousand Years in Exeter* (Chichester, 1979) 7
19. *ADL* 53
20. *PDAS* Hearne & Seager-Smith No 53 119
21. *ADL* 60
22. *PDAS* Weddell No 45 92
23. Hoskins, *Two Thousand*, 9
24. *TDA* Vol. 86 227
25. *PDAS* Weddell No 43 78
26. Hoskins, *Devon* 45
27. Cherry & Pevsner, *Buildings*, 349
28. *Concise Oxford Dictionary of English Place Names* (1960) xxiii
29. Kenneth Cameron, *English Place Names* (London, 1969) 38
30. *PDAS* Weddell No 45 75

31. Jeremy Haslam, *Anglo-Saxon Towns in southern England* (Chichester, 1984) 277
32. Haslam, *Anglo-Saxon*, 279
33. *PDAS* Weddell No 45 81
34. Hoskins, *Devon* 53
35. Kain & Ravenhill, *Historical Atlas*, 99
36. Bath, *Newton Abbot*, ch. 2
37. Stanes, *A History*, 37
38. *TDA* Vol. 85 137
39. John Morris (ed.), *Domesday Book Devon* (Chichester, 1985) ref. 16.163
40. Morris, *Domesday*, ref. 16.
41. *TDA* Vol. 97 106
42. *ADL* 99
43. Deryck Seymour (ed.), *The Exchequer Cartulary of Torre Abbey* (Torquay, 2000), 1
44. Bradley (National Trust, 1989) 9
45. Dates used are from Beresford *New Towns of the Middle Ages.*
46. *PDAS* Weddell Vol. 43 77
47. Maurice Beresford, *New Towns of the Middle Ages* (London, 1967) 423
48. Kain & Ravenhill, *Historical Atlas*, 400
49. Jones, *A book*, 13
50. Bradley, 10
51. A. J. Rhodes, *Newton Abbot its History & Development* (Newton Abbot c.1904) 83, 103
52. Trixie M. Lamb, *The Ancient Tower of St Leonard Newton Abbot, S. Devon, 1220–1973* (Newton Abbot, 1973) 1
53. *PDAS* Weddell No 43 78
54. DCRS Vol. 14 2
55. Kain & Ravenhill, *Historical Atlas*, 404–5
56. Bath, *Newton Abbot*, ch. 4
57. Cherry & Pevsner, *Buildings*, 588
58. Bradley, 10–11
59. *TDA* Vol. 81 234
60. R Harris, *King's Teignton* (nd) 15
61. Cherry & Pevsner, Buildings, 584
62. International Journal of Nautical Archaeology (2001) 30.2: 266–272
63. Maryanne Kowaleski, *Local markets and regional trade in medieval Exeter* (Cambridge, 1995) 265
64. Kain & Ravenhill, *Historical Atlas*, 328
65. Bradley, 12
66. Rhodes, *Newton Abbot*, 41
67. *TDA* Vol.129 160/1
68. *TDA* Vol. 34 208
69. Bath, *Newton Abbot*, ch. 4

70. *DCN & Q* Vol. 18 208/9
71. T.L. Stoate, *Devon Lay Subsidy Roll for 1524–1527* (Almondsbury, 1986) 200/1, 227
72. Jones, *A book*, 115
73. Bath, *Newton Abbot*, ch. 4
74. DRO 1638F/Z31
75. Rhodes, *Newton Abbot*, 114
76. Seymour, *Exchequer Cartulary*, 21
77. Jones, *A book*, 15
78. Seymour, *Exchequer Cartulary*, 21
79. *PDAS* Weddell No 43 78
80. T.L. Stoate & A.J. Howard, *The Devon Muster Roll for 1569* (Bristol, 1977) 234/5
81. Anthony Crockett, *Chudleigh a Chronicle* (Tiverton, 1985) 25
82. Kain & Ravenhill, *Historical Atlas*, 379
83. Mike Duffy *et al* (eds), *The New Maritime History* (London, 1992), I, 139–43, 163–70; Rhodes, *Newton Abbot*, 73; *TDA* Vols 66 363, 115 19–35
84. Bath, *Newton Abbot*, ch. 5
85. Mary O'Hagan, *A History of Forde House* (Newton Abbot, 1990) 14
86. Rhodes, *Newton Abbot*, 49
87. DCRS new series Vol. 33 34–5
88. DCRS new series Vol. 33 38
89. Jones, *A book*, 17
90. R.N. Worth, *A History of Devonshire* (London, 1886) 307
91. Jones, *A book*, 17
92. Bath, *Newton Abbot*, ch. 5
93. *TDA* Vol. 121 167
94. DCRS new series Vol. 38 xxx
95. DCRS new series Vol. 38 xxxvii
96. DCRS new series Vol. 38 xxxv, xxvii
97. Jones, *A book*, 116
98. DCRS new series Vol. 38 xxxv footnote
99. O'Hagan, *A History*, 39
100. O'Hagan, *A History*, 42
101. Mark Stoyle, *Loyalty and Locality* (Exeter, 1994) 176
102. Stoyle, *Loyalty*, 83
103. O'Hagan, *A History*, 44, 45
104. Joshua Sprigg, *English Recovery* (Oxford, 1845) 163, 176
105. Sprigg, *English Recovery*, 186
106. Judy Chard, *Along the Lemon* (Bodmin, 1980) 50
107. A.G. Matthews, *Calamy revised; being a revision of Edmund Calamy's Account of the Ministers and others ejected and silenced 1660 –2* (Oxford, 1934) 552
108. Jones, *A book*, 108
109. Calamy, *Nonconformist's* 53
110. *TDA* Vol. 16 491
111. Matthews, *Calamy revised*, 552
112. Roberts, *Recovery*, xvi
113. O'Hagan, *A History*, 46
114. O'Hagan, *A History*, 57
115. Peter Kay, *Exeter–Newton Abbot, A Railway History* (Sheffield, 1993) 2; *TDA* Vol. 28 197–215
116. DCRS new series Vol. 11 inventory 164
117. Bath, *Newton Abbot*, ch. 6
118. Bath, *Newton Abbot*, ch. 7
119. *TDA* Vol. 5 235/6
120. T.L. Stoate, *Devon Hearth tax 1674* (1982) 195, 221s
121. DRO Ilsington Overseers 122A/PO 410, 411, 414, 417
122. Anne Whiteman, *The Compton Census of 1676, a critical edition* (Oxford, 1986) xxiii
123. Whiteman, *Compton Census*, 281, 287/8
124. Jones, *A book*, 19
125. Rhodes, *Newton Abbot*, 51
126. Jones, *A book*, 56
127. Jones, *A book*, 56–7
128. Stephen Roberts, *Recovery and Restoration in an English County* (Exeter, 1985) 191
129. Rhodes, *Newton Abbot*, 69
130. Bath, *Newton Abbot*, ch. 7
131. *Universal British Directory c.*1794 App. 145
132. George Lipscomb, *A Journey into Cornwall* (London, 1799) 342
133. John Pike, *Torbay's Heritage Torquay* (Torquay, 1993) 14
134. *TDA* Vol. 122 48/9
135. *TDA* Vol. 122 67
136. *TDA* Vol. 57
137. *TDA* Vol. 109 59
138. Harry Unsworth, *A new Look at old Newton Abbot* (Coffinswell, 1993) 70/1
139. *TDA* Vol. 130 114
140. *TDA* Vol. 130 117
141. *White's* 1878 567
142. *Gentleman's Magazine* 1749 411/2; *Herald Express* 21 January 2003 24; Jones, *A book*, 76–79
143. DCRS Vol. 23 152
144. DCRS Vol. 23. 100–103
145. Chope, *Early Tours*, 148
146. Ian Maxted, *Bibliography of British Newspapers, Cornwall and Devon* (British Library, 1991) 158–9
147. *PDAS* Miles No 35 p
148. *TDA* Vol. 87 194/5
149. Helen Harris, *The Haytor Granite Tramway and Stover Canal* (Newton Abbot, 1994) 10
150. L.T.C. Rolt, *The Potter's Field* (Newton Abbot, 1974) 27
151. Harris, *King's* 24
152. Derek Beavis, *Britain in Old Photographs Newton Abbot* (Stroud, 2000) 61
153. Jones, *A book*, 37–44; *The Vicarian* 1928
154. *TDA* Vol. 55 86
155. Duffy, *New Maritime*, 167
156. J.K. Bellchambers, *Devonshire Clockmakers* (Torquay, 1962) 38
157. Helen Harris, *Devon's Century of Change* (Newton Abbot, 1998) 39
158. *EFP* 30 April 1773 2d
159. Ian Maxted, *Books with Devon Imprints* (British Book Trade History No 6, 1989) 115, 125, 127
160. Ian Maxted, *From Script to hypertext* (Exeter, 1999) 18
161. Greener, dissertation (2000) 50
162. O'Hagan, *A History*, 59
163. Jones, *A book*, 15
164. Jeremiah Milles, *Devonshire Survey* (Bodleian MSS, 1762).
165. Harris, *The Haytor*, 11
166. *EFP* 14 December 1844 2f; *Herald Express* 1 July 2003 32; Jones, *A book*, 62–4
167. Robert Bovett *Historical Notes on Devon Schools* (DCC,1989) 222
168. DCN &Q Vol. 14 259/60
169. Alan Everitt (ed.), *Perspectives of English Urban History* (London, 1973) 107
170. Everitt, *Perspectives,* 110

171. Bath, *Newton Abbot*, ch. 8
172. Unsworth, *A new Look*, 7
173. *EFP* 15 December 1791 2c
174. *EFP* 9 October 1794 3c
175. Todd Gray & Margery Rowe, *Travels in Georgian Devon* (Tiverton, 1998) Vol. 2 160
176. Gray & Rowe, *Travels* (1999) Vol. 3 107
177. Gray & Rowe, *Travels*, Vol. 3 142
178. Gray & Rowe, *Travels*, Vol. 1 xviii
179. Crockett, *Chudleigh* (1985) 90
180. Stanes, *A History*, 101
181. *EFP* 13 August 1795 3c
182. Richard Warner, *A Walk Through Some of the Western Counties of England* (Bath, 1800) 182
183. *The New British Traveller* Vol. 2 159
184. *Robinson's Directory c.*1838 160
185. *TDA* Vol. 129 160
186. Jones, *A book*, 81
187. DH no. 45 12
188. Maxted, *From Script*, 3
189. Ian Maxted, *Newspaper readership in south west England* (1996) 4
190. Harris, *The Haytor*, 33
191. Sellman, *Illustrations*, 42
192. Jones, *A book*, 56
193. Rhodes, *Newton Abbot*, 77
194. *EFP* 22 February 1838 2f
195. *WT* 28 January 1843 3c
196. *EFP* 20 December 1804 3d
197. *EFP* 29 May 1800 2c
198. DRO 335ME/EZ
199. Crockett, *Chudleigh*, 91
200. *EFP* 30 July 1807 1a
201. *EFP* 2 August 1810 1b
202. C.G. Scott, Series History of Photography 1988 v. 15: 1
203. Harris (2001) 3
204. Helen Harris, *Devon's Railways* (Launceston, 2001) 3
205. *EFP* 23 December 1841 2e
206. *EFP* 22 July 1841 3e
207. *EFP* 28 October 1841 1b
208. *TDA* Vol. 80 226/7
209. *EFP 18 May 1842 2c*
210. *EFP* 31 August 1826 1d
211. *EFP* 5 March 1840 3cd
212. *EFP* 4 March 1841 3c
213. Jones, *A book*, 57
214. Bath, *Newton Abbot*, ch. 7
215. Simon Dell, *Policing the Peninsula* (Newton Abbot, 2000) 10
216. *EFP* 28 September 1844 3a
217. Hoskins, *Devon* 442
218. DRO Wolborough Vestry minutes 17 December 1844
219. Rhodes, *Newton Abbot*, 197
220. *EFP* 20 July 1848 3c
221. *Woolmer's Gazette* 3 June 1848 8c
222. Unsworth, *A new Look*, 21
223. *EFP* 29 March 1821 4d
224. Rhodes, *Newton Abbot*, 183
225. DRO 924B/E1/18
226. Bath, *Newton Abbot*, ch. 6
227. Jones, *A book*, 118/9
228. Rhodes, *Newton Abbot*, 185
229. Kain & Ravenhill, *Historical Atlas*, 182
230. *White's Devon* 1950 457
231. Rhodes, *Newton Abbot*, 73

232. Rhodes, *Newton Abbot*, 92
233. Lamb, *Ancient*, 11
234. *EFP* 6 March 1834 2f
235. In a letter written by Keats to B.R. Haydon
236. Kay, *Exeter*, 1
237. Kay, *Exeter*, 1/2
238. *EFP* 18 May 1844 2c
239. *EFP* 1 August 1844 3e
240. *EFP* 12 June 1845
241. *WT* 6 June 1846 6b
242. Kay, *Exeter*, 15/16
243. Unsworth, *A new Look*, 16
244. R.H. Gregory, *The South Devon Railway* (1982) 8
245. Kay, *Exeter*, 16
246. *Woolmer's Gazette* 2 January 1847 3e
247. *EFP* 7 January 1847 2b
248. *E & SDA* 23 April 1847 5c
249. *EFP* 4 February 1847 1c
250. *EFP* 13 May 1847 2f
251. *WT* 24 July 1847 5d
252. *WT* 5 August 1847 5d
253. Kay, *Exeter*, 28
254. *WT* 12 August 1848 6b
255. J G Avery, *The Cholera Years* (Southampton, 2002) 29
256. *WT* 20 December 1849 8d.
257. *WT* 13 November 1847 4e
258. Cecil Torr, *Small Talk at Wreyland* (Cambridge, 1921) 14
259. E.T. Mac Dermott, *History of the Great Western Railway* (Paddington, 1931) 226
260. Mac Dermott, *History*, 240
261. *Western Times* 3 November 1848 7c
262. *Torquay & Tor Directory* 14 August 1846 8c
263. *Torquay & Tor Directory* 24 November 1847 8b
264. Les Berry & Gerald Gosling, *Around Newton Abbot* (Bath, 1994) 15
265. Bath, *Newton Abbot* ch. 8
266. Beatrix F. Cresswell, Newton Abbot & its neighbouring villages including Chudleigh (London, 1908) 31/2
267. *Woolmer's Exeter & Plymouth Gazette* 1839
268. *Woolmer's Gazette* 5 August 1848 5d
269. *Western Gazette 6 May 1843 3c*
270. *Western Gazette* 29 July 1843 3c
271. Rhodes, *Newton Abbot*, 209
272. *EFP* 9 September 1847 3e
273. *EFP* 28 August 1828 3a
274. *WT* 9 May 1846 5a
275. *WT* 7 February 1846 5b
276. *WT* 21 February 1846 5c
277. *EFP* 29 July 1847 3e
278. *Murray's Handbook For Devon & Cornwall* (London, 1851) 35
279. *Billing's Directory* 1857 517
280. *Morris's* 1870 526
281. *Murray's Handbook*, 1879 84
282. James John Hussey, *On the Box Seat* (London, 1886) 275
283. *EFP* 11 November 1852 4b
284. *EFP* 16 October 1851 4b
285. DRO Wolborough Vestry minutes 6 October 1853
286. Rhodes, *Newton Abbot*, 80
287. DRO Wolborough Vestry minutes 24 June 1852
288. *EFP* 25 August 1853 4b
289. Rhodes, *Newton Abbot*, 78/9

290. *EFP* 17 April 1856 7f
291. *EFP* 20 October 1853 3e
292. *EFP* 10 July 1861 7d
293. *EFP* 14 October 1863 7d
294. *EFP* 15 April 1885 7f
295. *EFP* 25 December 1895 3c
296. *EFP* 13 May 1858 7f
297. *EFP* 28 July 1859 7e
298. DRO Wolborough Vestry minutes 24 May 1860
299. *EFP* 25 November 1863 7d
300. DRO Minutes Wolborough Local Board 1864/74 1/2
301. DRO Minutes Wolborough Local Board 1864/7 43
302. DRO Minutes Wolborough Local Board 1864/74 51
303. DRO Minutes Wolborough Local Board 1864/74 7, 12/20, 33
304. DRO Minutes Wolborough Local Board 1864/74 106/7
305. DRO Minutes Wolborough Local Board 1864/74 124
306. DRO Minutes Wolborough Local Board 1874/84 218
307. Rhodes, *Newton Abbot,* 176
308. DRO Minutes Wolborough Local Board 1884/92 303
309. Avery, *Cholera,* 70
310. Harris, *King's,* 28
311. *DWT* 28 October 1898 7a
312. Bath, *Newton Abbot* ch. 1
313. Rhodes, *Newton Abbot,* 199–200
314. Beavis, *Britain,* 8
315. *EFP* 26 January 1895 6c
316. *EFP* 25 February 1893 2c
317. Derek Beavis, *Newton Abbot, The Story of the Town's past* (Buckingham, 1985) 82
318. DRO Minutes Wolborough Local Board 1874/84 205
319. DRO Minutes Wolborough Local Board 1874/84 64
320. DRO Minutes Wolborough Local Board 1874/84. 223/4
321. DRO Minutes Wolborough Local Board 1864/74 23
322. DRO Wolborough Vestry minutes 19 October 1866
323. DRO Minutes Wolborough Local Board 1864/74 167, 175
324. DRO Minutes Wolborough Local Board 1864/74 337
325. *EFP* 27 December 1871
326. *EFP* 13 December 1876 7f
327. *EFP* 5 September 1866 1b
328. Rhodes, *Newton Abbot,* 171
329. DRO Minutes Wolborough Local Board 1864/74 170
330. DRO Minutes Wolborough Local Board 1864/74 253
331. *EFP* 12 March 1873 7d
332. *EFP* 19 January 1876
333. *EFP* 21 January 1880 7f
334. DRO Minutes Wolborough Local Board 1874/84 100
335. *EFP* 14 March 1877 7e
336. Rhodes, *Newton Abbot,* 79
337. *EFP* 2 March 1887 3e
338. *EFP* 14 April 1888 7f
339. DRO Minutes Wolborough Local Board 1864/74 47
340. DRO Minutes Wolborough Local Board 1864/74 214
341. DRO Minutes Wolborough Local Board 1884/92 195
342. DRO Minutes Wolborough Local Board 1874/84 357
343. *EFP* 12 May 1888 8e
344. DRO Minutes Wolborough Local Board 1884/92 265
345. Rhodes, *Newton Abbot,* 177
346. DRO Minutes Wolborough Local Board 1864/74 60, 67
347. DRO Minutes Wolborough Local Board 1864/74 141
348. DRO Minutes Wolborough Local Board 1864/74 231
349. *EFP* 31 March 1869 7f
350. *EFP* 5 February 1873 3f
351. Jones, *A book,* 116/7
352. DRO Minutes Wolborough Local Board 1874/84 22
353. DRO Minutes Wolborough Local Board 1884/92 291
354. *DWT* 17 February 1899 7d
355. *DWT* 3 March 1899 7a
356. *EFP* 23 April 1857 4d
357. Jones, *A book,* 75; MDA 5 September 1973 4
358. *EFP* 16 August 1894 2d
359. Rhodes, *Newton Abbot,* 175
360. *EFP* 13 June 1896 8b
361. *EFP* 25 July 3e
362. *DWT* 21 April 1899 7d
363. DRO Newton Abbot Minutes 1897–1901 276
364. DRO Newton Abbot Minutes 1897–1901 402
365. Rhodes, *Newton Abbot,* 118
366. *E & SDA* March 1905
367. *EFP* 24 February. 1853 4d
368. Beavis, *Britain,* 59
369. *EFP* 2 February 1881 7e
370. *EFP* 20 November 1861 7f
371. *EFP* 11 May 1870 7e
372. *EFP* 16 February 1878 3c
373. *EFP* 20 March 1878 7f
374. *EFP* 14 August 1878 7d
375. *EFP* 5 July 1882 7e
376. *EFP* 3 January 1883 7e
377. *EFP* 25 July 1883 7f
378. *EFP* 26 September 1883 7d
379. *EFP* 17 May 1855 8b
380. *EFP* 1 May 1856
381. *EFP* 28 February 1877 7f
382. *EFP* 5 September 1877 7f
383. *EFP* 28 November 1877 7f
384. *EFP* 6 August 1883 7e
385. *EFP* 17 December 1887 3b
386. Jones, *A book,* 119
387. *WMN* 3 December 1952
388. LC *Western Morning News* 15/10/63
389. *EFP* 16 August 1894 2d
390. *EFP* 9 August 1894 4g
391. *EFP* 4 October 1894 5g
392. *EFP* 11 May 1985 6c
393. *EFP* 10 December 1892 2c
394. *EFP* 26 January 1895 7d
395. *EFP* 23 March 1985 6b
396. *EFP* 27 April 1895 6c
397. *EFP* 22 February 1896 7d
398. *EFP* 21 March 1896 3ed
399. *EFP* 4 April 1896 3d
400. *EFP* 11 April 1896 6d
401. *EFP* 7 November 1896 7b
402. *EFP* 12 December 1896 3e
403. *EFP* 19 June 2d
404. *DWT* 2 June 1899 7b
405. *EFP* 22 November 1855 7e.
406. *MDA* 22 August 1970
407. DRO Minutes Wolborough Local Board 1864/74 204
408. *Morris's* 1870 126
409. *EFP* 24 June 1874 7e
410. Rhodes, *Newton Abbot,* 193
411. *EFP* 17 August 1881 7e
412. *EFP* 4 May 1870 3d
413. *EFP* 14 August 1872 7d

414. *EFP* 1 January 1873 7f
415. *EFP* 22 May 1878 7e
416. *EFP* 25 May 1881 7e
417. *EFP* 5 January 1881 7e
418. Rhodes, *Newton Abbot*, 196
419. *EFP* 11 May 1889 6d
420. *EFP* 30 September 1893 7b
421. *EFP* 19 October 1895 3c
422. *EFP* 22 March 1865 3f
423. *EFP* 20 May 1852 4b
424. *EFP* 24 March 1853 4a
425. *EFP* 23 June 1853 3e
426. *EFP* 11 August 1853 3e
427. *EFP* 9 March 1854 4b
428. *EFP* 25 September 1856 7f
429. *EFP* 28 October 1858 5c
430. *EFP* 28 April 1859 7f
431. EFP 28 May 1862 7c
432. *EFP* 6 August 1862 7f
433. *EFP* 6 May 1863 7e
434. *EFP* 16 September 1863 7c
435. *EFP* 20 September 1865 7f
436. *EFP* 6 November 1867 3f
437. *EFP* 26 January 1870 3f
438. DRO Minutes Wolborough Local Board 1864/74 380
439. *EFP* 3 February 1875 7e
440. *EFP* 5 April 1876 7f
441. *EFP* 24 May 1876 7c
442. *EFP* 25 July 1877 7f
443. *EFP* 19 February 1879 7e
444. *EFP* 2 January 1884 7f
445. *EFP* 13 January 1886 7f
446. *EFP* 30 June 1888 3d
447. Unsworth, *A new Look*, 62
448. *EFP* 28 April 1891 4f
449. *EFP* 6 August 1892 6c
450. *EFP* 26 November 1892 2d
451. *EFP* 26 July 1894 5e
452. *EFP* 6 July 1895 6b
453. *EFP* 13 July 1895 6c
454. *EFP* 19 October 1895 3c
455. *EFP* 2 May 1896 8c
456. *EFP* 5 December 1896 5d
457. *EFP* 6 February 1897 2c
458. *EFP* 27 November 1897 8d
459. *DWT* 1 December 1899 8d
460. *EFP* 30 December 1852 4b
461. Hazel Harvey, *Exeter Past* (Chichester, 1996) 63
462. Rhodes, *Newton Abbot*, 126
463. *EFP* 12 May 1859 7f
464. *EFP* 8 February 1860 7c
465. *EFP* 12 June 1861 7f
466. *EFP* 2 October 1861 7f
467. *EFP* 5 September 1866 7b
468. *EFP* 21 November 1877 7e
469. Rhodes, *Newton Abbot*, 172
470. Sellman, *Illustrations*, 475
471. *EFP* 5 August 1885 7f
472. *EFP* 28 January 1885 7f
473. *EFP* 25 May 1889 6d
474. *EFP* 14 June 1890 5a
475. *EFP* 20 June 1891 4e
476. DRO 1508/M SS3/Wharfs etc; *EFP* 5 June 1851 8c
477. *EFP* 20 July 1850 3c
478. *EFP* 30 June 1859 7e
479. *EFP* 9 September 1858 5d
480. *EFP* 11 November 1858 5d
481. Cherry & Pevsner, *Buildings*, 584
482. *EFP* 23 October 1861 sup 2f
483. *EFP* 9. August 1871 3f
484. *EFP* 27 August 1862 7e
485. DRO Wolborough Vestry minutes 12 April. 1860
486. *EFP* 7 March 1860 7f
487. *EFP* 22 May 1867 7d
488. Beavis, *Newton*, 45
489. *EFP* 5 December 1883 7e
490. *EFP* 4 February 1893 2e
491. *DWT* 8 July 1898 7c
492. *EFP* 29 May 1878 7f
493. *EFP* 6 June 1896 7c
494. *DWT* 28 April 1899 8f
495. *EFP* 2 February 1854 3d
496. *EFP* 8 May 1856 7f
497. *EFP* 2 February 1870 3d
498. *EFP* 29 December 1886 8d
499. *TDA* Vol. 116 72
500. *EFP* 6 November 1861 7e
501. *TDA* Vol. 116 67
502. *EFP* 16 April 1892 6c
503. *EFP* 15 June 1854 4c
504. *EFP* 3 July 1861 7f
505. *EFP* 21 August 1856 7f
506. *EFP* 21 December 1854 5f
507. *EFP* 12 September 1855 8c
508. Kain & Ravenhill, *Historical Atlas*, 244
509. Chard, *Along*, 56
510. Jones, *A book*, 35
511. Unsworth, *A new Look*, 6
512. *EFP* 22 November 1876 1c
513. *EFP* 3 October 1877 7f
514. *EFP* 13 September 1882 7e
515. *Herald Express* 18 March 2003 24; History *Today* May 2002 3/4
516. *EFP* 9 June 1859 7e
517. *EFP* 25 March 1874 7f
518. *EFP* 5 August 1874 7f
519. Rhodes, *Newton Abbot*, 172
520. DRO Minutes Wolborough Local Board 1874/84 202
521. *EFP* 9 November 1881 7f
522. *EFP* 18 June 7c
523. *EFP* 17 December 1892 7g
524. Bath, *Newton Abbot*, ch. 8
525. *EFP* 1 May 1851 8c
526. *EFP* 21 August 1851 8c
527. *EFP* 28 August 1851 8c
528. *EFP* 11 September 1851 8c
529. James Walvin, *Beside the Seaside* (London, 1978) 37
530. *EFP* 26 August 1852 3f
531. *EFP* 20 January 1853 4b
532. *EFP* 21 February 1856 7f
533. *EFP* 10 June 1858 7f
534. *EFP* 25 July 1850 8d
535. *EFP* 13 May 1874 7f
536. *EFP* 19 May 8c
537. *EFP* 26 May 1875 7e
538. *EFP* 21 May 1887 5c
539. *DWT* 20 May 1898 2abc
540. *EFP* 8 June 1870 7f
541. *EFP* 20 August 1873 7f
542. DRO Minutes Wolborough Local Board 1874/84 132

543. *EFP* 4 August 1875 7d
544. *EFP* 2 February 1876 7f
545. DRO Minutes Wolborough Local Board 1874/84 224
546. *EFP* 2 March 1881 7f
547. *EFP* 1 December 1880 7f
548. *EFP* 20 September 1882 7d
549. *EFP* 13 December 1882 7f
550. *EFP* 25 June 1887 6f
551. Rhodes, *Newton Abbot,* 209
552. *EFP* 14 February 1883 7d
553. *EFP* 7 March 1883 7f
554. *EFP* 23 May 1883 7f
555. *EFP* 9 January 1892
556. *EFP* 24 December 1892 2c
557. *EFP* 25 March 1893 7b
558. *EFP* 2 December 1893 7b
559. *EFP* 26 June 1986 7d
560. Rhodes, *Newton Abbot,* 211
561. *EFP* 21 January 1888 8d
562. *EFP* 27 October 1888 6e
563. *EFP* 22 December 1888 3a
564. *E & SDA* 9 May 1891 8g
565. *DWT* 15 July 1898 7b
566. DRO *Newton Abbot Minutes 1897–1901.* 183
567. *DWT* 1 September 1899 7a
568. *DWT* 22 September 1899 8c
569. *DWT* 29 December 1899 8c
570. *EFP* 5 May 1875 7e
571. Richard Hall, *Lovers on the Nile* (London 1980); Audrey Hexter, personal communication; *E&SDA* 8 June 1901
572. Hall, *Lovers; Herald Express* 7 January 2003 21; Jones, *A Book,* 63; *Weekender* 5 April 2001 10
573. *EFP* 9. August 1871 7e
574. *WMN* 5 June 1871
575. *EFP* 31 January 1872 7e
576. *EFP* 19 March 1873 3c
577. *EFP* 6 May 1874 7f
578. *EFP* 17 September 1884 7f
579. EFP 3 September 1887 8d
580. *EFP* 5 February 1892 5b
581. *EFP* 10 September 1892 6d
582. Mary M Davenport, *Newton Abbot in old picture postcards* (Zaltbommel 1984) No 46
583. *DWT* 2 September 1898 7a
584. *Kelly's* 1883 293
585. *White's* 1890 608
586. Vile & Williams, *Newton Abbot as a tourist centre and Guide to South Devon* (Newton Abbot, 1898) 1
587. For further reading see *Devon Historian* No 65 'Towns in nineteenth century Devon.
588. Rhodes, *Newton Abbot,* 19
589. Kay, verbal information
590. *EFP* 27 February 1878 7f
591. *Devonia* Vol II 13/4
592. *E & SDA* 29 March 1901
593. Unsworth, *A new Look,* 22
594. Jones, *A book,* 123–8
595. *E & SDA* 16 November 1901; Copies of *Little Maid Marion, Robin of Sun Court,* are held in WSL.
596. *E & SDA* May 1904
597. *E & SDA* June 1904
598. Jones, *A book,* 59
599. *WMN* 15 September 1938
600. *E & SDA* October 1907
601. *MDT* 12 July 1924
602. Martin Pugh, *The Pankhursts* (Harmondsworth, 2001) 171
603. *E & SDA* January 1908
604. Berry & Gosling, *Around,* 14
605. *E & SDA* January 1909
606. *E & SDA* March 1909
607. *E & SDA* May 1909
608. Rhodes, *Newton Abbot,* 179–80
609. *E & SDA* January 26, February 2, 1901
610. *E & SDA* 26 June 1902
611. *E & SDA* 15 June 1901
612. Rolt, *The Potter's,* 148
613. *MDA* May 1962
614. Roger Grimley, *Motor Buses of Newton Abbot and District* (*c.*1994) 3
615. Jones, *A Book,* 74; Rhodes, *Newton Abbot,* 24; *Advertiser/Post* 23 March 2001 19
616. *E & SDA* 19 January 1901
617. *E & SDA* May 1908
618. *E & SDA* July 1906
619. *MDA* November 1909
620. *MDA* June 1913
621. *MDA* March 1948
622. NAHR Clay Industry
623. *E & SDA* 9 March 1901
624. *MDA* April 1911
625. *E &SDA* 7 June 1902
626. *E & SDA* 5 September 1903
627. *MDA* December 1912
628. *E & SDA* 29 August 1903
629. *E & SDA* December 1907
630. *E & SDA* July 1909
631. *MDA* June 1912
632. *MDA* August 1913
633. DRO 867B/S9
634. Jones, *A book,* 115
635. *MDA* November 1912
636. *MDA* August 1916
637. *MDA* January 1914
638. Rowena Forster, *Knowles Hill School* (nd) 8
639. Bovett, *Historical Notes,* 222
640. *MDA* October 1913
641. *MDA* February 1915
642. *MDA* March, April 1915
643. *MDA* June 1918
644. *MDA* February 1911
645. Rhodes, *Newton Abbot,* 228
646. *Memories of St Michael's 1918–1971* (*1995*)
647. Grimley, *Motor,* 39
648. *E & E* 7 April 1981
649. Cherry & Pevsner, *Buildings,* 586
650. *MDA* May 1914
651. *MDA* January 1920
652. *MDA* September 1912
653. *E & SDA* 5 January 1901
654. *E & SDA* 4 May 1901
655. *E & SDA* 1 February 1902
656. *E & SDA* 1 August 1903
657. *E & SDA* 28 November 1903
658. *E & SDA* September 1905
659. *E & SDA* October 1906
660. *E & SDA* September 1908
661. *MDT* 2 September 1924
662. *E & SDA* March & April 1908

663. *E & SDA* January 1909
664. *E & SDA* October 1908
665. *E & SDA* June 1909
666. *MDA* May 1911
667. *MDT* 20 May 1924
668. *MDT* 22 May 1934
669. *MDA* December 1913
670. *E & SDA* 1 March 1902
671. *E & SDA* 4 July 1903
672. *E & SDA* January 1904
673. Jones, *A book*, 68
674. Crispin Gill (ed.), *Dartmoor; a New Study* (Newton Abbot, 1977) 239
675. Bath, *Newton Abbot*, ch. 1
676. *E & SDA* 11 October 1902
677. *E & SDA* 1 February 1902
678. *E & SDA* February 1906
679. Hearder's Almanack 1906 15
680. *E & SDA* May 1907
681. *E & SDA* August 1907
682. *E & SDA* April 1909
683. Alan Heather, *Oliver Heaviside FRS,* (Torbay Civic Society 2002/3)
684. *MDA* April 1911
685. *MDA* February 1913
686. *MDA* April 1913
687. *MDA* November 1913
688. DRO R2361A/(5/4) Z7
689. Gerald Wasley, *Devon in the Great War* (Tiverton, 2000) 41
690. Wasley, *Devon in*, 125
691. *MDA* 1 August 1914
692. *MDA* 8 August 1914
693. *MDA* 15 August 1914
694. *MDA* December 1914
695. *MDA* January 1915
696. *MDA* 21 March 1973
697. Florence Farnborough's diaries are held by the Imperial War Museum ref. 87/18/1
698. *MDA* March 1916
699. *MDA* May 1916
700. *MDA* December 1970
701. *MDA* August 1916
702. *MDA* September 1916
703. *MDA* November 1916
704. *MDA* April 1917
705. *MDA* May 1917
706. *MDA* June 1917
707. *MDA* July 1917
708. *MDA* October 1917
709. *MDA* November 1917
710. *MDA* February 1918
711. *MDA* April 1918
712. *MDA* September 1918
713. *MDA* supplement 26 October 1918
714. *MDA* November 1918
715. *MDA* December 1918
716. *MDA* January 1919
717. *MDA* April 1919
718. *MDA* July 1919
719. *MDA* February 1921
720. Cherry & Pevsner, *Buildings*, 593
721. *MDT* 11 March 1922 6a, 23 July 1922
722. Berry & Gosling, *Around*, 13
723. DRO Devon Roll of Honour
724. *WMN* 23 May 1993
725. Chard, *Along*, 49
726. *MDA* August 1918
727. *MDA* July 1918
728. *MDA* February 1914
729. *MDA* September 1914
730. *MDA* April 1916
731. *MDA* June 1916
732. *MDA* January 1917
733. *MDA* January 1918
734. *MDA* April 1920
735. *MDT* 21 October 1922 3ab
736. *MDT* 24 November 1924
737. *MDT* 17 June 1933
738. *MDT* 29 July 1927
739. Ian Bulpin personal communication; records in private hands
740. Harris, *Devon's Century*, 34.
741. *MDA* 1 August 1931 18c
742. *MDT* 14 December 1938
743. Unsworth, *A new Look*, 46/7
744. *MDA* January 1970
745. *MDT* 4 January 1929
746. Berry & Gosling, *Around*, 108
747. *MDT* 22 December 1925
748. Chas F. Willis, *Newton Abbot and its Industrial Advantages* (Newton Abbot, 1920) 14,40
749. NAHR Clay industry
750. *MDA* December 1920
751. *MDA* June 1921
752. *MDA* October 1921
753. *MDT* 23 September 1922 2,7
754. *MDT* 20 February 1923
755. *MDT* 8 November 1926
756. *MDT* 1 January 1927
757. *MDT* 9 December 1929
758. *MDT* 11 December 1929
759. *MDT* 15 January 1933
760. *MDT* 8 June 1936
761. DRO 6435
762. NAHR Power station
763. *Municipal Journal* October 1924
764. *MDT* 3 May 1926
765. Porter, *Devon*, 336
766. Porter, *Devon*, 335
767. Porter *Devon*, 340
768. *MDT* 22 June 1922
769. Berry & Gosling, *Around*, 21
770. Beavis, *Britain*, 42/3
771. *MDT* 2 July 1928
772. *MDT* 27 January 1933
773. *MDT* 17 November 1928
774. *MDT* 13 June 1933
775. *MDT* 22 February 1936
776. Unsworth, *A new Look*, 90
777. Chard, *Along*, 34/5
778. Glenys Loder personal communication, Loder's ledger in private hands
779. Unsworth, *A new Look*, 40
780. *MDT* 12 November 1938
781. *MDA* May 1919
782. *MDA* June 1919
783. *MDA* October 1920
784. *MDA* November 1920
785. *MDA* May 1921

786. *WMN* 16 May 1933
787. *MDA* November 1921
788. *MDA* September 1921
789. J.H. Porter, *Devon and the General Strike 1926* (International Review of Social History Vol. XXIII 1978 part 3), 351
790. *MDT* 13 October 1926
791. *MDT* 4 December 1927
792. *MDT* 24 March 1929
793. *MDT* 14 May 1929
794. *MDA* 3 October 1931 5 bcde
795. *MDT* 16 November 1925
796. *MDT* 30 November 1925
797. *MDT* 20 November 1933
798. *MDT* 9 February 1927
799. *MDT* 19 May 1930
800. *MDT* 17 July 1933
801. *Devon & Exeter Gazette* 17 February 1931
802. *MDT* 21 February 1931
803. *MDT* 18 January 1925
804. *MDA* 7 November 15 bcde
805. *MDT* 1 July 1932
806. *MDT* 24 September 1932
807. *MDT* 19 November 1934
808. *WMN* 7 November 1937
809. *MDA* February
810. *MDT* 17 January 1938
811. *WMN* 10 August 1937
812. *MDT* 4 August 1938
813. DRO 547B/p3701
814. *WMN* 28 June 1936
815. Bradley NT 46/7
816. *WMN* 12 February 1968
817. *MDT* 28 October 1922 5bc
818. *MDA* 21 November 6 c
819. *MDA* April 1944
820. *MDT* 4 June 1938
821. *MDT* 21 October 1922 3ab
822. *MDT* 1 January 1930
823. *MDT* 20 January 1930
824. *MDT* 5 May 1924
825. NAHR Milber
826. NAHR Milber
827. *MDT* 13 June 1935
828. *E & E* 11 May 1953
829. *MDT* 17 June 1922 5c
830. *MDT* 31 January 1929
831. *MDT* 28 September 1927
832. *WMN* 9 June 1927
833. *WMN* 28 June 1936
834. *MDT* 7 February 1924
835. *MDT* 16 May 1929
836. *MDT* 17 January 1931
837. *MDT* 25 March 1933
838. *MDA* November
839. *MDT* 15 January 1938
840. *MDT* 7 February 1923
841. *MDT* 13 October 1923
842. *MDT* 11 March 1925
843. *Devon & Exeter Gazette* 27 March 1927.
844. *MDT* 16 May 1933
845. *MDA* January 1921
846. *MDA* April 1921
847. *MDT* 13 July 1922
848. *MDT* 10 December 1930
849. *MDT* spring 1922 especially January, 15 & 27 May
850. Forster *Knowles* (nd) 23/4
851. *MDT* 5 August 1927
852. *MDT* 11, 20, 24, 25 January 1932
853. *E & E* 19 May 1932
854. *MDT* 3 June 1926
855. Cherry & Pevsner, *Buildings,* 585/6
856. *WMN* 17 June 1963
857. Herald Express 22 April 2003 24; Jones *A Book,* 112; W. Keeble Martin *Over the Hills* (London, 1968)
858. *E & E* 16 February 1996
859. *MDA* January 1921
860. *MDT* 2 September 1926
861. *MDT* 23 June 1934
862. *MDT* 14 January 1925
863. *MDT* 29 March 1927
864. *Dictionary of National Biography;* Newton Abbot guide for 1952 51
865. K.A. Wescott, *Observation at St Mary's chapel Newton Abbot 1988* (Exeter, 1988) 1
866. *E & E* 12 September 1984
867. Beavis, *Newton,* 65
868. *WMN* 7 February 1985
869. *MDT* 30 April 1928
870. *MDT* 28 February 1931
871. *MDA* August 1919
872. *MDA* March 1920
873. *MDT* 26 April 1924
874. *MDT* 9 January 1925
875. *MDT* 7 August 1929
876. *MDT* 22 May 1930
877. *MDT* 21, 28, May 1928
878. *MDT* 6/7 May 1935
879. *WMN* 10 May 1935
880. *MDT* 17 June 1935
881. *The Times* 13 August 1936 7
882. *WMN* 1 Jan 1937 5
883. *MDA* January
884. *WMN* 7 March 1937
885. LC *WT* 13 March 1920
886. *MDT* 18 May & 24 August 1928, 25 October 1935
887. *MDT* 22 August 1936
888. *MDT* 19 January 1938
889. *Kelly Newton* 1939 PA 23
890. Unsworth, *A new Look,* 111
891. *MDA* December 1970
892. Brian Thomas, *Newton Abbot in the News* (Exeter, 1996) 9/10
893. *MDT* 10 July 1939
894. *MDT* 1 September 1939
895. *MDT* 17 October 1938
896. *MDT* 11 November 1939
897. Beavis, *Newton,* 97
898. A.R. Kingdom, *The Bombing of Newton Abbot Station No 1* (Newton Ferrers, 1991) 2
899. *MDT* 24 August 1939 1 cd
900. Beavis, *Newton,* 97
901. *E & E* 20 August 1993
902. Hoskins, *Devon* 309
903. DRO R2361A/(5/4) C92
904. *TDA* Vol. 122 20
905. *WMN* 30 March 1940
906. *MDA* 5 September 1970
907. *MDT* 15 June 1939 1 cd
908. *MDA* June 1945

909. Unsworth, *A new Look,* 48
910. Unsworth, *A new Look,* 103
911. Unsworth, *A new Look,* 107
912. *Newton Advertiser* 12 September 1983
913. *WMN* 23 April 1940
914. *WMN* 23 April 1934
915. Berry & Gosling, *Around,* 7.
916. *MDA* May 1942
917. Unsworth, *A new Look,* 99
918. *MDA* September 1948
919. *MDA* August 1943
920. *MDA* June 1945
921. *MDA* October 1943
922. *MDA* November 1944
923. Thomas, *Newton,* 14
924. DRO 867B/S38
925. *MDA* February 1948
926. Beavis, *Britain,* 11
927. NAHR Bovey Beds Lignite Deposit
928. *MDT* 8 July 2f
929. Bath, *Newton Abbot,* ch. 1
930. NAHR Gas works.
931. Beavis, *Britain,* 70
932. *MDA* August 1948
933. Cherry & Pevsner, *Buildings,* 584
934. Hoskins, *Devon* 309
935. Davenport, *Newton Abbot,* Introduction
936. LC *Western Morning News* 12 July 1963
937. Thomas, *Newton,* 15
938. *WMN* 19 September 1991
939. LC *Western morning News* 11 June 1977
940. *E & E* 24 April 1980
941. Thomas, *Newton,* 22
942. Thomas, *Newton,* 24
943. *Dawlish Advertiser* 21 April 1988
944. *WMN* 10 June 1998
945. *MDT* 19 May 1930
946. *WMN* 11 December 1995
947. Thomas, *Newton,* 19
948. LC *Western Morning News* 13 July 1960
949. LC *Western Morning News* 5 January 1961
950. LC *Western Morning News* 30 May 1969
951. *MDA* March 1966
952. LC *Western Morning News* 9/6/67
953. Elsie Townsend, *Memories of Newton Abbot* (Exeter, 1987) 6
954. *WMN* 3 October 1970
955. Thomas, *Newton,* 6
956. Thomas, *Newton,* 7
957. Unsworth, *A new Look,* 22
958. *WMN* 12 May 1979
959. *WMN* 10 August 1999
960. Thomas, *Newton,* 18
961. *WMN* 17 April 1975
962. *TP* 22 June 1975
963. Thomas, *Newton,* 22
964. Beavis, *Newton,* 60
965. Thomas, *Newton,* 29
966. *WMN* 26 July 1978
967. *WMN* 13 March 1981
968. *E & E* 20 April 1993
969. O'Hagan, *A History,* 68
970. Beavis, *Britain,* 115
971. Thomas, *Newton,* 21
972. *WMN* 27 January 1988
973. Jones, *A book,* 71
974. Chard, *Along,* 73/80
975. *WMN* 23 February 1980
976. District council Review October 1981
977. *WMN* 14 April 1982
978. *WMN* 24 October 1981
979. *WMN* 29 May 1981
980. *TP* 7 September 1984
981. *TP* 3 November 1989
982. *WMN* 9 August 1985
983. *WMN* 23 February 1987
984. *WMN* 2 October 1996
985. *WMN* 15 March 1997
986. Beavis, *Britain,* 75
987. *Teignmouth Post* 3 November 1992
988. *TP* 4 December 1992.
989. *E & E* 23 January 1993
990. *WMN* 24 March 1994
991. *E & E* 22 July 1995
992. *E & E* 23 July 1998
993. *WMN* 12 March 1998
994. *E & E* 5 June 1953
995. *MDA* February 1966
996. *E & E* 3 August 1982
997. *WMN* 7 June 1990
998. Asa Briggs, *Marks & Spencers 1884–1984, A Centenary History* (London, 1984); Hoskins, *Devon* (1954) 309; Austins, Marks & Spencer, Sainsbury's and Tesco all kindly provided information; numerous entries and advertisements in local papers.
999. *MDA* 27 September 1952 4
1000. Thomas, *Newton,* 5
1001. *MDA* 20 February 1971
1002. *E & E* 26 April 1979
1003. *WMN* 22 February 1980
1004. *E & E* 4 March 1982
1005. *E & E* 8 February 1983
1006. *WMN* 19 June 1987
1007. *E & E* 5 August 1987
1008. *E & E* 5 August 1987
1009. *WMN* 24 December 1997
1010. *MDA* December 1954
1011. Thomas, *Newton,* 4
1012. *WMN* 17 May 1985
1013. *WMN* 14 July 1989
1014. DRO 6435
1015. *E & E* 13 June 1974
1016. *WMN* 11 January 1985
1017. *WMN* 21 march 1974
1018. Thomas, *Newton,* 16
1019. NAHR Power station
1020. Thomas, *Newton,* 17
1021. LC *Western Morning News* 12 October 1968
1022. *WMN* 9 June 1980
1023. Beavis, *Newton,* 32
1024. *WMN* 8 December 1982
1025. *E & E* 20 September 1983
1026. Colin Willcocks personal communication, records in private hands
1027. *TP* 10 August 1984
1028. *WMN* 19 November 1985
1029. *E & E* 4 May 1998
1030. *WMN* 18 June 1986
1031. *E & E* 13 August 1986
1032. *E & E* 30 January 1988

1033. *WMN* 24 September 1990
1034. *WMN* 7 July 1992
1035. *E & E* 10 February 1999
1036. *WMN* 12 May 1983
1037. *TP* 16 March 1990
1038. *WMN* 6 April 1990
1039. *WMN* 18 October 1999
1040. *E & E* 28 January 1994.
1041. *E & E* 5 February 1994
1042. *WMN* 15 May 1998
1043. *E & E* 12 June 1999
1044. *WMN* 12 September 1996
1045. *E & E* 30 September 1998
1046. *WMN* 11 July 1997
1047. Bath, *Newton Abbot* ch. 8
1048. LC *Western Morning News* 10 September 1965
1049. Rolt, *The Potter's,* 146
1050. *WMN* 21 February 1977
1051. *WMN* 17 January 1978
1052. Unsworth, *A new Look,* 29
1053. *WMN* 13 July 1996
1054. *WMN* 19 June 1997
1055. *Express &Echo* 20 October 1994
1056. *WMN* 30 November 1998
1057. *E & E* 18 October 1999
1058. *E & E* 26 October 1983
1059. *E & E* I2 August 1984
1060. *WMN* 2 July 1994
1061. LC *Western Morning News* 15 October 1963
1062. Beavis, *Newton,* 83
1063. Bovett, *Historical Notes* 225
1064. *WMN* 2 February 1989
1065. Thomas, *Newton,* 12
1066. *WMN* 4 August 1990
1067. Bovett, *Historical Notes* 389
1068. *TP* 11 January 1985
1069. LC *Western Morning News* 15 May 1964
1070. LC *Western Morning News* 25 July 1966
1071. Beavis, *Britain,* 54
1072. *Dawlish Post* I November 1991
1073. *E & E* 3 June 1982
1074. *WMN* 9 April 1983
1075. Cherry & Pevsner, Buildings, 125
1076. *WMN* 14 June 1997
1077. *E & E* 10 April 1998
1078. Thomas, *Newton,* 20/21
1079. *WMN* 30 July 1980
1080. Thomas, *Newton,* 22
1081. LC *Devon & Cornwall Journal* Jan–Mar 1953
1082. *MDA* May 1963
1083. *MDA* March 1967
1084. Berry & Gosling, *Around,* 59
1085. Thomas, *Newton,* 25
1086. *WMN* 25 July 1977
1087. *WMN* 21 July 1980
1088. Beavis, *Newton,* 84
1089. *WMN* 17 March 1980
1090. *WMN* 17 June 1989
1091. *E & E* 12 September 1983
1092. *WMN* 31 September 1983
1093. *Dawlish Post* 23 June 1989
1094. *WMN* 29 April 1992
1095. *WMN* 21 December 1994
1096. Harris, *Devon's Century,* 38

BIBLIOGRAPHY

Bath, Edward, J. *Newton Abbot Roundabout* (1954) unpaginated.

Beavis, Derek, *Newton Abbot, The Story of the Town's Past* (1985)

Beavis, Derek, *Great Britain in Old Photographs, Newton Abbot* (2000)

Berry, Les & Gosling, Gerald, *Around Newton Abbot* (1994)

Bradley NT (1989)

Chard, Judy, *Along the Lemon* (1980)

Cherry, Bridget, and Pevsner, Nikolaus, *The Buildings of England Devon* 2nd edition (1997)

Clark, Arthur, *Newton Abbot, some places of interest* (n.d.)

Cooke, G.A. etc. *Topography of Great Britain or British Travellers Pocket Directory* (1818)

Creswell, Beatrix, F. *Newton Abbot & its neighbouring villages including Chudleigh* (1908)

Curtis, J. Sydney, *Devonshire Historical and Pictorial* (1897)

Davenport, Mary M. *Newton Abbot in old picture postcards* (1984)

Dunning, Martin, *Newton Abbot* (2002)

Forster, Rowena, *Knowles Hill School* (n.d.)

Granville, A.R. *Spas of England 2 The Midlands & South.* Reprint (1971)

Gregory, R. H. *The South Devon Railway* (1982)

Grimley, Roger, *Motor Buses of Newton Abbot and District.* c.1994

Harris, Helen, *The Haytor Granite Tramway and Stover Canal* (1994)

Harris, Helen, *Devon's Railways* (2001)

Harris, R. *King's Teignton* (n.d.)

Hearder, George H. *Hearder's Almanack 1906* (1906)

Hoskins, W.G. *Devon* (1954)

Jones, Roger, *A book of Newton Abbot* (1986)

Kay, Peter, *Exeter–Newton, A Railway History* (1993)

Kingdom, A.R. *The Bombing of Newton Abbot Station No 1* (1991)

Lamb, Trixie, M. *The Ancient Tower of St Leonard Newton Abbot, S. Devon 1220–1973* (1973)

Lysons, *Magna Britannia Devonshire* Vol. 6 (1822)

Mate's Illustrated Newton Abbot (1903)

Matthews A.G. *Calamy revised: being a revision of Edmund Calamy's 'Account of the Ministers and other ejected and silenced 1660-2.*

Memories of St Michael's 1918–1971 (1995)

O'Hagan, Mary, *A History of Forde House* (1990)

Rhodes, A.J. *Newton Abbot Its History and Development* (n.d.) c.1904)

Rice, Ian, (ed.), *Newton Abbot 150 Years a Railway Town* (1996).

Rolt, L.T.C. *The potter's field, a history of the south Devon ball clay industry* (1974)

Scott, C.G. *Richard Beard, Newton Abbot and the growth of photography* (1988)

Stirling, D.M. *A History of Newton-Abbot and Newton-Bushel* (1830)

Thomas, Brian, *Newton Abbot in the News* (1996)

Townsend, Elsie, *Memories of Newton Abbot* (1987)

Unsworth, Harry, *A New Look at Old Newton Abbot* (1993)

Vile & Williams *Newton Abbot as a tourist centre and Guide to South Devon* (1898)

Westcott, K.A. *Observation at St Mary's chapel Newton Abbot 1988* (1988)

Willis, Chas. F. *Newton Abbot and its Industrial Advantages* (1920)

Woolner, Diana, *Herzogin Cecille* (c.1975)

Young, Christine, *The Story of Stover* (n.d.)

Census

Census Enumerator' Books in Westcountry Studies Library

1851 Highweek HO 1071871 Folios 594–641, Wolborough HO 107 1871 Folios 490–593

1891 Haccombe & Combeinteignhead RG 12/1699 Folios 12–22, Highweek RG 12 1699 Folios 34–84, Kingsteignton RG 12/1700 Folios 1–31, Ogwells RG 12/1699 3–33, Totnes RG 12 1711 Folios 67–144. Wolborough RG 12 1700 Folios 56–117

Cuttings

Lamb's Cuttings File 56 at the Devon & Exeter Institute from *Devon & Cornwall Journal, Western Morning News,* and other publications.

Directories

Billing's Directory of Devon 1857 M. Billing, Steam Printing Offices, Birmingham

Deacon's Court guide, Gazetteer and County Blue Book London C.W. Deacon & Co. 1882

Harrod. *J.G. & Co Royal County Directory of Devonshire 1878* Norwich

Kelly, Newton 1939

Kelly, Post Office directory of Devonshire and Cornwall 1856, 1866, 1873, and 1883 London Kelly & Co.

Morris's Directory of Devonshire 1870

Robinson's London & Western Counties Directory 1838

Slater's 1844 and *1852* Printed in London I Slater

The Universal British Directory of Trade, Commerce and Manufactures *c.*1 794, original publishers Peter Barford and John Wilkes (1988) microfiche Buntingford by Microfi Ltd

Whites 1850, History, Gazetteer and Directory of Devonshire (1968) Reprint New York, Augustus M. Kelly, also *1878* and *1890* Sheffield

Documents

PRO; South Devon Railway documents

264 177, Loco and carriage Dept employees 1857–97.

630 2, Establishment report 1873.

631 1, Directors Meetings 1844–1846.

631 44, I.K. Brunel's Reports and Correspondence concerning Atmospheric system 1844–1840

631 87, Ledger personnel 1857–63.

PRO, all Rail

1005 86, Some historical notes on the County of Cornwall, also of Devon.

1005 109, South Devon Railway Remains.

1005 138, South Devon & Cornwall Railway Photographs.

1008 12, Workings of South Devon and Cornwall Railway 1850–1865.

Devon Record Office DRO

1508M/Devon adds Special Subjects/SS3/Wharfs etc Devon Wharfs.

    1 Devon Wharfs Newton Abbot Exports 1860–1906.

    2 Devon Wharfs Newton Abbot Imports 1860–1910.

    Devon Special Subjects/Harbours/Others/No 16 "Devon Wharfs" Newton Abbot 1851–1862.

    Special Subjects /Harbours/ Others/ No 17 "Devon Wharfs" Newton Abbot 1881–1908.

Other papers

122A/PO, Ilsington Overseers apprenticeship indentures.

1638F/Z31, Gilbert's Almshouses orders & directions .

21310X/LR6, Registration of Motor Cars & Motor Cycles.

335M/EZ, Summary & report building of new Globe 1844.

547B/P 3701, Sale Catalogue Ford House, Newton Abbot 1936.

547B/P2224, Sale *Globe* January 31st 1924.

867B/S9, Sale Catalogue for Ogwell and Bradley Manor Estates in Wolborough. 1909.

R 2361 A/C5/4, Wolborough General Rate Books .

R2361A/(5/4) Z7, Register of wounded Newton VAD hospital.

R2361A/(5/4)Z, Evacuation scheme Newton Abbot.

6435 Records of Devon Leathercrafts and New Devon Pottery.

At Newton Abbot Museum

Notice 'Newton Abbot and Newton Bushel Building Company in 1841'

Guides

Newton Abbot as a tourist centre and Guide to South Devon, 1898.

Mate's Illustrated Newton Abbot, 1903 unpaginated.

Newton Abbot & its neighbouring villages including Chudleigh, 1908.

Newton Abbot and its Industrial Advantages, 1920.

Newton Abbot, The Gateway of Dartmoor, *1935.*

Newton Abbot, the Official Guide, *1950.*

Newton Abbot, Venue of Royal Agricultural Show, 1952.

Journals

Devon and Cornwall Notes & Queries DCNQ

Devon and Cornwall Record Society DCRS

The Devon Historian DH

Devonia

Devonian Year Book

District Council Review

Gentleman's Magazine

History of Photography

History Today

International Journal of Nautical Archaeology

International Review of Social History

Municipal Journal

Proceedings of Devon Archaeological Society PDAS

Transactions of the Devonshire Association TDA

The Vicarian

Minutes at DRO

Wolborough Local Board, later NAUDC 1864–1901

Wolborough Vestry Minute Book 1839–1866

Miscellaneous

The Railway at Newton Abbot Compilation made 1993 and held in Newton Abbot at specialist Railway Library.

Newton Abbot Humanities Records NAHR in Newton Abbot Reference Library on *Bovey Beds Lignite Deposit, Clay Industry, Conditions, Gas Works, Leather Industry, Market and Mills, Milber, Power Station, Road Transport, Tucker's Maltings, Woollen Industry.*

Newspapers

Dawlish Advertiser

Dawlish Post

Devon & Exeter Gazette

Devon Weekly Times DWT
East & South Devon Advertiser E & SDA
Express & Echo E & E
Herald Express
Mid-Devon Advertiser MDA
Mid-Devon Times MDT
Newton Advertiser
Teignmouth Post TP
The Times
Torquay and Tor Directory and General Advertiser
Trewman's Exeter Flying Post EFP
Weekender
Western Gazette
Western Morning News WMN
Western Times WT
Woolmer's Exeter & Plymouth Gazette

Official papers

House of Commons Papers 1852–53 Volume LXXXVIII
House of Commons Papers 1852 Volume XLII Census
British Parliamentary papers 1891 census England and
    Wales Vol. CVl Population 23

Dissertation

Investigating the Role of the Devon Gardener Clare
    Greener unpublished (2000)

INDEX

Bold numbers = insets
Italic numbers = illustrations

Hamlin, Mrs Viola, wreath-layer; 124
Hamlyn, George; dangerous driver; 76
Hammett Mr, inspector; 59
Hammond, Rev. John; 145
Hampshire; 98
Handley, Tommy, comedian; 160
Hansom, Joseph, architect; 190
Hardy, Keir, politician; 109
Harris; Helen, historian; 45, Mr, public nuisance; 62
Hart, Tony, bridegroom; 195
Hartland; 51, 93
Harvey; Len, boxer; 146, Mr, builder; 62
Haslam Jeremy, historian; 4
Hatherley, esq.; 40
Hawkmoor; 113, 128, 142
Haydon, Dr E; 142
Hayman, Robert, benefactor; 14
Hay-on-Wye, Wales; 145
Haytor; x, 34, 44, 144, 158, 190, Granite Tramway; 34, 44
Heathfield; 1. 78, 87, 111, 144, 165, 176, 177, 179, 180, 188
Heaviside, Oliver, scientist; **121**
Hennock; 17, 97, 138
Henry III; 8
Henry VIII; 14
Hereford; 174
Heward, George, offender; 76
Hexter Humpherson; 110, 132, 180
Hicks, George, builder; 89
Hill, Dr Charles, MP; 192
hills; Break Neck; 58, 168, Chapel Hill; 8, 173, Ess Hill; 86, 118, Knowles Hill; *59, 86,* 89, 94, 180, Telegraph Hill; 194, Treacle Hill; 8, Wolborough Hill; 59, 68, 88, 89, 94, *118*
historiography; ix–x
Hitler, Adolph; 149
Hobbs, Mr, railway officer; 53
Holbeam, Dam; 58, 170, Domesday; 6
Hole, Mrs Gladys, absentee concealer; 156
Holsworthy; 93
Holwill, Thomas Samuel, casualty; 126
Home Guard; 153–154
Honeybun, Gus, mascot; 192
Honiton; 8, 93
hooter, railway; 187
Hoskins, W.G., historian; ix, 174
hospital; 61–62, 78, 89, 106, 122, 142, 155, 159, 188, 189, American at Stover; 155, 159, 194, Isolation; 61, 113, 159, Naval; 152, 153, 159, 189, Newton Hall (VAD); 120, 122, 123, 124, Stover; 121, Torbay; 70, 188
hotels see inns
houses; 172–173, Abbotsbury; 61, 63, 117, Abbotsleigh; 81, *81,* Bradley Manor; 2, 6, *11,* 12, 26, 113, 114, 141, Bradley View; 121, Bradley Wood; 33, 113, 144, Broadlands; 64, 188, courthouse; *25,* Darracombe; 116, 142, Devon Villa; 126, Dyrons (later school); 32, 62, 189, 190, East Park; 140, Fishwick; 40, Forde; 14, 16, 19, *19,* 21, 22, 26, 33, 39, 45, *45,* 52, 124, 166, 169, 172, 194–195, Georgian; 167, Hometeign; 182, 188, Lake View; 191, Laurels, The; 159, Lower Marsh; 76, Manor; *14,* 184, Marlborough; 166, Minerva; *55,* Morely; 113, Ogwell; 113, *114,* Park; 152, Priest's; 169, Rose-hill; 86, Round; 161, Sandford Orleigh; 35, 45, 75, 89, 90, 155, 172, Somerset Lodge; *47,* Stover; 35, 61, 118, 121, Stowford Lodge; 35, Tudor; *13,* Whitehill Lodge; 11

housing; Pioneer; 173, prefabricated; 172–173
Howton; 33
Hull, Robert, landscape gardener; 33
Hussey, James, traveller; 56
Hyner, Hennock; 79
Hymenophyllum, a fern; 90

Iberia; 17
Ideford; 6, 31
Ilford Park see Polish Camp
Ilfracombe; 174
Ilsington; 37, 97, 138
India; 35, 73, 90, 98, 126, 160
Ingsdon; 6, 116, 192
Inns & hotels; 36, Barge's see *Half Moon; Bear,* 40, Beazley's see *Globe; Cider Bar,* 30, *Commercial;* 31, 54, 82 84, 110, 113, 157, 167, *Dartmouth Inn;* 17, 42, 110, *Globe;* 23, 36, 39, 40, 42, *42,* 46, 47, 48, 51–52, 55, 56, 63, 64, 66, 80, 81, 85, 86, 87, 89, 110, 112, 113, 125, 138, 140, 155, 160, 167, 169, 192, 197, *Golden Lion;* 40, 51, *Greene Man (Devon Arms); 47, Half Moon Inn;* 59, 85, *Imperial Hote,* Torquay; 172, *Jolly Farmer (Bradley Hotel);* 31, 75, 113, 193, *Jolly Sailor;* 76, 84, 192, *London Inn;* 36, *Market House Inn;* 76, Magor's see *Commercial; Mercer's Arms;* 23, *Newfoundland Inn;* 17, 52, 166–167, *Old London,* Exeter; 50, *Passage House Inn,* Hackney; 40, 41, 194, *195, Penn Inn (Penguin);* 140, *156, Plough (Drive Inn);* 167, *Plymouth Inn;* 61, *Queen's Hotel;* 31, 167, *Railway Tavern;* 155, *Richard Hopkins;* 154, *Royal Oak Inn;* 76, *Seven Stars Inn;* 59, 144, 169, *Sun;* 32, 36, 122, *Swan Inn;* 172, *Turk's Head;* 31, 40, *50,* 62, 76, 140, *Union; 47,* 89, *Week House Inn;* 167, *Wharf House, (Passage House Inn),* Newton Abbot; 79, *White Hart;* 31, 36
Invertere; 183, *184*
Ipplepen; 1, 31, 46, 70, 97, 121, 131, 174
Ipswich; 113
Ireland; 23, 98, 193
Iron; Age; 1, 2, mine; 83
islands; Falkland; 183, Scilly; 179, Shetland; 179

Jacobs, Mr, dog owner; 62
Jackman, Albert, petty offender; 76
Jackson, Mary Ann, sand hawker; 91
James I; 16
Japan; 157
Jetty Marsh; 34, 82, 140, 166, 172, 177, 188
Johnny, nom de plume; 67, 69, 70
John O'Groats; 193
Jones, Roger, historian; x, 8, 19, 22, 66
jubilees; *88,* Victoria Gold; 87–88, Victoria Diamond; 89, George V Silver; 146, Elizabeth II Silver; 193
Julius Caesar; 3
Just You; *104*

Kanefsky, John, historian; 30
Kay, Peter, railway writer; 49, 94
Keats, John; 48
Kelly Bray, Cornwall; 182
Kennford; 8
Kent, county; 44, 98, Duke of see George, Prince
Kent's Cavern; 1, 3
Keyberry; 28, 30
King; Charles B., entertainer; 76, Coffee; 69
Kingsbridge; 4, 9, 93, 98, 112, 175, 182
Kingskerswell; 2, 14, 30, 97, 115, 162, 166, 174, 193, arch;